FRANCE

MENORCA

MALLORCA

IBIZA

FORMENTERA

MEDITERRANEAN SEA

THE SPANISH

MEDITERRANEAN

ISLANDS

COOKBOOK

THE SPANISH

MEDITERRANEAN

ISLANDS

COOKBOOK

JEFF KOEHLER

CONTENTS

At the Thursday Market

For over 700 years there has been a weekly food market in my village in Menorca. In 1301, the ruling king decreed the establishment of a *mercat*, giving the recently founded town at the geographic centre of the island its name: Es Mercadal, meaning the square or location where a market is held. It takes place on Thursdays. While it happens during the morning for most of the year, from the beginning of June until the end of September, it starts at 7 p.m. and goes on until late. The summer market significantly expands to include stalls belonging to jewellery makers and various types of artisans. It remains Menorca's largest and most popular weekly market.

Historically, Menorca – an isolated island in the Mediterranean, with land that offered little for the cook – was largely self-sufficient because it had no choice. It developed a cuisine adapted to its circumstances, with lessons in growing, gathering and preserving passed down for generations. The fruits of these traditions can be found at the Thursday market. Most who sell food are *pagesos*, farmers or those who work the land (or people from the countryside), and this reflects an artisanal approach based on knowledge, skill and hard work.

Running end-to-end down the single-lane main street and a number of connecting side ones, long tables supported by sawhorse legs offer an abundance of fresh produce, preserved items and traditional baked goods. Bundles of long, matchstick-thin wild asparagus in spring, red-blushed apricots in June, round yellow melons in the summer heat, a range of figs beginning in late August and deep-gold wild chanterelles in autumn. Red-skinned potatoes, burgundy-veined green beans, small, thick-skinned tomatoes for rubbing on bread, pale purple aubergines (eggplant), violet-tinged artichokes, light green courgettes (zucchini). Boxes of lemons and garlic. Eggs in various sizes and colours, handed over inside twists of newspaper if you didn't bring your own egg carton. Jars of capers foraged on the rocky headlands, salted and preserved in vinegar. Spreadable, paprika-rich pork sobrassada sausage and denser (paprika-free) *carn i xua*. Square cow's milk cheeses with rounded corners and orangish-brown rinds. Loaves of country bread that will keep for a week. Flaky, lard-rich savoury pastries stuffed with spinach, pine nuts and raisins, with fish, with lamb or with fresh cheese. Sheet pans of *coca* flatbreads topped with roasted vegetables and sponge cakes dimpled with apricot halves. Jams – melon, fig, apple, tomato – and thick honeys.

With a broad wicker basket slung over your shoulder, shopping can feel like a feast regarding certain items such as apricots, quince or broad (fava) beans. When these are in season, they are at their best – their most flavourful, most abundant and least expensive moment of the year. Such a seasonal glut also compels the widest variety of preparations and the need or desire for preserving. And therein lies the pleasure for the home cook as well as those around the table.

* * *

Located just off Spain's eastern coast are the country's four Mediterranean islands: Mallorca, Menorca, Ibiza (or Eivissa in the local dialect) and Formentera. (In English, Mallorca is sometimes called Majorca and Menorca is called Minorca.) Collectively they are known as the Balearic Islands, or Illes Balears in Catalan and Islas Baleares in Spanish. At the centre of the chain is Mallorca, by far the largest and most populated of the islands, with Ibiza and Formentera to its southwest and the closest to the mainland, and Menorca to its northeast and the most distant.

Menorca is 48 km/30 miles long, 16 km/10 miles wide and still strikingly rural. Alaior, Ferreries, Es Migjorn Gran and Es Mercadal form a quartet of interior villages surrounded by rolling hills, sprawling fig trees and rock-strewn fields divided by stacked dry-stone walls. Charcoal-grey lizards bask on small limestone outcroppings among Bronze-age ruins, grazing dairy cows and shimmering silver wild olive trees (*ullastre*, which produce little oil but have highly valued wood).

In 1996, I settled in Barcelona and then married the Catalan woman whom I had met in a London residence hall for foreign postgraduate students and followed home. A few years later we made our first visit to Menorca, and by 2010, with family in tow, we were renting a small hilltop house in Es Mercadal in summer. Set on the edge of town, the generous tract of farmland had a coop with a dozen chickens whose eggs our two young daughters would gather each morning, garden plots of yellow melons, courgettes and dry-farmed tomatoes that we were welcome to pick, and a dozen fig trees that ripened at the summer's end. (The hammock strung between two of those shady fig trees was a much fought-over spot for afternoon reading.) The town was friendly and open, and making friends came easy.

Set at the foot of the island's highest point, Es Mercadal (population 5,000) is not a summer tourist place but a thriving town with a pair of busy hardware shops, a school and well-stocked library, a concert hall/theatre, tennis and paddleball courts and a new swimming pool with a retractable roof. There are five bakeries, two butcher's shops and an excellent produce shop that gets supplemented by the Thursday market. A fish supplier sells from a cubbyhole in one of the town's two grocery shops, while a family that owns a fishing boat in a nearby port sells some of the day's catch, often limited to just scorpion fish, skate and a few other options.

Restaurants have a line on Fridays, even in January, while café tables edging the two squares are busy year-round. The streets around the central square frequently get closed off, tables and chairs fill much of the space and live music floats through the warm evening air.

On such summer nights, the two dozen members of the town's ball dancing club occupy a long centre table in the lower square, and by the third or fourth song of the two-hour set, they have finished their dinner and begun to dance everything from waltzes to country line dancing. Memories of watching this during the first summers that we spent in the village remain vivid. As the dancers twirled and spun in unison under long strands of lights that stretched from the corners of the square to the illuminated clocktower that loomed above it, and couples (and reluctant kids) gradually joined in, it felt like we were witnessing scenes from a charming old movie. My wife and kids and I knew it was where we wanted to be.

We all fell hopelessly in love with the island and the village, and in 2014 we bought a place of our own in the centre of the town.

Our home is a traditional three-storey nineteenth-century townhouse made of a type of porous sandstone quarried on the island called *marés*. It stays cool in summer but is hard to heat in winter. The houses around us appear mostly identical: whitewashed inside and out, with terracotta floor tiles, brilliant forest-green wooden shutters and doors, and red-tiled roofs. Our narrow street rises gently up to the church, which stands at the highest point in Es Mercadal, and ends in a tiny, tree-shaded square given over in summer to evening lectures and the occasional student orchestra performance. As the street is essentially pedestrian, some of our neighbours set their chairs outside on summer evenings and talk until midnight in the breeze. Being near the church means that all of the village festivities, fiestas and processions pass by our door, as the scattered drops of candle wax from silent Holy Week processions can attest.

When we bought the house, it had a large cistern under the living room for captured rainwater and a well in the garden but no running water from the city beyond a recently installed brass spigot beside the front door. (As residents, we also had the right to collect 10 litres/2½ gallons of drinking water every Saturday morning from the town cistern.) Sturdy beams in the high-ceilinged attic held hundreds of hooks to hang and cure sausages in winter, and a screened-off room for other types of preserved goods. As the vast number of nails showed, the sheer quantity of charcuterie that once hung in our attic was a mark of wealth. According to its past owner, the variety of shapes and flavours they prepared – from classic deep red sobrassada to round, blood-black *cuixots* seasoned with aniseed, cinnamon and black pepper – also demonstrated deep culinary creativity that accompanied the traditional necessity of preserving a pig after butchering.

In the back behind the house, the walled-in yard was filled with tomato plants and backed by a pair of sheds that held coops for numerous *perdiu* (red-legged partridge). The tomatoes were largely cooked into sauce and canned for the winter, while the partridges were used for an ancient, pre-Roman method of hunting called *reclamo*. During a six-week-long season that opens around Christmas, hunters carry male partridges in cages into the field to attract with their song other partridges, who get caught live in lasso traps made of string. (The other classic animal to hunt on the island is rabbit. Wild rabbit slowly braised to tenderness with lots of onions, garlic and fresh herbs is one of Menorca's classic dishes.)

In a remodel the following year to install new wiring and plumbing in the house, we converted the tomato patch to a grassy yard lined with traditional herbs (rosemary, thyme, sage, oregano, lavender, mint), planted a pair of mulberry trees for summer shade and dismantled the partridge coops. But the rainwater cistern was left untouched, as was the ample *rebost* (pantry or larder) on the ground floor under the stairs.

While our girls were still in school, I tended to open the house around Easter, go as much as possible during spring and then, at the end of June, once school had finished, we'd move there for the summer, returning in early September before school restarted. But since they both started university, my visits have extended, with longer and more frequent stays in spring (for foraging wild asparagus) and autumn (for wild mushrooms), while the summer stay now stretches from June through to October.

Moving for the summer means a sharp change in the routine and rhythm from Barcelona, where we live in a small, central apartment. Village life is more social. Walking the block to the *plaça* to buy bread or the Menorcan newspaper takes at least fifteen minutes because you see a dozen people you know – and there is always time to chat.

It also means a shift in our approach to cooking. Barcelona's food markets are among the finest in the world, with Asian, Latino and North African speciality shops supplementing those offerings with global ingredients. I can usually find whatever I need – or crave.

When I am in Menorca, meals rely heavily on local produce and preserves, and they have fewer ingredients. I head to the municipal Mercat de Peix (fish market) in Ciutadella or Maó, hoping rather than planning to buy a specific item. I know that what ends up in my shopping basket will depend on what the sea has supplied that morning: you get what looks good and go from there. It changed me as a cook. I have gained a stronger dependency on the highly local seasons, but also a deeper appreciation for them. (I've also gained more support in the kitchen. I just step next door, apron on and wooden spoon in hand, to ask my neighbours about any sudden doubts.)

After we bought the house, the first thing we did was have one of the carpenters in the village build us a traditional Menorcan table made from pine wood for our covered back terrace. With few exceptions, it is here that we eat all of our meals. If there is a centre to the house, it is this sturdy, 2-metre (6½-feet)-long, well-varnished table with long benches.

What we eat at that table is a keen reflection of the island. One of our favourite dishes is *caldereta de peix*, a fish soup served over very thin slices of dried bread. Today it's a classic (alongside its more expensive sibling prepared with spiny lobster, *caldereta de llagosta*), but it began as a humble fisherman's dish, prepared using fish that got tangled in the nets or small, bony specimens with little value at the market. Of course, it was a way to utilize day- (or days)-old bread, which also makes it more filling.

Such is the trajectory of so many dishes. Developing in isolation as a small island in the Mediterranean required ingenuity – initially to survive with the available foodstuffs and then, eventually, to create gastronomic delights. First came the need to eat, and then the desire to eat well. That is a defining tenet for Menorca and all of Spain's Balearic Islands.

Introducing the Balearic Islands

Despite being only 80–250 km/50–150 miles off the mainland, the Balearic Islands are remarkably distinct from the Spanish peninsula. Today it's an easy (and frequent) thirty-minute flight from Barcelona or an overnight ferry ride across the Balearic Sea, which stretches between the islands and the mainland. But Mallorca, Menorca, Ibiza and Formentera remained insular until the mid-nineteenth century or later. Perhaps even more surprising is how the islands themselves are strikingly distinct, each with its own landscape, traditions and even dialect of Catalan.

The Balearic Islands fall historically under the Catalan linguistic area. While Spanish is widely spoken and shares co-official status, Catalan, brought here during the Christian Reconquista of the islands from the thirteenth century onwards, is the main language of the region. There is a Balearic dialect, with each of the islands having their own sub-dialect: *mallorquí* (on Mallorca), *menorquí* (on Menorca) and *eivissenc* (on Ibiza and Formentera). (Some people on the islands argue that these are not dialects but separate languages.) I have largely used Catalan or the local dialect (rather than Spanish) throughout this book, and also give the Spanish name for a number of dishes. One exception is the spelling of Ibiza. While its name is Eivissa in *eivissenc*, Ibiza is commonly used on the island and abroad.

In many respects more akin to other nearby islands such as Corsica and Sardinia than mainland Spain, the Balearic Islands' classically Mediterranean landscape is often rugged and frequently rocky, with pine, juniper, holm oak and some buckthorn, wheat and barley, olives, vineyards, almonds and carob, apricots and sprawling fig trees, thorny capers, rosemary, thyme and chamomile. With most of the Balearic population of around 1.2 million living in a few main cities, the islands continue to feel overwhelmingly rural outside this handful of urban areas.

The diet in the Balearic Islands is among the most representative of Mediterranean diets anywhere, with olive oil, wine, fish, rice, garlic and plenty of fruits, vegetables and pulses (legumes) at the heart of the kitchen. It is the Mediterranean distilled to its essences on the plate.

Sitting on key trade routes that criss-crossed the Mediterranean and endowed with protective natural harbours, the islands have borne witness to the comings and goings of an array of the region's empires and occupiers, beginning with the Phoenicians and Carthaginians, then the Romans and Vandals, and then the Byzantines from the east of the Mediterranean. From 902 CE, Moors (the general name for the Muslim inhabitants in Spain) ruled for over three centuries. The Catalan empire, under the Crown of Aragón – which also included, at various times, Sicily, Sardinia, southern Italy, Corsica, Malta and parts of Greece – controlled them from the early thirteenth century. With the dynastic union of the Crown of Aragón and the Crown of Castilla in the late fifteenth century, the islands came under the control of the Spanish monarchy and eventually democratic Spain. In Menorca, during the eighteenth century, there were also interludes of British and (very brief) French occupations.

All of these invaders, outsiders and settlers left marks on the culture and character of the islands. They introduced crops, livestock and cooking methods and impacted the always evolving cuisines. The Roman period, for instance, is notable for the widespread introduction of olives and grapes, and new traditions in curing meats, using vinegar for stews and preserving. Along with creating countless confections and the blending of sweet and savoury flavours, Muslim Moors were notable for their mastery of irrigation. The numerous new crops planted can be seen clearly in the many names with Arabic roots: *albercoc* (from *al-birqûq* or *barqûq*, apricot), *carxofa* (from *ḥáršafa*, artichoke), *albergínia* (from *al-bedenǧéna*, aubergine/eggplant), *llimona* (from *lāimûna*, lemon), *arròs* (from *ar-ruzz*, rice), *safrà* (from *za 'fârân*, saffron), *espinacs* (from *ispinâḫ*, spinach) and so on, while corn is called *blat de moro*, literally 'Moor's wheat'. The Catalans introduced new ways of cooking, using crushed almonds to flavour and thicken savoury stews and introducing a host of Lenten salt cod dishes. Jewish influences, the maritime trade from Italy and new ingredients from the Americas – peppers! tomatoes! potatoes! – were fundamental in transforming the cuisine.

Ultimately, though, these islands were long secluded and, while incorporating new ingredients and techniques, they still developed a distinctive Mediterranean gastronomy strongly marked by seasonality and isolation. They were self-sufficient because they had to be. Their cuisine is a combination of what could be grown or preserved, the heritage of those who had passed over a long and complex history, and creativity at the stove. It took patience in the kitchen to eke out flavours.

Humbled – or least limited – by its geography, rocky soil and frequent lack of water, the food of these islands is essentially Mediterranean comfort cooking with flashes of refinement. It is deeply rooted in the individual islands, in the ways of the people, in the markets and vegetable gardens, in the hills where foraging takes place, and in the bays when the sea is calm. Most of all, it is influenced by what the seasons offer.

While differences can be found from island to island, there are many constants. Large, round country loaves of bread are a staple on the table. Olive oil might be the main fat, but lard remains key to many baked goods, while some use a blend of the two: deeply popular *coca* flatbreads today still call for equal amounts of olive oil and lard. Baked in large sheet pans, *coques* have a range of toppings, from roasted red peppers and olives (page 42) to Swiss chard, spring onions and parsley (page 41). Pulses (legumes) are a pillar of the diet, as are vegetables in their various guises – raw, grilled, roasted, steamed, boiled, baked. Stuffing vegetables is particularly common, as it is a way to create a full meal from a few aubergines (eggplant) (page 84 and page 87), courgettes (zucchini) or onions. Figs are a key fruit, both for people – eaten fresh as well as baked with some wine (page 314) or preserved as a smooth jam called *figat* (page 343) – but also for livestock, who eat the fallen fruit. Citruses and almonds find their way into countless savoury dishes, and sweet ones. Capers add zest to salads, fish dishes and stewed meats (most famously tongue, page 235). And fresh herbs – parsley, thyme, rosemary, marjoram – consistently enliven dishes. Rice is essential, extremely common and cooked with just about any other ingredients imaginable, from vegetables and snails, fish (pages 131–138) and pork (pages 138, 143 and 156) to salt cod with cauliflower during Lent (page 146). Indeed, nothing absorbs or adjusts to what a season offers better than short-grain white rice. (Some rice is grown in the paddies that border the protected Albufera wetlands in north-eastern Mallorca, but most comes from fields around Valencia, just across the Balearic Sea.) Fishing provides for the kitchen, from sardines grilled over embers until their scales turn tinny and eyes go white, to squid (calamari) braised in its own ink (page 202), to lobster served with fried potatoes and topped with a fried egg (page 201).

While sheep, rabbit and chicken are mainstays, pork is iconic, and the *matança del porc* or *matances* (butchering of pigs) in late autumn and early winter is a key part of the culture. Nearly the entire animal is used in *embotits* (charcuterie) during the *matança*. Preparing *embotits* began back in the Roman era and remains so popular that it gives the islands something of a culinary identity. The most famous is the spreadable sobrassada pork sausage. Minced (ground) raw pork, paprika, cayenne pepper and plenty of salt are stuffed into casings, hung from beams in attics and dry-cured. While Mallorca makes a strong claim to it, with official protected Denominación de Origen (DO) status from the Spanish government to back it up, it is equally prevalent on the other islands, as both something eaten as charcuterie and an ingredient, from being stuffed into squid (*calamar*, page 207) and brioche-like buns (page 46) to giving meatballs added flavour (page 249). It's even found in some sweet pastries.

Another local favourite that's frequently present is allioli. Along with some cracked green olives, many restaurants set down a generous bowl of this garlic and olive oil emulsion to slather onto bread as people look over their menu. The name is a compound of its ingredients: garlic (*all*) and (*i*) oil (*oli*). (In Spanish it is spelled with a single *l* – *alioli* – and the English aioli borrows from the French *aïoli* and Occitan *aïoli*.) It is also frequently dolloped on rice dishes (spectacularly with black rice, page 134), eaten with grilled meats (page 269) or boiled fish, whisked with stock (broth) as a fish sauce (page 168), and spooned onto salt cod fillets that get slid into the oven and baked until the dish has a golden gratin top (page 188). It feels at times an omnipresent part of the Balearic table.

Many of the elaborate (and now expensive) classics began as much simpler fare to be prepared by those working in the fields or on fishing boats. A soupy rice in Mallorca called *arròs brut* ('Dirty' Rice, page 140), made with the produce from the fields and hunted game (plus, in the old days, a bit of blood to cloud the stock and give the dish its descriptive name) is one such dish. On Ibiza, the classic two-course fish stew is another. In this, fish and potatoes are boiled and served as one course (*bullit de peix*, page 160). The saffron-rich broth from that is used to make another course, most famously *arròs a banda*, or 'rice on the side' (page 131), which is cooked with some cuttlefish in a wide paella pan. The intensely flavoured rice, which is no more than a single grain deep, is set down in the middle of the table and eaten directly from the pan. The grains of rice are tender and plump with flavour, and in a properly prepared pan, there is a thin layer of slightly caramelized rice on the bottom known as *socarrat*. The only noise is spoons scraping the pan.

The islands also all have an unabashed devotion to sweet treats. Along with year-round favourites like sheet pans of cake made with boiled potato in the spongy dough and topped with fresh apricots (page 283) and aromatic rice pudding (page 311), there is a venerable calendar of sweets that marks the year: spiral-shaped ensaïmades with sobrassada and caramelized pumpkin in Mallorca for Carnival, *flaó* cake (page 278) made with fresh goat's or sheep's milk cheese and mint leaves (with some aniseed and anise liqueur in the crust) for Easter in Ibiza and Formentera, cookies like jam-filled *crespells* (page 294) and lard-rich, floral-shaped *pastissets* (page 291) during the summer fiestas in Menorca, *panellets* (round marzipan cookies made from ground almonds, sugar and boiled sweet potato and covered in pine nuts, page 297) for All Saints' Day in Ibiza, homemade almond nougat at Christmas, and so on.

Overall, a strong sensibility towards food and an attitude of taking little for granted remains. Nowhere is resourcefulness more keenly glimpsed (or tasted) than in the pantry, which, in many homes, still retains culinary pride of place. Along with oil, honey, pulses (legumes), rice and assorted other staples, pantries tend to hold plenty of homemade preserves. Rows of tomato preserves, from chunky tomato and pepper and puréed tomato sauce (both page 342) to tomato jams (with hints of lemon and cinnamon, page 343). Other jams, too, from fig (page 343) to melon, apricot and even lemon. Sobrassada and other types of cured sausage. Fried almonds with sea salt. Wide-mouthed jars of wild capers soaking in vinegar. Pickled shoreline sea fennel (see page 23). Dried mushrooms to add to stews or rice dishes. *Galletes d'oli* (rich, savoury olive-oil biscuits). Dried aromatic herbs gathered on spring walks. Dried chamomile. Figs dried and packed with bay leaves and anise. Tall bottles of bright green liquor with a half dozen local herbs steeped in a blend of sweet and dry anise liqueur (*herbes*, page 331).

Today, preserves remain a key element in the islands' cooking. Only some of what is grown, harvested, butchered or caught is enjoyed fresh: the rest is preserved for later. Some might consider pantries to be humble, but they demonstrate hard work, creativity and know-how, as well as a commitment to the conscientious habit of keeping them stocked.

So closely linked to the land and sea are the people and their foods that each of the four islands has its own distinctive flavours. At times they feel so avidly original that any specific influence from their complex pasts has been cooked off into something truly unique – and exquisite.

Mallorca

At 3,640 sq km/1,405 square miles, Mallorca is the largest of the Balearic Islands, and, with a population of some 950,000 people, by far the most populous. The island is roughly diamond-shaped, stretching some 100 km/62 miles north to south and 70 km/43 miles west to east. It is the only one of the Balearics with highly distinctive regions.

Running protectively across the island's northwest side are the rugged Serra de Tramuntana mountains, named after the fierce northern winds. With soaring peaks reaching 1,436 m/4,711 feet in elevation, they are visible from across the island (also usually from Menorca and occasionally even from Barcelona, some 200 km/125 miles away). Along the range's northern side, the land plunges down towards the sea, forming a rocky, cove-riddled coast; to the south, the flanks ease down through terraced slopes of olives and almonds, apricots and figs. These south-facing slopes, protected from the cold northern winds and capturing abundant sunshine, are home to the important citrus groves, with Sóller (and nearby Fornalutx, further up the slopes) at the centre of the industry. Known as the Valley of the Oranges, production dates back over seven centuries. So emblematic is the industry here that Sóller has given its name to a popular variety of orange.

A second range runs along the southeastern side of Mallorca, the smaller, lower and more rolling Serres de Llevant. The east of the island is well known for its melons and charcuterie. (And for tennis: Manacor is home to Rafa Nadal and his tennis academy.) Between these two ranges lies the central depression known as Es Pla (*pla* means 'flat'), which measures some 600 sq km/230 square miles, about 21.5 per cent of Mallorca's total area. Flour mills, windmills and old waterwheels dot an agriculture-rich landscape extensively planted with crops that generally need little irrigation – olives, grapes, almonds, cereals, non-citric fruits. Summers here are dry and winters cold and damp, with most of the rain falling in autumn. And while the climatic statistics are similar to much of the island, Es Pla lacks the moderating effects of the sea. Morning fog is common and rain downpours tend to be short and particularly strong. Each of the fourteen small villages scattered throughout Es Pla has an important weekly market (see page 37). Once (or in some cases twice) a week, the narrow streets of these quiet towns huddled around a large parish church bustle with activity. The fertile, well-watered transition area that runs between Es Pla and the Tramuntana range is known as Es Raiguer, and on its slopes grow olives, carob and almonds. Around Binissalem and Inca, Mallorca's main wine-producing area, there are vineyards. And in the south, sitting on a wide, curving bay, is the island's capital city, Palma. A key Mediterranean port founded during the Roman era, Palma's stunning old city is home to the magnificent gothic La Seu cathedral (begun in 1230, almost immediately after the Christian Reconquista, on the site of a mosque, but only finished and consecrated in 1601), as well as narrow, picturesque historic streets and a pair of particularly fantastic covered food markets (Mercat de l'Olivar and Mercat de Santa Catalina). With a population of around 425,000, it is by far the largest city in the Balearics. For perspective, the second is the abutting municipality of Calvà, while the third largest is Ibiza Town, with just 50,000 people. Maó and Ciutadella in Menorca both have populations of around 30,000 each.

Among the conquerors to arrive on Mallorca, one of the most significant was initially accidental. In 902 CE, a storm blew the fleet of a powerful Muslim leader named Isam al-Jawlani to Mallorca. At the time, the Umayyad dynasty, with their Caliphate of Córdoba, ruled well over half of the Iberian Peninsula. After seeing the rich potential of the island, al-Jawlani returned to raid and then, with the support of the Emir of Córdoba, commanded a fleet to conquer it. Renamed Madina Mauyurqa, Palma grew in importance as Mallorca prospered.

The 300 years of Moorish rule mark a rich period for the island's culinary development. During this period, many of Mallorca's prosperous farm estates were developed and villages established. Advances took place in the building of dry-stone walls, terraces, and, along with novel irrigation techniques (some of the water systems remain in use today), numerous new crops were planted. The Muslims introduced sweetening with sugar, blending sweet and savoury flavours and seasoning with a larger array of spices. Saffron, for instance, is comparatively more common in Mallorca, and the spice blend generally known as *quatre espècies* (four spices), of black pepper with cloves, cinnamon and nutmeg, remains widely used.

Mallorca's cooking is a fusion of its rich gastronomic heritage – from Roman-era sausage-making, Jewish influences in pastries and spices, and lamb dishes during the Muslim period to Catalan allioli (page 338). In the Middle Ages, the Catalans also introduced two key cooking techniques: *sofregit*, a slowly sautéed base of onions, tomatoes, often garlic and sometimes peppers that forms the foundation of many stewed dishes; and *picada*, a paste pounded from almonds, garlic and a few other ingredients that gets stirred into the dish at the end. A *picada* draws the flavours together, gives the sauce body and boldness and changes the texture and even the colour of the dish. (See pages 174 and 175 for more on these two key techniques.)

Until the mid-1950s, when Mallorca became one of the first Spanish destinations for package tourism, the island's economy was based on agriculture, livestock and fishing. Among the most important products was olive oil.

Olives and olive oil have long been a symbol and source of income for Mallorca. The production of oil dates far back to the island's ancient past, and the average age of its groves is around 500 years old (see page 36). That was a period of a massive increase in plantings and the growth of the industry. Until the mid-nineteenth century, olive oil accounted for up to 80 per cent of the island's exports in terms of value. Today, *oli* remains absolutely fundamental in the kitchen and on the table.

In 1837, Mallorca was finally connected to the mainland by steamships. At the end of the nineteenth century, vast groves of almonds were planted and many of the island's vineyards expanded, and the island experienced prosperity from the almond and wine trades, which supplemented its olive oil exports.

The sea, of course, also offers its bounty to Mallorcan cooks. From along the shoreline comes a loose collection of species called *peix de roca* (rockfish), which is used in soups, stews and for stock (broth), bream and red mullet for the frying pan (skillet), and in summer, shoals of sardines to grill over embers with friends. Fishing boats also bring back giant *anfós* (grouper) that lope along the seabed with their mouths agape, John Dory, skate (or ray) and dogfish sharks. Calamari, cuttlefish and octopus are frequently found in the pan, often stewed with plenty of onions (page 214) or in rice dishes. And the celebrated (and expensive) Sóller red prawns caught in the deep waters off Mallorca's north coast are one of the region's gastronomic highlights – and culinary icons. There is even a large sculpture of the prized crustacean in the Port de Sóller. They are grilled simply and with great devotion (page 197).

Despite being an island, pork and lamb tend to dominate, but the most famous meat comes in preserved form. Indeed, one of the things most identified with Mallorca is sobrassada, a smooth, paprika-rich sausage (the finest from the indigenous breed of black-footed pig). While often eaten on bread, it is a common ingredient in a wide assortment of dishes and sometimes even tops ensaïmades.

The flat, snail-shaped ensaïmada is the Balearic Islands' most emblematic sweet. In the 1970s, Josep Pla (1897–1981), Spain's greatest food writer, called it the 'lightest, airiest and most delicate thing in this country's confectionery'. The Mallorcan ensaïmada is considered so unique that the Spanish government awarded it Protected Geographical Indication status (Indicación Geográfica Protegida, or IGP) . Mallorca might claim to be the original creator of the delicacy, but differences on neighbouring Menorca, Ibiza and Formentera are minimal and its status on the other islands equally iconic.

While the standard ensaïmada is plain (*llisa*), *pastissers* also prepare them with *cabell d'àngel* ('angel hair', a stringy sweet made from squash pulp), creamy chocolate, apricot halves in summer or, as mentioned above, sobrassada, which offers a highly unique (and delicious) sweet-and-savoury combination. Locals and visitors alike eat them for breakfast, as an afternoon snack and for dessert.

Menorca

The furthest northeast of the Balearics, Menorca (population 100,000) is the most exposed of the four islands and catches the full force of the frequent *tramuntana* winds that blow from the north. The importance of these winds is hard to overestimate; Menorca is sometimes even called the 'island of winds'. Each direction has its own name – and character. The eight winds of Menorca, named for the direction from which they have come (not where they are heading): *tramuntana* (north), *gregal (northeast), llevant* (east), *xaloc* (southeast), *migjorn* (south), *llebeig* (southwest), *ponent* (west) and *mestral* (northwest).

Being the most distant from the mainland and having the (relatively) poorest weather meant that Menorca was largely spared the package tourist development that Mallorca and Ibiza experienced in the 1960s and 1970s, with very little development on the island's 120 beaches. In 1993, UNESCO declared Menorca a biosphere reserve. This also means that the island's original identity has remained strongly intact.

Measuring some 700 sq km/270 square miles in size, Menorca is bean-shaped, with a city at each end: the elegant one-time Muslim capital Ciutadella to the west and, to the east, Maó (Mahón in Spanish), which has been the capital of the island since the British moved it there in the eighteenth century. The island's road system looks something like the skeleton of a fish, with the vertebrae connecting these two cities and small roads that run to the sides like bones. The north coast has wind-battered headlands, doubled-over trees, dark or reddish coloured sand, and cliff-top lighthouses that sit atop sheer drops to the rolling sea, while the protected south coast is riddled with calm bays of white sand edged with pine trees. The ancient coastal path known as the Camí de Cavalls (horses' path) roughly follows the shoreline and encircles the island. The trail system has existed since 1330, when the ruling king obliged all settlers on the island to keep horses at the ready to help defend Menorca. The trail connects watchtowers, fortresses and armaments. In 2010, the trail opened in its 186-km/115-mile entirety with public right of way, passing through farms, pine forests and behind beaches. Inland, Menorca is largely farmland. Zigzagging through the fields and hedges are a staggering 11,200 km/7,000 miles of dry-stone walls, built mostly to protect the fields from *tramuntana* winds. At the centre, hovering above Es Mercadal, is Monte Toro, the island's highest peak, which reaches 358 m/1,170 feet.

Without lakes, year-round rivers, mountains or snow, and with few springs, water scarcity has always been a vital issue for Menorca, and roofs have a system of funnelling rainfall into a cistern under the house. The first big rain of the year is not collected, nor the second, but from the third onwards it is. In 1735, when Menorca was under British rule, the island's governor Richard Kane ordered a large cistern built in Es Mercadal at the centre of the island, the only town along the main road connecting Ciutadella and Maó. The *aljibe* can hold 273,000 litres/72,000 gallons and dispensed water to the town's residents until 2018, when a corner of the water-capturing roof collapsed during a particularly strong storm. (While it has been refurbished, villagers are awaiting the return of their right to collect drinking water from it every Saturday.)

Frugality rather than excess marks the cooking of Menorca, with nothing wasted, and fresh produce combined with a handful of staples dominating meals. The emphasis is on patiently coaxing out flavours and tenderness from ingredients. Legumes, root vegetables, bone-in cuts of meat, small bony fish and plenty of soups are daily meals. The most classic soup is *oliaigua* (combining the words for 'oil' and 'water', page 60), a watery *sopa* with a chunky base of onions, tomatoes and peppers that gets ladled over thin slices of dried bread and served with fresh figs. Eggs take the flavours of any season and are cooked with vegetables, sometimes as a thick tortilla with skinny and somewhat bitter stalks of wild asparagus (page 117) or scrambled with wild mushrooms (page 124). Wide slices of low-salt country *pa de pagès* fill breadbaskets, and rice and legumes are fundamental. So are potatoes, which are often sliced and baked under a layer of sliced tomatoes in a dish known as *perol* (page 88). Between those layers of potatoes and tomatoes, cooks often put all manner of other things, from lamb shoulder (page 238) to seafood. Inners and extremities are never discarded – tongue with capers (page 235) is a classic – while foraged herbs and pieces of cured sausage frequently add flavour. Tomatoes are essential to Menorcan cuisine and are often farmed without irrigation, just humidity and morning dew, yielding deeply concentrated flavours. These tomatoes get preserved for the remainder of the year, and jars of sauce (page 341) are, for many homes, the most important item in the traditional Menorcan pantry.

From the wet winters and springs comes an important dairy (and cheese) industry (by far the most significant in the Balearics), and with that a number of popular milky desserts, including rice pudding scented with lemon peels and cinnamon (page 311) and *menjar blanc* (literally 'white food', page 304), a mediaeval pudding today prepared with milk, sugar and cornflour (cornstarch).

There is also a deep love of often elaborate (or at least laborious) sweet treats, from ensaïmades and lard-rich cookies to the popular spongy cake with apricot halves on top (page 283). In 1887, the island, with a population of 35,000, had forty *patisseries* and three chocolate factories with their own shops – and one dentist.

* * *

Menorca was home to the mysterious Talayotic people, who lived on the island from 2100 BCE. The roughly 1,600 megalithic sites they left speak of a people who lived from agriculture, and they ceremoniously buried their dead in caves beside the sea or under large stacks of rocks in the form of inverted boats. The island has one of the world's highest concentrations of prehistoric archaeological sites in an inhabited area, with ruins found in fields, along walking paths and beside farms, where some still shelter livestock – a living part of the landscape. In 2023, Menorca's prehistoric Talayotic sites were inscribed on the UNESCO World Heritage List.

Rome took control of Menorca in 123 BCE, when Barbary pirates were using the island as a base for raids around the region, and established the ports of Ciutadella, Maó and Sanitja (in the north). After the collapse of the Roman Empire, Menorca was ruled (and plundered) by the Vandals and then the Byzantine Empire. In 903 CE, Muslims from the Caliphate of Córdoba on the Spanish peninsula conquered the island. Considerable Muslim and Jewish emigration to Manûrqa (as the island was known) followed. The island's only significant city was Madînat al Jazîra (modern-day Ciutadella), with the majority of the population living on large farmsteads. After Catalan Christian forces took the island in 1287 (they had already been ruling Mallorca for six decades, and been happy enough until then with just an annual tribute from the Muslims on Menorca), the Muslim and Jewish populations either converted or emigrated.

Uniquely in the Balearic Islands, Menorca has historical links with Great Britain, which ruled the island from 1708 to 1802, with a brief mid-century break when the French wrested away control for seven years. The British introduced pigs from Sardinia and sheep from North Africa, and instilled a tradition of using butter, a particular affinity for cucumbers and a range of puddings and jams. The first British governor, Richard Kane, moved the island's capital from Ciutadella to Maó and had a road built connecting the two cities. He also introduced new varieties of apples and plums, as well as black-and-white Friesian cattle, which could produce more milk than the native breed of cow.

The British also established gin-making, which remains the island's most important spirit (see page 329). Much of the production goes into the island's drink of choice, the *pomada*. Prepared with lemon juice (or lemon soda) and sugar, it gets popped in the freezer and is served slushy. Drinking small cups of *pomada* is synonymous with summer and the fiestas when each town celebrates its patron saint, beginning with Sant Joan (in Ciutadella) at the end of June, opening the calendar of festivities, and finishing with Sant Nicolau (in Es Mercadal and Monte Toro) in mid-September.

Ibiza (Eivissa)

Considering its small size – 572 sq km/221 square miles, or a touch smaller than Menorca – and popularity in summer, when its population of 160,000 swells to around 1 million, Ibiza continues to feel surprisingly rural outside of a handful of areas. The Greeks called Ibiza, neighbouring Formentera and a couple of uninhabited islets between them the Pityusic Islands, which meant 'covered in pine trees'. The description, at least for Ibiza, still holds true, with generous parts of the island still covered with vibrant green pine trees.

Ibiza Town – the island's capital (population 50,000) – was founded by Phoenician settlers in 654 BCE and then fell to Carthaginians, who ruled from their base in Carthage on the southside of the Mediterranean in modern-day Tunisia. While Mallorca and Menorca continued with their local Talayotic culture, Ibiza became a satellite of Carthage and an important trade centre for salt and olive oil. After Carthage was destroyed by the Romans in 146 BCE, Ibiza was the only remaining Punic city. That didn't last long, though. Romans conquered the Balearics less than two decades later.

Under the Romans, Ibiza (known then as Ebusus) exported salt, oil, honey, wine, dried figs and raisins, and was a key place to prepare barrels of Rome's beloved fermented garum fish sauce for export. The arrival of the Vandals (in 424 CE) followed by the Byzantines (in 535) saw the island gradually shrink in regional stature and agricultural productivity. But under Moorish control from 902, Yebisah (as it was called in Arabic) developed into a fertile island, with improvements in the island's agriculture, irrigation and salt pans. Many of these innovations remain in place. One that can still be seen today is in Es Broll de Buscastell, a valley in the central north of the island. From the Es Broll spring, water flows through a series of canals and pools to irrigate the valley's crop-filled terraces built up with stone walls. The system was built about a thousand years ago.

In 1235, Jaume I (King James I of Aragón) conquered Yebisah after a long siege. Catalan replaced Arabic as the main language, Catholicism became the official religion and the island's name changed to Eivissa. War and the Black Plague of 1348 reduced the population to just 500 people. In the centuries that followed, those who arrived to repopulate the island carried with them pigs as well as the tradition of bookending many stewed dishes with a sautéed vegetable *sofregit* base at the beginning and stirring in a *picada* of pounded nuts and herbs at the end. Ibiza retained semi-autonomy until it was abolished by King Phillip V of Spain in 1715, and Madrid and the Catholic Church took over many of the island's affairs.

Apart from the ancient capital founded nearly 3,000 years ago, nearly all of the island's towns were established in the eighteenth and nineteenth centuries. Centred around a whitewashed church, with rustling palms that throw sharp afternoon shadows on the smooth walls, each town took the name of a Catholic saint: Sant Josep, Sant Antoni, Santa Agnès, Santa Eulària, Sant Joan and so on. Regular ferry service from the Spanish mainland arrived in the 1930s, and the first wave of tourists not long after. The likes of Brigitte Bardot, Truman Capote and Errol Flynn were among the early celebrities diving into its clear waters and lounging on yachts anchored just offshore (and partying onshore). Today, A-list actors, musicians and sport's biggest global stars stroll its sandy beaches, dine in its restaurants and dance all night to its beats in renowned clubs.

Ibiza's warm climate and high number of hours of sunshine is not only a boon when it comes to attracting visitors, but also means that a wide range of fruit can grow here, with plenty of lemons, watermelons, pomegranates, melons, apples, pears, grapes, apricots, plums and quince. Figs are perhaps the most emblematic, especially in dried form known as *xereques* (see page 207). Sun-dried and packed into ceramic pots with thyme and other spices, *xereques* are traditionally left until Christmas and then enjoyed over the months that follow for dessert with some of Ibiza's crunchy toasted almonds.

That powerful sun is also vital to two of Ibiza's ancient and important industries. In the very south of Ibiza, there are some 400 hectares/988 acres of still-working *salines* (salt pans) that the Phoenicians built as far back as 540 BCE.

(For perspective, New York City's Central Park is 341 hectares/843 acres.) Sea water is pumped into the loose grid of shallow pans in May and left to evaporate for about three months. During the extreme heat of August, workers rake out crystals from the now pinkish-tinted pans. It is a pure product with nothing added, just clean sea flavours and naturally white crystals created with the aid of the sun and wind. Salt is good for health and seasoning dishes but – more importantly in the past – is also key to preserving food. Salt was *or blanc* ('white gold'), and Ibiza's pans are among the most important in the entire Mediterranean. For 2,500 years – until tourism arrived in the second half of the twentieth century – salt was the island's only steady source of revenue.

In 122 BCE, the island – and its valuable salt pans – fell under the control of the Romans, who paid their soldiers partly in salt, called *salarium argentum* or 'salt money'. (This is the source for the modern-day term 'salary'.) The Romans, Vandals and then Byzantines maintained the pans over the next centuries, but it was the Muslims, arriving in the tenth century, who introduced hydraulic technology with a sophisticated system of channels, sluice gates and mills. Following the Christian Reconquista of the island in 1235, production rose to as much as 25,000 tons a year, or some 55 million pounds of salt. After the War of Spanish Succession (1701–1715), the Spanish Crown in Madrid put Ibiza and its saltworks firmly under its control. Extracting salt and maintaining the pans was gruelling work, and in seventeenth-century Ibiza, it was done in part by enslaved people and in the eighteenth century by prisoners. New ways to preserve foods in the nineteenth century drove down demand and production fell to just 7,000 tons. The pans were sold to a private company in 1871, and after new investment in the 1880s, production quickly shot up to 50,000 tons a year. At the beginning of the twentieth century, some 800 men were employed for the harvest. Today, tall piles of white salt gleam in the sun, and it remains a vital industry – and a key element in preserving Ibiza's olives, capers, charcuterie and cheeses. The salt pans are also an important wetland. Home to over 200 species of birds, including bright pink flamingos, the pans were declared part of a national park in 2001.

Ibiza's olive oil is another ancient industry that was gradually improved over the years and remains key today. Excavations and historical evidence show that olive oil production dates back to at least 450 BCE. In the third century BCE, there were almost two dozen 'agricultural operations' on Ibiza that produced between 30,000 and 60,000 litres/8,000 and 16,000 gallons of olive oil. In the first century CE, records show how important it was to the economy of the island. Today, Ibiza's fruity green olive oil remains exceptional. 'Aceite de Ibiza' with IGP status is made from three varieties of olives (arbequina, picual and koroneiki), either alone or blended. The island's mild springs are particularly conducive to flowering and pollination, while the long hours of sunshine and high temperatures help form high-quality oils.

Along with the important use of olive oil, cooking on Ibiza has many similarities to the other Balearic Islands. Lamb and pork are key meats, legumes and produce from the fields form an important part of the diet, and there is a strong love for fish and seafood. Seasonings can taste distinctive, though, with plenty of spices (cinnamon, nutmeg, aniseed, saffron) and herbs (bay leaf, mint, rosemary, fennel). Among the most popular fresh herbs in the kitchen are a local variety of wild thyme collected around the island and *moraduix* (marjoram).

The island's emblematic cake is *flaó* (page 278), which has its origins in the Middle Ages. Traditionally it is eaten on Easter Sunday, but it has recently become a year-round favourite. Another popular dessert is a version of bread pudding made with pieces of days-old ensaïmades soaked in a blend of milk, eggs and cinnamon and baked in a *greixonera* (page 308), a wide, deeply concave terracotta dish that gives the beloved dish its name.

In late spring, people across the island can be seen picking wild herbs, such as rosemary, fennel, lemon verbena, oregano, juniper, English lavender and sage. They aren't destined for the cooking pot as much as for glass bottles to make the island's deeply popular herb liqueur, *herbes eivissenques* (or *hierbas ibicencas*, page 331). The herbs are trimmed and laboriously pushed down through the neck of glass bottles with the help of a long, skinny stick called a *fura*. They are then filled with a blend of sweet and dry anise liqueur, corked and left to macerate for four to six months, during which time they take on their brilliant golden colour and the aromas (and goodness) of the herbs (see page 330 for more on this tradition). If a small tipple of chilled *herbes* is the classic entrance to an Ibizan meal, then a cup of flaming, fortified *café caleta* has become a popular way to end it.

In the 1950s, to fight off the high humidity and cold nights at sea, fishermen in a small *caleta* (cove) just west of the island's main city began to brew coffee in a terracotta pot. The drink was fortified with brandy and rum, sweetened with sugar and infused with lemon and orange peels and cinnamon. The likely inspiration was a local who did his compulsory military service in Galicia and saw *queimada*, a flaming punch with ancient Celtic traditions made with aguardiente (a spirit distilled from the remains of winemaking), and, back home on a damp winter evening, adapted the flaming drink to spirits favoured by Ibiza's fishermen. In the years since, it has become incredibly popular. Sipped in one of the island's boho-chic beachside bars, a glass of *café caleta* makes a particularly pleasing way to finish a meal with friends.

Formentera

Nearly attached to the southern tip of Ibiza is the tiny island of Formentera. Measuring just 83 sq km/32 square miles in size, it has no airport. Everything comes by boat from Ibiza. The frequent high-speed ferries make the Ibiza–Formentera run in 25 minutes, while slow ones carrying cars and cargo do it in one hour.

While Formentera lacks the geographic diversity of the other Balearic Islands, the jewelled blue and green waters around it are the clearest in all of Spain. That comes from being surrounded with meadows of *Posidonia oceanica* (Neptune grass), an endemic protected seagrass responsible for the crystal-clear water by filtering sediments, while providing a home to more than a thousand marine animals. From nearly any place on Formentera, the Mediterranean is just minutes away.

Some 19 km/12 miles long and a mere 2 km/1 mile wide in places, the flat island, with the tilted-z shape of a seahorse, is etched with coves and dune-backed beaches and lagoons. Juniper and pine trees dominate the flora, along with, on the south side of the island, its iconic fig trees with their low, sprawling crowns. On the north side of the island near the port are ancient salt pans that date from the Phoenician era. The island's name comes from the Latin *frumentairum*, meaning granary. Yet the arid, low-lying island has very little agriculture. It is so small that, essentially, people had to be both farmers and fishermen. With its dry summers, lack of rainfall and problems of salinity in the unproductive soil, Formentera was the most challenging of the Balearic Islands for cooks, who had the most limited pantries. Outside of the few towns, people lived in isolated farmhouses that were traditionally self-sufficient. Raising sheep, goats, pigs, chickens and rabbits complimented the crops they could grow.

Formentera's population of 12,000 lives largely in or around the island's six villages (Sant Francesc Xavier, with 3,000 inhabitants, is the largest). While there are signs of settlements dating back to the end of the third millennium BCE, it has never been densely populated. From 1403 until 1651 it was uninhabitable and completely abandoned due to Barbary pirate raids from North Africa and the Black Plague. Used largely for grazing flocks of sheep, the island didn't have a stable population living on it again until the eighteenth century.

Such extreme isolation meant that islanders were forced to depend heavily on what local products they could catch, forage or grow. The scarcity of these required people to find ways to use the limited resources to their fullest. The

way they produce figs is among the most unique. Sprawling fig trees with broad canopies created by propping branches on poles have long provided an important and prized staple. In the summer sun, figs are dried, packed into clay pots with aniseed and bay leaves and eaten throughout the year as a snack or as dessert with almonds. Poor ones, or figs that have fallen to the ground, are used to feed pigs. Fig trees remain emblematic on the island. (For more on Formentera's unique fig traditions, see page 307).

Salted and dried fish called *peix sec* is another example of self-sufficiency and nearly unwavering tradition, the same today as it was thousands of years ago. Scaleless, cartilaginous fish – most commonly *rajada* (skate) and *el gat* (dogfish sharks) – are salted, then hung on the sharpened branches of savin juniper trees to dry for three or four days. Warmed for a few minutes on a hot frying pan (skillet) to soften, the pieces are cut up and flaked, then stored in jars covered in olive oil. It takes about 80 kg/175 lb of fish to get 30 kg/65 lb of finished dried fish. Still deeply popular, it goes most famously into *enciam pagès* (farmer's salad, page 82) with pieces of crusty bread (baked until dry and crispy for longer preservation), tomatoes, peppers and onions. When tomatoes are at their peak in summer, this is often simplified to a perfect trio of flavours with the tomatoes, thin slices of onions and some *peix sec* (page 78).

A few decades ago, the salt used for drying fish came from the saltworks in the northwest of the island. Until exploitation was abandoned in 1983, the pans had been in operation for thousands of years. Historians speculate salt production began during the time of the Phoenicians, who had a small naval base nearby. During the Roman area, there was a settlement beside one of the salt lakes. When the Catalans looked at conquering neighbouring Ibiza in the thirteenth century, Formentera's saltworks were included in discussions of compensation. The Spanish Crown took control of them in 1715 and eventually sold them off to a private company in 1871. Today the ancient pans form part of the Parc Natural de Ses Salines and are not currently in use for producing salt.

Some fishermen still prepare *peix sec* for their own use, and drying fish can occasionally be seen hanging near the dry docks of *llaüts* (small boats) in sheltered coves like Es Caló. But a new law now prohibits the selling of it without a proper licence, and there is now just a single commercial company, Peix Sec de Formentera. The small family company follows ancient methods for drying skate but in a more controlled environment (after soaking the fish in brine, the pieces are hung up in a space completely enclosed with fine mesh). A jar of this is the top culinary souvenir to carry off the island.

Formentera has superb honey from bees that have pollinated wild thyme and rosemary, delicious apricots in early summer, excellent dense breads and fresh cheese made from a blend of goat's and sheep's milk. Among the typical dishes from the Formentera kitchen are broad (fava) beans (often in an egg tortilla, page 118), fish stews (page 57), lamb chops with red peppers and potatoes (page 242), stuffed squid, squid stewed in its own ink (page 202) and fish boiled with potatoes and served with a loose sauce of allioli and minced parsley whisked into some of the stock (broth) (page 168). The classic fisherman's breakfast on Formentera (as well as Ibiza) is a plate of *frit de pop* (page 217), octopus with fried potatoes, onions and peppers, eaten with plenty of bread, a hearty glass of wine and followed with a cup of coffee (not uncommonly spiked with brandy). *Frit de pop* remains a beloved classic that today is eaten any time. Seafood rice dishes are popular, and remain something celebratory and eaten among friends and family.

To end a meal, the most famous sweet is *flaó* cheesecake (page 208). It is so popular that almost the entire production of the island's cheese heads to bakeries for *flaó*.

Notes

ALLIOLI As the name of this widely used emulsion indicates, it is made from garlic (*all*) and (*i*) olive oil (*oli*) when prepared in the traditional method in a mortar. Today, most versions are made with an immersion hand blender and include an egg to help it bind, as well as some vinegar and a pinch of salt. See also page 339.

BAY LEAF (*llorer*) Bay laurel trees are found widely around the islands, including growing wild. Local bay leaves tend not to be overly large in size. They are frequently added to soups, stews, braised dishes and many sauces.

BOTIFARRÓ (pl. *botifarrons*) Rather than being dry-cured, these large sausages are boiled after being stuffed. *Botifarrons* can be sliced and eaten, grilled or stewed. In Menorca, there are two distinctive versions: *negre* (black) include blood to give them their colour, and are seasoned principally with fennel and black pepper, while *blanc* (white) omit blood, are seasoned with cinnamon, nutmeg and black pepper and are wrapped in a thin layer of natural fat. In Mallorca, *botifarró* gets seasoned with paprika, black pepper and cinnamon, and sometimes includes pine nuts, while blood is often added to the stuffing to give it a blackish colour. There are sweet and spicy versions in Mallorca.

CAPERS (*tàperes*) Capers add zesty, tangy notes to salads and sauces. Capers are the unopened, immature flower buds of the caper berry, picked with care from the thorny shrubs. (The Latin name indicates these spiny thorns: *Capparis spinosa*.) *Tàperes* grow wild on all of the Balearic Islands among rocks and walls near the sea. They are also cultivated commercially on each island. As with olives, they need to be pickled first to become edible. Vibrant green when freshly picked, the buds get washed and then soaked in brine for two or three days as they soften and turn a darker shade of green. (Traditionally, enough salt was added until a fresh egg could float in the water.) Once drained, the capers are put into glass jars and covered with vinegar. After a couple of weeks, they are ready to eat. They can keep for about two years but are best used within one year, as the quality fades. Rinse before using.

DRIED FISH (*peix sec*) Made using skate (ray) or a local dogfish shark, Formentera's famous *peix sec* is salted, dried, shredded and stored in olive oil. When removing pieces of fish, let the oil drain back into the jar, gently pressing the shreds of fish with two spoons or forks to help. The flavour of *peix sec* is milder than anchovies but bolder than canned tuna. The best substitute is high-quality tuna or *bonito del norte* in olive oil with an anchovy or two.

FOUR SPICES (*quatre espècies*) The Mallorcan spice blend of black pepper with clove, cinnamon and nutmeg is widely used in a number of the island's classic dishes, including *arròs brut* (Dirty' Rice, page 140) and *sopes mallorquines* (Mallorcan Soups', page 101). Black pepper is the principal component. Substitute with individual spices, leading with black pepper and using small amounts of the other three.

LARD (*seu de porc* or *saïm*) Rendered pork fat remains the fat of choice in many of the classic Balearic dishes, from flatbread *coca* bases to certain cookies and stuffed pastries. While using for frying is nowadays rare, lard continues to be widely used in many traditional pastries for the incomparable flakiness it gives and the subtle pork flavour it adds. *Llard* is the general name in Catalan, though in Menorca it is called *seu de porc* and in Mallorca *saïm*, where it gives its name to the region's most famous pastry, ensaïmada. In Spanish, it is called *manteca*. (See page 306 for more.) There are some easy substitutions, but as lard is pure fat (100 per cent), not all are 1:1. You can substitute:

* Vegetable shortening, in equal amounts.
* Butter, which is about 80 per cent fat, so use slightly more. For 100 g (½ cup) lard, use 120 g (½ cup plus 2 tablespoons) butter; for 200 g (1 cup) lard use 240 g (¼ cup) butter.
* A neutral vegetable oil, using around three quarters of the amount: for 100 g (½ cup) lard, use 75 ml (⅓ cup) oil.

MARJORAM (*moraduix*) This oregano-like herb has sweet, piny and citrus notes, and is more floral and woodsy than oregano. Used fresh, it is particularly popular in Mallorca and also Ibiza to flavour soups, legumes and snails. Substitute with fresh oregano.

MENORCAN CHEESE (*formatge de Maó* or *queso de Mahón*) Menorca's cow's-milk cheeses are sold in various levels of maturation. The best-known is a dense, semi-cured cheese with small holes, buttery texture and nutty aromas. See page 90 for more.

OLIVE OIL (*oli*) Many pantries have bottles of two types of olive oil on the shelf: extra-virgin and a milder one for frying and using in cakes. The latter is usually a blend of refined olive oil (which has no colour or flavour) with some extra-virgin oil added. Bottles of these often read '*suave*'.

PAPRIKA (*pebre bord*) As a key ingredient in sobrassada, a significant amount of paprika is used in preparing charcuterie. In Menorca, it is mixed with olive oil and rubbed on the rinds of the island's famous cheese when preparing. But cooks use it in a wide range of dishes. Mallorca's paprika uses the *tap de cortí* variety of pepper, and the final orangish-red spice has a sweet creaminess to it that lacks both spiciness and bitterness. It is hard to understate the importance of paprika on the cuisine – for flavour, preservation and even colour. See page 91 for more.

PICKLED SEA FENNEL (*fonoll marí*) Called sea fennel for the aroma that is reminiscent of fennel, *Crithmum maritimum* grows in the rocky crevices along the shoreline, where it catches moisture-laden sea breezes. The tender leaves and shoots are picked between spring and summer before it flowers (in Mallorca, June is considered the best month), and stored in vinegar. It is eaten alongside olives and pickles, most famously with slices of bread (*pamboli*, page 28). Rich in Vitamin C, it was used in the past to help fight scurvy.

RICE (*arròs*) Cooking with rice on the islands is about soaking up the flavours of the pot or pan: the stubby grains act as absorbent vehicles. (This is as opposed to boiling the rice plain and then adding sauce on top.) The rice should be short- or medium-grain white rice. Do not use long-grain, parboiled or instant rice, which will not be able to absorb as much liquid as short- or medium-grain varieties.

ROCKFISH (*peix de roca*) The generic name for smallish varieties of fish that live in the rocks around the seabed. Few are large enough to eat alone, and they tend to be bony – but they are flavourful and are key to soups and stocks (broths). And assortment of varieties is sometimes sold in the market together as *peix de sopa* (fish for soup).

SAFFRON (*safrà*) When buying saffron, look for threads that are deep red to almost purple. Avoid buying saffron powder, which might be adulterated. Powder also loses its potency more quickly. Store away from the light, which will damage saffron's delicate flavours. See opposite for details on using saffron.

SOBRASSADA The spreadable, paprika-rich cured sausage is one of the region's most iconic products. It is eaten on bread as a charcuterie and widely used as an ingredient to various dishes. See page 208 for more on sobrassada. Note that in Spanish, it is spelled with a single *s* (sobrasada). Substitute non-spicy chorizo with the casing removed. For some of the colour and flavour properties, make a paste with paprika, salt and either lard or olive oil.

SOUP BREAD (*pa de sopes*) In Menorca, it is typical to serve the island's most famous soups – from the tomato-based oliaigua (page 60) to the fish or lobster caldereta (pages 54 and 52) – over very thin (5-mm/¼-inch-thick) slices of day-old bread. These are generally strips about 5 cm (2 inches) wide and two or three times that in length. The pieces are often broken up, but this doesn't matter. Bakeries sell bags of them under the name *sopes* or *pa de sopes*. In Menorca, they are usually the typical low-salt white bread. In Mallorca, where they can also be made with brown bread, they are key to the island's famous *sopes mallorquines* (page 101), cooked vegetables served atop the *sopes*, which absorb all of the liquid. To make at home, very thinly slice pieces of a long loaf or baguette and gently toast on a baking sheet in the oven until dry but still quite pale in colour.

SQUID OR CALAMARI AND CUTTLEFISH (*calamar* and *sípia*) Although calamari are technically a type of squid – calamari tend to be smaller and more tender while squid have arrow-shaped fins – the two names are often used interchangeably in English. In Catalan, they are called the same thing, *calamar*. Cuttlefish are shorter and less cylindrical than calamari, and have a brittle, Styrofoam-like bone on the inside rather than the transparent, plastic-like quill found in squid. Importantly, cuttlefish tubes are thicker and more common to use in stews and rice dishes. See opposite for cleaning instructions.

SQUID OR CUTTLEFISH INK (*tinta de calamar* or *tinta de sípia*) Mercury-coloured ink sacs are found beneath the tentacles of squid and cuttlefish. These can be used in cooking for not only their colouring properties but also the flavour they add. When cleaning, remove carefully to avoid breaking (or ask your fish supplier to reserve them when cleaning). The ink is also sold separately in shops, often in 4-gram/½-ounce packets. Generally, two packets are enough for a dish for 4–6 people.

TOOLS

IMMERSION HAND BLENDER (*batedora de braç* or *minipimer*) An immersion hand blender is the workhorse of the Balearic kitchen, used for everything from puréeing soups or jams right in the pot to making quick allioli and mayonnaise emulsions.

MORTAR AND PESTLE (*morter i mà de morter*) While there are also wood and metal ones, most mortars are glazed ceramic with a thick wooden pestle (in Catalan, *mà* means 'hand'). These are used for pounding nuts and spices and to make a picada – of nuts, garlic and herbs; see page 175 for more on preparing a picada. Mortars are also the traditional tool for preparing allioli and mayonnaise emulsions.

PAELLA PAN Wide paella pans are used for making *arròs sec* (dry rice), such as the Ibizan classic *arròs a banda* (page 131). Wide pans need a wide, powerful

and uniformly distributed heat source so the rice can cook evenly. This can be done by using a wide gas ring that fits into the burner, cooking over multiple burners and turning the pan frequently, or cooking over a barbecue.

SHALLOW CASSEROLE PAN The most traditional cooking pot in the Balearic Islands is a shallow, round casserole dish that can be used on the stovetop and in the oven. It is both flameproof and ovenproof. They are used for making a range of dishes, from rices, stews and braised recipes to cakes and puddings baked in the oven. While the general Catalan name is *cassola* (*cazuela* in Spanish), in Mallorca they are called *greixonera* and in Menorca *tià*. Traditional ones are made from terracotta. If using a terracotta casserole dish, soak it first overnight in water and let it dry well before using for the first time.

TECHNIQUES

BLANCHING AND PEELING RAW ALMONDS
Put the almonds in a bowl, cover with boiling water and let sit for a few minutes until the peels loosen. Drain, slip off the peels with your fingers and spread out the almonds on paper towels to dry.

DRY-TOASTING PINE NUTS To fully draw out their rich, nutty flavours, pine nuts should be dry-toasted in a small ungreased frying pan (skillet) over medium–low heat for a couple of minutes until aromatic and golden. Stir frequently while toasting and immediately transfer to a plate to stop them from cooking further.

CLEANING WILD MUSHROOMS To clean foraged wild mushrooms, simply brush and wipe clean, using a lightly moistened towel if needed. Cultivated mushrooms can be quickly dunked in cold water, drained and patted dry with paper towels.

CLEANING ARTICHOKES To keep artichokes from darkening while cleaning, fill a bowl with cool water and drop in a couple of lemon wedges. To clean, work with one artichoke at a time. Cut or pull away the tough outer petals and trim away any fibrous parts. With a paring knife, trim the stem and peel away the outside if tough. Cut the artichoke into quarters or eighths as desired and immediately drop into the water with the lemon wedges. Repeat with the remaining artichokes. Leave the artichokes in the water until ready to use. When ready, drain and pat dry with paper towels.

BUYING AND CLEANING SQUID AND CUTTLEFISH When buying, be sure that the squid (calamari) or cuttlefish have a pleasant sea smell, and that the skin, head and arms are all intact and fresh looking.

To clean a squid, hold it in one hand, firmly grab the tentacles with the other and pull out from the tube. Trim the head below the 'beak' and discard. Gently cut away (and reserve if desired) the mercury-coloured ink sac behind the eyes. Pull out and discard the transparent quill from the tube and then run a finger through the tube to remove any gelatinous substance. Gently wash, rubbing away the purplish membrane on the outside of the tube (a clean dish towel can make this easier). Remove the 'wings' on the tube and reserve. Cut the tube, tentacles and wings as desired.

To clean a cuttlefish, make a superficial cut along the back and remove the brittle white bone. Using your thumbs, separate the body from the insides. Gently pull the insides away by grasping the tentacles. Carefully remove the ink sac without breaking. Rinse the body with water. Peel away the skin. Trim the legs below the eyes and remove the hard beak in the tentacles. Rinse and cut into pieces as desired.

BUYING AND CLEANING OCTOPUS Frozen octopus is usually sold already cleaned. Once thawed, rinse thoroughly and check the suction cups for any sand or grit. When buying fresh octopus, be sure that the octopus has a pleasant sea smell, and that the skin, head and arms are all intact and fresh looking. Remove and discard the eyes. Push the beak out from between the arms and discard, and carefully remove the ink sac. Remove everything from inside the sack-like head and discard. Rinse the body and legs under running water, making sure that any sand or grit is removed from the suction cups.

GRATING TOMATOES Rather than peeling and chopping tomatoes, grate them by cutting in half crosswise. Working over a bowl, gently squeeze out the seeds and run a finger through the seed cavity. Strain the liquid, pressing to get all of the juices, and reserve. Cup a tomato half in your palm and slowly grate on a box grater until the skin peels back flat and all the flesh has been scraped away. Discard the flattened skin. Repeat with the remaining tomato halves. Add the reserved juices to the grated pulp.

USING SAFFRON To tap the full colour and aroma properties of saffron, the threads should be lightly dry-toasted for 2–3 minutes in a small, ungreased frying pan (skillet) over medium–low heat and then crushed with dry fingers or in a mortar with a pestle. Alternatively, steep for about 20 minutes in hot liquid. Incorporate the golden, highly aromatic liquid into the dish (along with the threads themselves, too, if desired). A small pinch of threads is enough in most cases.

DESALTING SALT COD Salt cod needs to be desalted in water before it can be used. The water removes the salt, rehydrates the fish and softens the flesh. Depending on the size of the piece, the process takes 1–4 days, and you will need to change the water a few times a day. Pieces of boneless fillets cut from the *llom* (loin) that are about 2.5 cm/1 inch thick should take 2–3 days. Smaller boneless and skinless pieces can take as little as 24–36 hours.

To desalt: Rinse the pieces of salt cod under cool running water. Put the cod in a large bowl and cover with fresh water. Wait a few moments and drain. Rinse the bowl and refill with cool water. Set the pieces in the water skin-side up, put the bowl in the refrigerator and let soak for 12 hours. Drain, rinse out the bowl and refill with water. Soak in the refrigerator for another 12 hours. For the next 24 hours, change the water every 6–8 hours. Set the pieces with the skin-side down during the final 12 hours. Drain, rinse the cod and gently squeeze out some of the excess water. With the skin-side facing up, set in a strainer and let drain for at least 30 minutes. To check if it is ready, taste a pinch of the fish. It should be slightly salty but not disagreeably so. If it is still too salty, change the water and soak for longer. Check the fish for bones and remove before using in a recipe.

CHAPTER 1

BREADS, FLATBREADS & SAVOURY PASTRIES

'Bread with Oil'

Preparation time: 10 minutes
Serves: 4

4–8 large slices of country-style bread,
    preferably brown or wholegrain
3–4 small very ripe tomatoes
Extra-virgin olive oil, for drizzling
Slices of cured cold cuts or cheese,
    to taste
Pickled olives, preferably cracked green
    ones, to garnish, optional
4 tablespoons capers (see page 23),
    rinsed, optional
4–8 whole pickled green peppers
    (ideally Spanish guindilla), optional
Pickled sea fennel (*fonoll marí*, see
    page 23), optional
Flaky sea salt

30 ✳

One of Mallorca's most iconic foods, *pa amb oli* – 'bread with oil' – usually goes by *pamboli.* The name is slightly misleading as there is plenty more than oil on the bread. In Catalunya they call it 'bread with tomato', though it is the same as the Mallorcan 'bread with oil'. Wide slices of country bread get rubbed with tomato, drizzled with olive oil and topped with *embotits* (local charcuterie) or cheese, and are eaten accompanied by a quartet of preserves: cracked green olives, pickled sea fennel, capers and small pickled peppers. The Mallorcan friar Jaume Martí Oliver documented a recipe for *pa amb oli* in the mid-1700s, and it is so beloved today that there are even songs about it. *Pamboli* is more than a snack – it's a meal.

✳ Toast the bread, if desired.

✳ Halve the tomatoes and rub firmly on one side of each slice of bread, very lightly squeezing to help release the juices (but not too much of the pulp), until the bread is moist and reddish. Place one or two slices on each plate. Generously drizzle the bread with oil and sprinkle with a pinch of salt. Cover with slices of charcuterie or cheese.

✳ Serve with some pickled olives, capers, peppers and/or sea fennel (if using) on the plate beside the bread.

Toasted Bread
with Sobrassada & Honey

Preparation time: 5 minutes
Cooking time: 5 minutes
Serves: 4

200 g/7 oz sobrassada (see page 208),
　preferably mature, cut into slices
　about 5 mm/¼ inch thick
4 thick slices of country-style bread
　(about 1.5 cm/⅔ inch thick)
Slices of cured cheese, preferably
　Queso Mahón-Menorca, to taste,
　optional
4 teaspoons honey, or as needed

5 ✳ 30

Few trios of ingredients go together as perfectly as a wide slice of toasted country-style bread, sobrassada – cured, paprika-rich pork sausage – and honey. This classic Balearic treat is perfect for a late breakfast, an afternoon snack or as part of a meal. The honey should be a bit runny (put the jar in a bowl of hot water if needed). A popular addition is Menorcan cheese. Lay some thin slices on top at the end and slide it back under the oven grill (broiler) for a moment, to soften rather than melt.

✳ Preheat the oven grill (broiler) to medium.

✳ Remove the casing from the sobrassada. Lay the bread on a baking sheet. Lightly toast under the grill on both sides for a few minutes, turning as needed. Top the slices with sobrassada and return the baking tray to the oven. Cook under the grill until the sobrassada begins to sweat its oil, about 1 minute. Add the cheese (if using), slide back into the oven and grill for a few more minutes until the cheese begins to soften.

✳ Remove from the oven, drizzle with the honey and serve immediately.

Sobrassada with Apple,
Honey & Thyme on Toasted Bread

Preparation time: 10 minutes
Cooking time: 15 minutes
Serves: 4

2 tart green apples
100–120 g/3½–4 oz sobrassada
    (see page 208), cut crosswise into
    slices about 1 cm/½ inch thick and
    casing removed
4 tablespoons honey
4 large slices of country-style bread
Extra-virgin olive oil, for drizzling
Sprigs fresh thyme, leaves stripped
    from the stalk, to garnish

DF ✳ 5 ✳ 30

Sobrassada with honey on toasted bread (page 30) is a quintessential and simple Balearic combination. Sobrassada's flavours also combine perfectly with cooked fresh fruit, and pairing it with sweetened apple slices is commonplace. While sometimes the bread is omitted, I like to use slices of the island's darker breads as a base and sprinkle plenty of fresh thyme from my garden over the top. This is one variation of the household favourite that all our guests eventually get.

✳ Peel the apples, quarter lengthwise and remove the core. Cut into slices about 5 mm/¼ inch thick and set aside.

✳ Heat an ungreased frying pan over medium heat, add the sobrassada and cook, turning once, until it changes colour, about 2 minutes total. Transfer to a plate.

✳ In the same pan with the oil left behind by the sobrassada, add the apple slices, honey and 4 tablespoons water. Cook, turning the slices gently, until tender but not yet mushy or breaking apart, about 10 minutes. Remove from the heat.

✳ Toast the bread. Arrange the slices on plates and drizzle with oil. Arrange the apple slices on the toast and place pieces of sobrassada on top. Spoon over some of the oil from the pan, generously sprinkle with thyme leaves and serve immediately.

Bread with Wine & Sugar

Preparation time: 5 minutes
Serves: 1

1 large slice of country-style bread
Red wine, for drizzling
Sugar, for sprinkling

V ✳ VEG ✳ DF ✳ 5 ✳ 30

While it hardly requires a proper recipe, and is certainly less popular than it was in the past, it's impossible to imagine a collection of traditional Balearic recipes that doesn't include *pa amb vi*, slices of one- or two-day-old bread given a sprinkling of red wine and sugar. This simple item was once the classic *berenar* (mid-morning or afternoon snack) for many, kids included. For a standard slice of country loaf that is about 25 cm/10 inches wide, use 3 or 4 tablespoons of wine.

✳ Set the bread on a plate. Slowly drizzle over just enough wine to fully moisten the slice. Sprinkle with sugar and serve.

Olive Oil
in Mallorca

Located at the foot of Mount Teix on the north-facing slopes of Mallorca's Serra de Tramuntana range, Deià is a stunning village of 600 people nestled 300 m/ 1,000 feet up in the cusp of limestone cliffs. It came to international attention for its artistic and bohemian residents (chief among them was the celebrated English writer and poet Robert Graves, who lived here from 1929 until his death in 1985), and while today it is decisively more upmarket, it remains one of the most breath-taking towns in Mallorca. A highlight of any visit is walking about an hour down to the small *cala* (cove) for a swim, dropping through terraces of gnarled, centuries-old olive trees with silvery leaves and sheep standing in their shade.

The long history of growing olives in Mallorca dates back to before the Roman period. In the island's Mediterranean climate – mild temperatures, dry summers, soft breezes, humidity to aid growth – the trees thrived. There was an improvement in techniques during the Roman era (123 BCE–465 CE), and another major improvement during the period of Muslim rule (903–1229 CE); as masters of irrigation, they tapped the Tramuntana's agricultural potential. Records show oil being shipped from Mallorca to North Africa in the thirteenth century. By the mid-fifteenth century, it was a regular export from the Port of Sóller. From the sixteenth century, plantings increased substantially and became widespread, particularly in the Serra de Tramuntana. Olive oil was the island's dominant export until the first half of the nineteenth century.

While the average age of the groves in the Serra de Tramuntana is around 500 years old, some trees were planted centuries before that. A few years ago, on the range's southern slopes, a thousand-year-old olive tree in the Sóller Valley near Fornalutx was named Mejor Olivo Monumental de España (Best Monumental Olive Tree in Spain). Planted at the beginning of Muslim rule of the island, the tree has a perimeter of more than 6.5 metres/21 feet. It is the empeltre variety, also known as Mallorquina. Older trees seem to be less dependent on each season's climate and the shifts in climate change, and this millennium-old one still gives 120 kg/265 lb of olives a year – significantly more than the average.

In an environment with scarce resources, a millennia of agricultural activities transformed the Tramuntana landscape with terraces, dry-stone walls and interconnected waterworks that include water mills that support orchards, vegetable gardens and, most importantly, olive groves. For this, UNESCO named the 'Cultural Landscape of the Serra de Tramuntana' a World Heritage Site in 2011.

Emblematic of the Tramuntana range, the hillside terraces that follow the contours of the landscape made it possible to grow olives on such steep slopes. Trees planted like this have a lower yield – they are harder to fertilize, maintain and harvest, and it is virtually impossible to use any sort of mechanical means of getting olives off the branches. The olives are generally picked riper, leading to a milder, sweeter oil that lacks bitter or spicy notes.

Olives and olive oil remain constants in Mallorca, and nothing better follows a swim in Cala Deià than sitting at a shaded table in the café at the back of the cove and ordering *pamboli* (page 28) – bread rubbed with tomatoes, generously soaked with olive oil from these hills and served with cracked green olives, pickled sea fennel and some capers. Like the trees themselves, enjoying their fruits is an integral part of the experience.

Mallorca's
Weekly Markets

Almost every town in Mallorca has a weekly *mercat* (market). In the small notebook that I carry when I am in Mallorca, there is a list of them and their corresponding days pasted inside the front cover. I try to make it to one each day. The list includes dozens of options. Among the ones that I find of particular interest for the variety of goods on offer are: Arta (Tuesday), Sineu and Santanyí (Wednesday), Inca (Thursday) and Alcudia, Pollensa and Santa María del Camí (Sunday).

Especially in the fourteen villages that make up the central agricultural region of Es Pla, these markets remain an important part of life.

The largest and most famous *mercat* in Es Pla (and indeed in Mallorca) is the Wednesday one in Sineu, a village in the very centre of the island with a population of fewer than 4,000 people. A weekly market was gathering in Sineu by the early 1200s in what the Muslims who controlled the island called *Suq al-arba'a* – *suq* means market, and *al-arba'a* means Wednesday. Traders, craftsmen and farmers gathered, turning the town into a thriving meeting place once a week. After the Christian conquest of the town in 1230, the Wednesday market continued, as records from 1252 show. In 1306, King Jaume II established it as a royal market, ensuring its permanence. It continues today, and is the only market in the Balearic Islands (and one of the few in Spain) that still sells live farm animals, including various types of poultry, rabbits, sheep, goats and even some horses.

The market runs from 8 a.m. until 1 p.m., and traders begin arriving in the preceding hours to set up. A line forms early outside Forn Ca'n Toni, a century-old family-run bakery with a wood-fired oven on the main *plaça*. People come for its ensaïmades and slices of *coca* flatbread – on one recent September day, there were large trays of *coca de trempó*, with tomatoes, onions and green peppers (page 38) and of *coca de verdures*, with Swiss chard, green onions and parsley, and tomato slices arranged on top (page 41). These are nibbled on while setting up stalls and arranging goods, or else taken to one of the village cafés to eat with *café amb llet* (milky coffee) for breakfast.

During the course of the morning, the narrow streets of the town, on Sa Plaça facing the thirteenth-century church and the large, shady square below, are gradually taken over by hundreds of stalls selling produce, jewellery and textiles.

The line at Ca'n Toni never really disappears. By mid-morning, people return for another slice of *coca* and some much-needed energy before heading back to their stalls.

Coca Flatbread with Vegetables

Preparation time: 30 minutes
Cooking time: 45 minutes
Serves: 6

1 quantity Dough for Coca Flatbread
  Base (unleavened or leavened, page
  341)
1 teaspoon sweet paprika, plus extra
  for dusting
1 yellow onion, diced
2 long sweet green peppers or 1 green
  bell pepper, stemmed, seeded and
  diced
3 large plum tomatoes, diced
3 tablespoons olive oil
Salt

DF ✳

There have been recipes for thin-crusted *coca* flatbreads appearing as far back as the fifteenth century, with New World ingredients being incorporated into the dish. *Trempó* (page 76) is Mallorca's iconic mix of tomatoes, green peppers and onions, served as a salad and eaten just about any time of day in summer. Here that same medley of vegetables tops the island's most popular *coca*. The classic base doesn't include yeast, but there are recipes for both leavened and unleavened (both page 341). The yeast makes it a bit spongier, though the firmer base is nice, as the moisture of the ingredients on top doesn't allow it to get completely dry.

✳ Put the flatbread dough in the middle of a 30 × 40-cm/12 × 16-inch baking sheet and spread it out with your fingers, trying to make it as even and thin as possible. Use the tines of a fork to shape the edges. Lightly sprinkle with paprika. Let the dough rest while preparing the toppings.

✳ Preheat the oven to 200°C/400°F/Gas Mark 6.

✳ Put the vegetables in a mixing bowl, add the oil and paprika, season with salt and toss to blend. Using your hands, and leaving the liquid in the bottom of the bowl, transfer the vegetables to the dough base and spread evenly across the surface.

✳ Bake in the hot oven until the base is cooked through, firm and somewhat flaky (it will come away easily from the baking sheet) and the edges of some of the vegetables are taking on colour, about 45 minutes.

✳ Remove from the oven and let cool before cutting into rectangular pieces using a pizza wheel, scissors or knife.

Coca Flatbread with Swiss Chard, Spring Onions & Tomatoes

Preparation time: 30 minutes
Cooking time: 50 minutes
Serves: 6

1 quantity Dough for Coca Flatbread
    Base (unleavened or leavened,
    page 341)
450 g/1 lb trimmed Swiss chard,
    chopped
1 large bunch (about 300 g/11 oz) spring
    onions (scallions), trimmed, white and
    tender green parts cut crosswise into
    1-cm/½-inch pieces (100 g/3½ oz/
    1 cup trimmed weight)
20 g/¾ oz (¾ unpacked cup) finely
    chopped flat-leaf parsley
1 heaped tablespoon sweet paprika
3 tablespoons olive oil
2 plum tomatoes, cut crosswise into
    1-cm/½-inch-thick slices
Salt and pepper

DF ✳

Along with *coca de trempó* (with tomatoes, green peppers and onions topping the flatbread base, page 38), one of the most popular *coques* in Mallorca has Swiss chard, spring onions (scallions) and plenty of parsley, a combination that is usually called, somewhat generically, *coca de verdures* (vegetables). The fresh greens get tossed with olive oil and sweet paprika before being spread across the *coca* base, and take on a lovely dark green colour when baked. Brilliant red tomato slices across the top of this add flavour, but also a visual appeal. These last summers, this has become a particular favourite in my house. Scatter some pine nuts across the top for the last few minutes of baking, if desired.

✳ Put the flatbread dough in the middle of a 30 × 40-cm/12 × 16-inch baking sheet and spread it out with your fingers, trying to make it as even and thin as possible. Use the tines of a fork to shape the edges. Let the dough rest while preparing the toppings.

✳ Preheat the oven to 200°C/400°F/Gas Mark 6.

✳ Put the Swiss chard in an extra-large mixing bowl. Add the spring onions (scallions) to the bowl, followed by the parsley, paprika and oil. Season with salt and pepper and toss to blend well.

✳ Spread the mixture evenly across the dough base. Arrange the tomato slices across the top.

✳ Bake in the hot oven until the base is cooked through, firm and somewhat flaky (it will come away easily from the baking sheet), the greens wilted and darker and the tomatoes soft, about 50 minutes.

✳ Remove from the oven and let cool before cutting into rectangular pieces using a pizza wheel, scissors or knife.

Coca Flatbread
with Roasted Red Peppers

Preparation time: 30 minutes
Cooking time: 1 hour 10 minutes
Serves: 6

3 red bell peppers (at least 800 g/
    1¾ lb total)
2 cloves of garlic, thinly sliced crosswise
1 teaspoon sweet paprika, plus extra for
    dusting
2 tablespoons olive oil, plus extra for
    brushing the peppers
1 quantity Dough for Coca Flatbread
    Base (unleavened or leavened,
    page 341)
12–16 black or green olives
Salt

DF ✳

The most iconic *coca* flatbread on Ibiza and Formentera is topped with strips of roasted red peppers and a handful of black olives. That is of little surprise, as there is deep love here for *pebres torrats* (roasted peppers). Some people add chunks of high-quality tuna preserved in olive oil or pieces of fried fish as well. When peeling the roasted peppers, avoid any temptation to rinse to ease the task at hand, as it will wash away some of those lovely flavours of the peppers. Roast the peppers over embers for added smoky notes.

✳ Roast and peel the peppers following the directions on page 95, 10–30 minutes depending on method.

✳ Tear or cut the peppers into long strips. Set in a flat bowl, add the garlic and paprika, season with salt and drizzle with the olive oil. Gently turn over. Set aside to let the garlic flavour the peppers.

✳ Meanwhile, preheat the oven to 180°C/350°F/Gas Mark 4.

✳ Put the flatbread dough in the middle of a 30 × 40-cm/12 × 16-inch baking sheet and spread it out with your fingers, trying to make it as even and thin as possible. Use the tines of a fork to shape the edges.

✳ Lightly dust with paprika. Lay the strips of pepper and garlic across the base to completely cover.

✳ Bake in the hot oven until the base is cooked through, firm and somewhat flaky (it will come away easily from the baking sheet), about 40 minutes.

✳ Remove from the oven. Arrange the olives on top. Let cool before cutting into rectangular pieces using a pizza wheel, scissors or knife.

Spinach-filled Pastries

Preparation time: 45 minutes
Cooking time: 40 minutes
Makes: about 15 (13-cm/5-inch) stuffed
    pastries

FOR THE FILLING
700 g/1½ lb trimmed fresh spinach
    leaves
1 tablespoon olive oil
1 yellow onion, finely chopped
2 tablespoons seedless raisins (about
    20 g/¾ oz)
2 tablespoons pine nuts (about 15 g/
    ½ oz), dry-toasted (see page 25)
Salt

FOR THE DOUGH
500 g/1 lb 2 oz (about 3½ cups) plain
    (all-purpose) flour, sifted
2 egg yolks
150 g/5 oz (⅔ cup) lard, at room
    temperature
60 ml/2 fl oz (¼ cup) mild olive oil
Pinch of salt
1 egg, beaten, for brushing

DF ✳

Filled Mallorcan half-moon pastries called *robiols* tend to be sweet – like those with jam on page 298 – and a favourite at Eastertime. But in Menorca, these pastries of mediaeval origin are more often savoury. The two most popular *robiol* fillings are fish and spinach. The latter is often blended with sautéed onions as well as pine nuts and raisins. Some even add chopped hard-boiled eggs to give the filling more body. Prepare the filling first, so it can cool down while you prepare the dough. There are two ways that *robiols* can be shaped, either by using a round cutter and then folding in half, or folding over and then tracing out the shape with a knife or pasta wheel.

✳ Prepare the filling: bring a large pot of lightly salted water to a boil, add the spinach and boil until wilted, 2–3 minutes. Drain well in a colander and let cool, gently pushing out the excess moisture as it cools.

✳ Heat the oil in a frying pan or sauté pan over medium heat, add the onion and cook until soft, 8–10 minutes. Stir in the raisins and pine nuts and remove the pan from the heat.

✳ In a mixing bowl, combine the spinach and the onion mixture, then toss together and season with salt. Set aside.

✳ Prepare the dough: put the flour in a large bowl and make a well. Add the egg yolks, lard, oil and salt, and begin mixing, with either a spoon or your hands, gradually adding 120 ml (4 fl oz/½ cup) water. Knead until it forms a smooth and supple ball.

✳ Preheat the oven to 180°C/350°F/Gas Mark 4. Line several oven sheets with baking (parchment) paper. Put the beaten egg in a cup.

✳ On a clean work counter, lay out a large sheet of baking paper. Take a piece of dough (about 70 g/2½ oz/¼ cup) and roll it out on the baking paper until 5 mm/ ¼ inch thick. Use a smallish round bowl (12–13 cm/4 ½–5 inches in diameter) to press out a circle. Trace around the circle with a knife and pull away the excess dough.

✳ Place about 30–35 g (1 oz/scant loosely packed ¼ cup) of the filling in the centre. Moisten the edges of the pastry with water and, lifting up the baking paper, fold over to form a half-moon. Lightly press the edges together with your fingers. Using the tines of a small fork, press down along the edges. Gently place on one of the baking sheets. Repeat until you have used the remaining dough and filling.

✳ Prick the tops of the pastries in a few places with the tines of a small fork. Brush with the beaten egg.

✳ Bake the pastries in the hot oven until golden (don't let them darken too much), about 25 minutes. Remove from the oven and let cool.

✳ Store in sealed containers. Best eaten within 3 days.

Sobrassada-filled Rolls

Preparation time: 30 minutes,
    plus rising time
Cooking time: 15 minutes
Makes: 16–18 rolls

120 ml/4 fl oz (½ cup) milk
2 tablespoons mild olive oil,
    plus extra for oiling
3 tablespoons sugar
2 large (US extra-large) eggs
12 g/½ oz fresh baker's yeast or
    4 g/1½ teaspoons instant
    (easy-blend) dried yeast
300 g/11 oz (2 cups) plain (all-purpose)
    flour
175 g/6 oz sobrassada (see page 208),
    casing removed

The village fiestas in Menorca are an enormously important part of summer, with plenty of social calls. A handful of things are mandatory to offer guests: *panets* with sobrassada for those who want something savoury, *pastisset* cookies (page 291) for those who want something sweet, and *pomada* (page 332), the slushy gin and lemon cocktail, for everybody. *Panets* are brioche-like rolls (made with olive oil rather than butter and very little egg). While plain ones (page 49) are popular all year, when it's fiesta time they should have some sobrassada. Because sobrassada is quite salty, these filled buns generally don't have salt in the dough, but you can add a pinch when crumbling in the yeast if desired.

∗ To a large mixing bowl, add the milk, oil, sugar and 1 of the eggs and beat together until well combined. Crumble in the yeast and slowly work in the flour. Using your hands, work into a sticky dough. Cover snugly with clingfilm (plastic wrap) and let rise in a warm place for 1 hour.

∗ Line baking sheets with baking (parchment) paper.

∗ With lightly oiled hands, take a piece of dough weighing about 25–30 g (1 oz/ 2 tablespoons) and roll into a ball about 4 cm/1½ inches in diameter. On a clean, lightly oiled work counter, flatten out with your fingers to form a disc 10 cm/ 4 inches in diameter. Take about 10 g (¼ oz/2 teaspoons) of sobrassada, form into a slightly cylindrical shape and lay across the middle of the dough disc. Roll up the dough so that it is slightly overlapping. Pinch the ends closed. Arrange spread out on the baking sheets and let rise in a warm place, uncovered, for 1 hour.

∗ Preheat the oven to 165°C/325°F/Gas Mark 3.

∗ In a cup, beat the remaining 1 egg. Using a pastry brush, lightly paint the rolls with the eggwash.

∗ Bake in the hot oven until golden, about 12 minutes. Remove and let cool. Store in a sealed container. They are best eaten within a couple of days.

Anytime Buns

Preparation time: 30 minutes,
    plus rising time
Cooking time: 15 minutes
Makes: about 30 buns

250 ml/8 fl oz (1 cup) milk
60 ml/2 fl oz (¼ cup) mild olive oil, plus
    extra for oiling hands
80 g/3 oz (⅓ cup) sugar
2 large (US extra-large) eggs
25 g/1 oz fresh baker's yeast or 8 g/
    3 teaspoons instant (easy-blend)
    dried yeast
Generous pinch of salt
600 g/1 lb 5 oz (4 cups) plain
    (all-purpose) flour

VEG *

Plain, round *panets* (buns) are a favourite to eat with cured cold cuts or local cheese, and make a tasty breakfast with some butter and marmalade. These are brioche-like, but less rich and less sweet. The classic recipe doesn't call for any salt, but I use a pinch to smooth out the flavour a touch. Secrete a small tablet of chocolate in a couple of the buns before baking for a surprise treat.

* To a large mixing bowl, add the milk, oil, sugar and 1 of the eggs and beat until well combined. Crumble in the yeast, add the salt and slowly work in the flour. Using your hands, work into a sticky dough. Cover snugly with clingfilm (plastic wrap) and let rise in a warm place for 1 hour.

* Line baking sheets with baking (parchment) paper.

* With lightly oiled hands, take a piece of dough weighing about 40 g/1½ oz (roughly 5 cm/2 inches in diameter) and gently roll into a smooth ball. Arrange spaced out on the baking sheets and let rise in a warm place, uncovered, for 1 hour.

* Preheat the oven to 165°C/325°F/Gas Mark 3.

* In a cup, beat the remaining 1 egg. Paint the buns with the eggwash using a pastry brush.

* Bake in the hot oven until golden, 12–14 minutes. Remove and let cool. Store in a sealed container. They are best eaten within a couple of days.

CHAPTER 2

SOUPS, STEWS & PULSES

Spiny Lobster Stew

Preparation time: 45 minutes
Cooking time: 1 hour 10 minutes
Serves: 2

1 kg/2¼ lb fresh or thawed frozen
    lobster, preferably spiny lobster
4 tablespoons olive oil
2 cloves of garlic, peeled
1 yellow onion, finely chopped
1 small sweet long pepper, stemmed,
    seeded and finely chopped
2 plum tomatoes, halved and grated
    (see page 25)
1 tablespoon finely chopped flat-leaf
    parsley
12 toasted peeled almonds
    (see page 25)
Very thin slices of day-old country-style
    bread, cut into 2.5-cm/1-inch-wide
    strips (pa de sopes, see page 24)
2 tablespoons brandy or cognac
Salt and pepper

DF ✳ 1 POT

Menorca's most celebrated dish, *caldereta de llagosta*, is chiefly associated with Fornells, a small fishing village in the north of the island. Having a *caldereta* at one of its seafood restaurants remains something of a summer ritual. Preparing one at home is worthy of any celebratory occasion. There are two kinds of lobsters. The classic local one in Menorca is the clawless spiny lobster (*llagosta* in Catalan, *langosta* in Spanish), a smaller and sweeter-tasting crustacean than its more common relatives with large front claws (called *llamàntol* in Catalan, *bogavante* in Spanish). Both are delicious. Calculate about 500 g/1 lb 2 oz of lobster per person. *Caldereta* is served over *sopes*, very thin slices of dried bread (see page 24). Some pass the *sofregit* through a food mill or purée for a smoother final texture to the stew. That step is included in the directions below, but skip (as I usually do) if desired. Traditionally, the dish is left to sit for an hour or two before serving, to let the flavours deepen.

✳ If using fresh lobster, place it in the freezer for 15 minutes (this numbs the lobster). Remove it from the freezer, then lay it, stomach-side down, on a chopping (cutting) board. Insert the tip of a large, heavy knife into the cross on the back of its head and firmly plunge it through the shell with a sharp blow, through to the chopping board.

✳ Scoop out the dark matter and discard. If the lobster is female, remove the roe (coral) and set aside. Remove and set aside the stomachs and livers (tomalley). Split the head in half lengthwise and discard the dark green matter. Rinse the halves and set aside. Cut the body crosswise into pieces with a heavy knife or kitchen scissors, leaving the meat attached to the shell. Crack the large claws so they remain intact but the meat will be easily accessible when served.

✳ Heat the oil in a large, flameproof casserole pan (see page 25), heavy sauté pan or Dutch oven over medium heat. Add the garlic and cook until aromatic, 1–2 minutes. Remove and reserve. Add the onion and pepper and patiently cook until the onion is soft and translucent, about 15 minutes. Add the tomatoes and cook over low heat until darker and pasty, about 15 minutes, adding a few tablespoons of water during cooking. If desired, pass the sauce through a food mill and then return it to the pan. Season.

✳ Set the lobster pieces in the pan and cook until the meat turns pearly, turning a few times in the sauce, 2–3 minutes. Stir in 1 litre (34 fl oz/4¼ cups) water. Bring to a boil over high heat, then reduce the heat to low and gently cook for 20 minutes.

✳ Meanwhile, prepare a picada. To a large mortar with a pestle, add the reserved garlic, the parsley, the almonds, a small piece of the dried bread (about 10 g/¼ oz), the reserved tomalley and roe from the lobster and the brandy or cognac, and pound to a paste. Or blend, in brief pulses, in a food processor, adding a touch of liquid from the pan as needed. (See page 175 for more on making a picada.)

✳ Loosen the picada with some liquid from the pan and stir into the sauce until well integrated. Gently cook for about 10 minutes. Turn off the heat and let the stew rest for 1–2 hours for the flavours to deepen. Just before serving, gently reheat.

✳ To serve, put some slices of bread in each wide soup bowl. Ladle over some soup and serve with the remaining bread in a basket.

Fish Stew

Preparation time: 30 minutes
Cooking time: 40 minutes
Serves: 4

1–1.5 kg/2¼–3¼ lb scaled and cleaned
    whole medium fish, such as scorpion
    fish, bream, sea bass or red snapper,
    or another firm-fleshed variety
3 tablespoons olive oil
2 medium yellow onions, finely chopped
1 clove of garlic, minced
3 medium tomatoes, halved and grated
    (see page 25)
60 ml/2 fl oz (¼ cup) dry white wine
2 litres/68 fl oz (8½ cups) Fish Stock
    (page 338)
1 teaspoon sweet paprika
Small pinch of saffron threads,
    crumbled
Very thin slices of day-old country-style
    bread, cut into 2.5-cm/1-inch-wide
    strips (pa de sopes, see page 24),
    for serving
Salt and pepper

DF ✳ 1 POT

This Menorcan speciality is the more affordable – but equally delicious – alternative to the better-known lobster *caldereta* (page 52). While it can be prepared using water, fish stock (broth) will greatly heighten the final flavours of the dish. *Caldereta* is served over very thin slices of dry and brittle day-old bread called *pa de sopes*. If making your own *sopes*, toast them before adding (see page 24). For a less rustic presentation, some like to remove the fish before serving and flake it back into the pan before ladling into wide bowls over the bread slices.

✳ Cut the fish crosswise into thick steaks. Reserve the heads and tails.

✳ Heat the oil in a Dutch oven or large, heavy pot over medium heat. Add the onions and cook until soft, 8–10 minutes. Stir in the garlic and then add the tomatoes. Cook until pulpy and deeper red, about 10 minutes, adding a few tablespoons of water (or stock) from time to time to keep it moist. Add the wine and cook for 2 minutes to burn off the alcohol. Stir in 250 ml (8 fl oz/1 cup) of the stock.

✳ Pass the sauce through a food mill, or purée in a blender, and return to the pan. Stir in the paprika and saffron, and season with salt and pepper.

✳ Season the fish steaks and reserved heads and tails with salt and pepper and add to the pan. Pour over the remaining 1.75 litres (60 fl oz/7½ cups) of stock. Bring to a simmer over medium heat and simmer, uncovered, for 15 minutes, without letting it reach a strong boil, to keep the fish from breaking apart.

✳ Remove the pot from the heat. Remove and discard the heads and tails. Cover the pot and let sit for 10 minutes.

✳ Meanwhile, if the slices of bread for *sopes* are not crunchy, toast. Preheat the oven grill (broiler), arrange the bread on a baking sheet and place under the grill until toasted. Transfer to a bread basket.

✳ To serve, put a couple of pieces of bread in each of 4 wide soup bowls. Ladle over the soup with 1 or 2 pieces of fish per bowl. Serve with the remaining bread in a basket to add as desired while eating.

Fish Stew with Potatoes
& an Almond Picada

Preparation time: 20 minutes
Cooking time: 1 hour 15 minutes
Serves: 4

1 kg/2 ¼ lb thick steaks of monkfish,
    scorpion fish, grouper or John Dory
3 tablespoons olive oil
2 cloves of garlic, skins on
1 large onion, finely chopped
1 long sweet green pepper, stemmed,
    seeded and chopped
2 medium tomatoes, halved and grated
    (see page 25)
Pinch of saffron threads, crumbled
4 medium white potatoes (about
    800 g/1 ¾ lb total), peeled and cut
    crosswise into 4 pieces
750 ml/25 fl oz (3 cups) Fish Stock
    (page 338)
Handful flat-leaf parsley, minced
15–20 toasted peeled almonds
    (see page 25)
½ teaspoon sweet paprika
Generous pinch of ground cinnamon
Salt and pepper

DF ✳ GF

This *guisat* (stew) from Ibiza and Formentera is a close cousin to the two-course *bullit de peix* (page 160). One main difference is that this is eaten as a single course rather than two. There should be some broth, but just enough to keep the dish moist. The flavours should be as concentrated as possible. While fishermen would often use water when preparing their fish stews, using stock (broth) improves the dish. While basically any kind of fish will work for this dish, firm-fleshed fish like scorpion fish, John Dory and grouper are especially appreciated. I find monkfish is a particularly good choice because, along with its fine flavour and texture, the only bone it has is the backbone, making it easy to eat. The *picada* stirred in at the end gives the *guisat* its body, while some aromatic cinnamon at the end brings it together.

✳ Season the fish with salt and pepper and set aside.

✳ Heat the oil in a shallow, flameproof casserole pan (see page 25), heavy sauté pan or Dutch oven over medium heat. Add the garlic, onion and green pepper and cook until the onion is soft, about 10 minutes. Add the tomatoes and cook until thicker and pulpy, about 10 minutes, adding a couple of tablespoons of water (or stock) as it cooks.

✳ Add the saffron and potatoes and cover with 500 ml (18 fl oz/2 cups) of the stock. Cook until the potatoes are nearly done, about 20 minutes. Remove the garlic and set aside to cool. Set the fish in the pan and cover with 175 ml (6 fl oz/¾ cup) of the stock. Cook for 15 minutes, gently turning the pieces once, being careful not to break up the fish.

✳ Meanwhile, remove the skin from the cooled garlic. Prepare a picada: in a large mortar, combine the garlic, parsley, almonds and paprika, and pound with a pestle to a paste with 2–3 tablespoons of simmering broth. Season with salt. (See page 175 for more on making a picada.)

✳ Loosen the picada with the remaining 5 or so tablespoons of stock so that it will integrate more easily into the stew. Stir the picada into the stew, add the cinnamon and cook over low heat for a final 5 minutes.

✳ Serve in wide bowls.

Fisherman's Broth with Fideo Noodles

Preparation time: 5 minutes
Cooking time: 20 minutes
Serves: 4

8–16 mussels, cleaned, optional
1.5 litres/50 fl oz (generous 6 cups)
   stock (broth) from *bullit de peix*
   ('Boiled' Fish, page 160) or Fish Stock
   (page 338)
Pinch of saffron threads, crumbled,
   optional (see above)
160 g/5½ oz thin fideo noodles
   or another small soup pasta

DF ✳ 5 ✳ 30

Cooking some *fideus* (short, thin fideo noodles) in the broth made from Ibiza and Formentera's classic *bullit de peix* (page 160) is a typical second dish. It's generally not very complicated, and is often just the flavourful broth with the soup pasta. Sometimes, though, cooks also include cuttlefish (cut up small and sautéed first), shrimp, a few mussels and so on. But this isn't a seafood dish, per se: these additions are there just to bring more flavour to the broth. This recipe is a basic one with a few mussels. For a more elaborate version of this, see Fisherman's Brothy Rice (page 132). If using broth from *bullit*, it will have saffron already; if using fish stock, you will need to add a pinch of crumbled saffron threads when bringing it to a boil.

✳ To steam the mussels (if using): put the mussels in a saucepan, cover with 60 ml (2 fl oz/¼ cup) water and bring to a boil over high heat. Lower the heat, cover the pot, and simmer, shaking the pot from time to time, until the mussels have opened, about 2 minutes. Discard any mussels that didn't open. Twist off and discard the 'empty' half of each shell. Set aside.

✳ Bring the stock to a boil in a large pot, and add the saffron (if needed) and the pasta. Reduce the heat and boil until tender, 6–12 minutes, following the timing on the package. Add the mussels for the last 1 minute of cooking. Divide among soup bowls and serve.

Tomato Soup with Fresh Figs

Preparation time: 20 minutes
Cooking time: 30 minutes
Serves: 4–6

1 kg/2 ¼ lb ripe plum tomatoes or
    another variety of medium–small
    tomatoes
4 tablespoons olive oil
1 yellow onion, chopped
1 long sweet green pepper or ½ green
    bell pepper, stemmed, seeded
    and roughly chopped
2 cloves of garlic, minced
1 heaped tablespoon minced flat-leaf
    parsley
Salt

TO SERVE
Very thin slices of day-old or toasted
    bread
Fresh figs, chilled, peeled if desired

V ✳ VEG ✳ DF ✳ 1 POT

In a testament to the humbleness of Menorca's cuisine, its most famous dish alongside lobster stew (page 52) is a simple tomato and onion soup whose name literally translates to 'oil water'. It is served over thin slices of dried bread (*pa de sopes*, see page 24). The most common piece of advice given when preparing this comes as more of a warning: 'Don't let it boil!' Serve it warm and not scalding hot. As peak tomato season coincides with that of figs, a plate of figs is traditionally served alongside. Following local style, alternating bites of the soup with the fresh, soft sweetness of figs makes for a magical combination of flavours and textures.

✳ Put a strainer over a bowl. Quarter the tomatoes lengthwise. Remove the hard core and seeds and put in the strainer in order to catch all of the juices. Cut the quarters into 2 or 3 pieces. Set aside with the reserved juices.

✳ Heat the oil in a shallow, flameproof casserole pan (see page 25), Dutch oven or heavy sauté pan over medium heat. Add the onion and cook until it begins to soften, about 5 minutes. Add the green pepper and cook for 5 minutes more. Stir in the garlic and parsley, add the tomatoes and reserved juices, season with salt and cook for 20 minutes, stirring from time to time, until the tomatoes have softened but still retain their texture. Add a touch of water, if needed, to keep it moist.

✳ Add 1 litre (34 fl oz/4 ¼ cups) water and slowly heat, about 10 minutes. It is important that it does not reach a boil. When the whitish foam comes to the surface, remove the pot from the heat. Let cool for 10 minutes.

✳ To serve, put some slices of bread in bowls and ladle over some warm soup. Serve with more bread slices and the figs on the side.

Two-course Winter Soup

Preparation time: 10 minutes
Cooking time: 2 hours 20 minutes
Serves: 4

1 bone-in chicken leg (drumstick and
    thigh)
1 ossobuco (about 250 g/9 oz)
1 beef bone (about 300 g/11 oz)
3 carrots, halved lengthwise
1 yellow onion, halved
1 leek, trimmed
1 turnip, halved lengthwise
1 parsnip, halved
1 teaspoon black peppercorns
1 celery stalk with leaves, folded in half
sprigs of fresh thyme
2 medium white potatoes, peeled
    and halved
175–200 g/6–7 oz small soup pasta
Extra-virgin olive oil, for drizzling
Salt

DF ✳

Many Christmastime tables in the Balearics serve two-course soup. A hearty broth is prepared from a broad selection of meats, vegetables and legumes. For a first course, pasta is boiled and served in that broth, with the reserved meats, vegetables and legumes served as the second course. It is similar to *escudella i de carn d'olla* in Catalunya and *cocido* around Madrid. In Menorca, it is sometimes called *sopa de la reina*, 'the queen's soup'. There is a simpler version also prepared during the winter with vegetables and herbs, plus a piece of chicken (with the skin on, as this gives flavour) and a slice of ossobuco. These elements get served after the broth, but are eaten as a topping of a meal rather than being considered a full second course. In such soups, the work of the ingredients is to give up their flavour for the broth. That means that for some tastes, these components might need some olive oil and salt to enliven when served.

✳ Bring 2.5 litres (generous 2½ quarts/10½ cups) water to a boil in a large soup pot over high heat. As it nears a boil, add the chicken, ossobuco and beef bone. Bring to a rolling boil and skim off any foam that comes up to the surface. Add the carrots, onion, leek, turnip, parsnip and peppercorns. Tie the celery and thyme together with cotton string and add. Generously season with salt. Once it returns to a boil, reduce the heat to low, cover the pot and gently boil for 1 hour. Add the potatoes and boil until the potatoes are very tender, about 45 minutes.

✳ Strain the broth into a large saucepan, discarding the bones and bundle of herbs. Bring the broth to a boil over high heat. Add the pasta, cover the pot and boil until done, following the time indicated on the package.

✳ Meanwhile, arrange the meats and vegetables on a large serving platter. Cover to keep warm.

✳ Serve the soup with pasta in bowls as a first course. Follow this with the platter of meats and vegetables as a second course. Serve the meats and vegetables with olive oil to drizzle and salt on the side.

Stewed Lentils with Green Beans

Preparation time: 10 minutes
Cooking time: 1 hour 10 minutes
Serves: 5–6

400 g/14 oz (2 cups) dried brown lentils
2 tablespoons olive oil
½ yellow onion, thinly sliced
2 cloves of garlic, minced
2 medium tomatoes, halved and grated
    (see page 25)
150 g/5 oz green beans, trimmed and
    cut into 2–4-cm/¾–1½-inch pieces
1 teaspoon sweet paprika
1 white potato, peeled and cut into
    bite-size pieces
1 carrot, cut into 5-mm/¼-inch-thick
    circles, optional
Salt and pepper
Finely chopped flat-leaf parsley,
    to garnish

V ✳ VEG ✳ DF ✳ GF ✳ 1 POT

The abundance of stewed lentil dishes across the islands is dazzling. Simple, economical and healthy, they can incorporate all manner of ingredients. This is one of the popular vegetarian versions with green beans. Add some generous pieces of pumpkin squash if desired. To add some pork for added flavour, I would recommend sautéing some chopped pork belly (150 g/5 oz should be enough) in the beginning with the onion. Served with a green salad – ideally with thinly sliced onions and olives and dressed with olive oil, a dash of vinegar and salt – it makes an excellent meal. Don't worry if this recipe makes more than you can eat for one meal. Lentils make perfect leftovers.

✳ Put the lentils in a large bowl and pick them over for any debris. Rinse.

✳ Heat the oil in a large, heavy pot over medium heat. Add the onion and cook until pale, about 6 minutes. Stir in the garlic, add the tomatoes and cook until dark and pasty, about 10 minutes. Add the green beans and cook for 2 minutes, stirring frequently. Stir in the paprika and lentils, then add the potato and carrot (if using) and season with salt and pepper.

✳ Cover with 1.5 litres (50 fl oz/generous 6 cups) water and bring to a boil. Reduce the heat to low, cover the pot and gently boil until the lentils are tender but not mushy, about 40 minutes. Add more water if necessary to keep the lentils loose.

✳ Ladle into bowls, garnish with parsley and serve hot.

Simply Lentils

Preparation time: 5 minutes
Cooking time: 45 minutes
Serves: 4

400 g/14 oz (2 cups) small dried brown
    lentils
Paprika, for seasoning
Finely chopped flat-leaf parsley,
    to garnish, optional
Extra-virgin olive oil, for drizzling
Vinegar, for dashing
Salt and pepper

V ✳ VEG ✳ DF ✳ GF ✳ 5 ✳ 1 POT

While there are plenty of ways of cooking lentils with a long list of ingredients, at home, they are often prepared in a much more straightforward and simple manner: boiled and dressed with good olive oil and vinegar, and seasoned with paprika, salt and pepper. Like this, the lovely nuttiness of the lentils is on full display. Use small brown Spanish Pardina lentils, which hold their shape, and don't overcook them. They shouldn't be mushy; they should have a firmness to their body.

✳ Put the lentils in a large bowl and pick them over for any debris. Rinse.

✳ Bring the lentils and 1.5 litres (50 fl oz/generous 6 cups) water to a boil in a large, heavy pot over high heat. Reduce the heat to low, cover the pot and gently boil until the lentils are tender but not mushy, about 40 minutes. Add more water if necessary to keep the lentils loose.

✳ Ladle into bowls. Season with paprika, salt and pepper, and stir in some parsley (if using). Generously drizzle over some oil, dash in some vinegar and serve.

Stewed Chickpeas

Preparation time: 10 minutes,
 plus resting time
Cooking time: 1 hour
Serves: 4–6

525 g/18½ oz (2⅔ cups) cooked or
 canned chickpeas (garbanzo beans)
3 tablespoons olive oil, plus extra for
 drizzling
1 yellow onion, finely chopped
2 cloves of garlic, minced
3 tomatoes, halved and grated (see
 page 25)
1 teaspoon sweet paprika
1 litre/34 fl oz (4¼ cups) Vegetable
 Stock (page 339) or water
2 medium white potatoes (about
 400 g/14 oz total), peeled and cut into
 generous cubes
250 g/9 oz peeled and seeded pumpkin,
 cut into generous cubes
250 g/9 oz cabbage (about ½ smallish
 one or ¼ larger one), chopped
200 g/7 oz trimmed fresh spinach
 leaves, roughly chopped
Salt and pepper

V ✳ VEG ✳ DF ✳ GF

Often, stewed legume dishes – chickpeas (garbanzo beans), lentils, white beans – in the Balearic Islands use seasonal vegetables rather than meat to give them flavour, making for an economical and healthy meal. That said, a variety of non-vegetarian embellishments are common. Add some pieces of desalted salt cod at the end of cooking, add black sausage (*botifarró*) during stewing or fry some chopped pork belly (*panxeta*) at the beginning with the onion. At home, we generally omit meat, but often serve this with a poached egg on top, another popular local combination. This recipe calls for cooked or canned chickpeas, but you can boil dried beans that have been soaked overnight. See page 341 for directions on that.

✳ If using chickpeas (garbanzo beans) that have just been prepared from dried beans, leave them in the liquid until ready to use. If using canned ones, drain, rinse and put in a saucepan with about 750 ml (25 fl oz/3 cups) water, bring to a boil, remove the pan from the heat and leave in the liquid until ready to use.

✳ Heat the oil in a large, heavy pot over medium heat. Add the onion and cook until soft, about 8 minutes. Stir in the garlic, add the tomatoes and cook until dark and pasty, about 10 minutes. Stir in the paprika. Add the stock and bring to a boil. When it reaches a boil, add the potatoes, pumpkin and cabbage, partly cover the pot and gently boil until tender, 20–30 minutes.

✳ Strain the chickpeas, reserving some of the liquid, and add to the pot. Season with salt and pepper. Cook, uncovered, for 5 minutes. It should be quite saucy but not watery. Add a touch of the reserved liquid, if needed, or reduce. Stir in the spinach. Turn off the heat, cover the pot and let rest for 15 minutes for the spinach to soften and the flavours to firm up.

✳ To serve, ladle into wide bowls, then drizzle with olive oil.

Chickpeas with Spinach

Preparation time: 20 minutes
Cooking time: 35 minutes
Serves: 4–6

600 g/1 lb 5 oz (4 cups) cooked
    (page   341) or canned chickpeas
    (garbanzo beans)
500 g/1 lb 2 oz trimmed fresh spinach
    leaves
3 tablespoons olive oil
3 cloves of garlic, peeled
1 yellow onion, finely chopped
4 hard-boiled eggs, peeled and halved
15 toasted peeled almonds
    (see page 25)
1 heaped teaspoon sweet paprika
1 small bay leaf
Salt and pepper

VEG * DF * GF

Spinach pairs particularly well with chickpeas (garbanzo beans). In this stewed chickpea recipe, a pounded *picada* of garlic, almonds and a hard-boiled egg yolk also gets stirred into the dish for both flavour and body. For an even more soothing final texture, scoop out some chickpeas at the end, mash (or purée) and then stir back into the pot.

* If using chickpeas (garbanzo beans) that have just been prepared from dried beans, leave them in the liquid until ready to use. If using canned ones, drain, rinse and put in a saucepan with about 750 ml (25 fl oz/3 cups) water, bring to a boil, remove the pan from the heat and leave in the liquid until ready to use.

* To a large pan with a lid, add the spinach. Cover the pan and cook over medium heat until just wilted, about 5 minutes. Remove the pan from the heat and set aside.

* Heat the oil in a large, flameproof casserole pan (see page 25), heavy sauté pan or Dutch oven over medium heat. Add the garlic and cook until golden, 1–2 minutes. Do not allow the garlic to burn. Remove and reserve as soon as it is done. Add the onion to the pan and cook until soft, 8–10 minutes.

* Meanwhile, prepare a picada. In a large mortar, combine the reserved garlic, the yolk from 1 of the hard-boiled eggs, the almonds and about 2 tablespoons of liquid from the chickpeas, then pound to a paste. Or blend, in brief pulses, in a food processor, adding a touch of liquid as needed. (See page 175 for more on making a picada.)

* Drain the chickpeas, reserving at least 750 ml (25 fl oz/3 cups) of the liquid. Add the chickpeas to the pan, stir in the paprika and the picada, add the bay leaf and season with salt and pepper. Add about 500 ml (18 fl oz/2 cups) of the reserved chickpea liquid. Reduce the heat to low and simmer, partly covered, for 15 minutes. The dish should be loose and moist. Stir in more reserved liquid if needed.

* Drain off any excess liquid from the spinach and add the leaves to the pan. Stir well and cook, uncovered, for about 3 minutes.

* Spoon into bowls, garnish each with a hard-boiled egg half and serve hot.

Stewed White Beans
in Tomato Sauce with Pork

Preparation time: 10 minutes
Cooking time: 30 minutes
Serves: 4

750 g/1⅔ lb (about 3 cups) canned
    white beans, such as cannellini or
    white lima beans
2 tablespoons olive oil
200 g/7 oz trimmed fresh pork belly or
    shoulder, cut into bite-size pieces
3 cloves of garlic, skins on, lightly
    crushed under the palm
200 g/7 oz fresh or cured pork sausage,
    cut into bite-size pieces
1 packed teaspoon minced fresh
    marjoram leaves, oregano or parsley,
    plus 4 sprigs to garnish
1 small hot red chilli (chile), optional
250 ml/8 fl oz (1 cup) tomato sauce,
    preferably homemade (page 342)
Salt and pepper

DF ✳ GF

This warming winter dish with white beans from the interior of Mallorca includes some pork sausage, often a local blood one called *botifarró* (see page 23). The popular fresh herb *moraduix* (marjoram), with its warm and piney notes, gives the dish its characteristic flavour. Fresh oregano is the best substitution if you don't have marjoram. Often, a small dried red chilli (chile) gets added to the beans for a bite of heat.

✳ Drain and rinse the beans. Put in a saucepan with about 500 ml (18 fl oz/2 cups) water. Bring to a boil, cover the pan and remove from the heat. Leave them to sit in the liquid until ready to use.

✳ Heat the oil in a flameproof casserole pan (see page 25) or Dutch oven over medium heat. Add the pork belly and garlic, season with salt and pepper and cook until the pork is browned, 6–8 minutes. Stir in the sausage and cook for 2 minutes. Add the minced herbs, chilli (chile), if using, and tomato sauce, and cook for 2–3 minutes, stirring well. Drain the beans and add to the pan. Cover with 250 ml (8 fl oz/1 cup) water. Bring to a gentle simmer over low heat and simmer for 10 minutes. It should be loose enough to require a spoon to eat.

✳ Ladle into bowls, garnish each with a sprig of marjoram, oregano or parsley and serve hot.

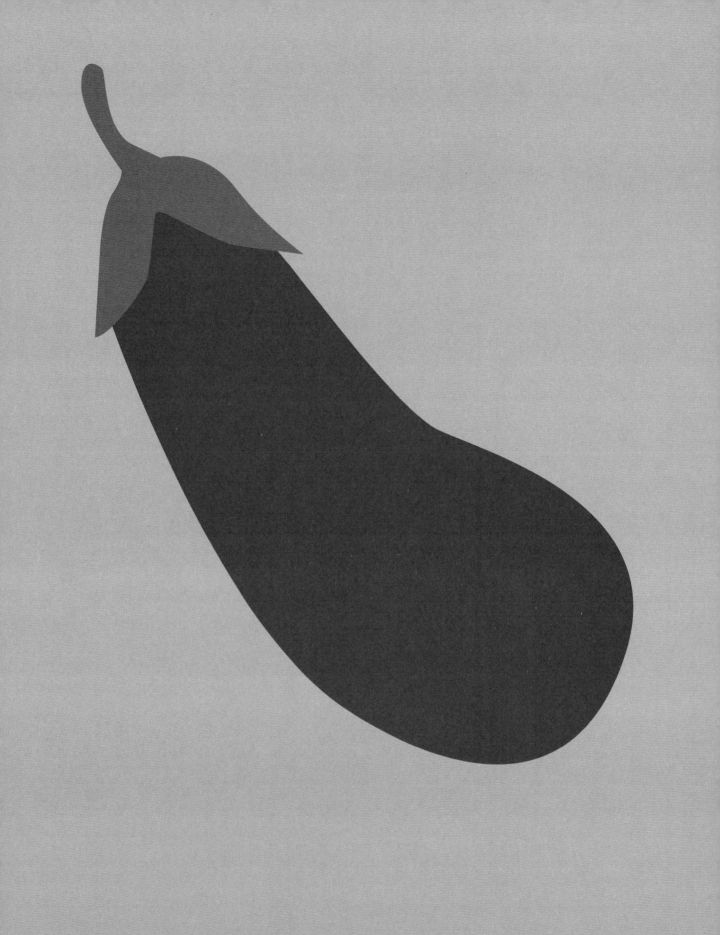

SALADS
& VEGETABLES

Summer Tomato, Onion & Pepper Salad

Preparation time: 10 minutes
Cooking time: 1 minute
Serves: 4

3 ripe tomatoes
2 long sweet green peppers, stemmed, seeded and finely diced
1 white onion or 2 bulbous spring onions (scallions), finely diced
Red or white wine vinegar, for dashing, optional
3–4 tablespoons extra-virgin olive oil
Salt

V ✳ VEG ✳ DF ✳ GF ✳ 5 ✳ 30

One of Mallorca's most famous dishes is a modest summer salad prepared with the island's tomatoes, long green peppers (they are a paler shade of green than typical ones) and sweet white onions, seasoned with only salt and dressed with olive oil and occasionally – for an individual touch – a dash of vinegar. *Trempó* (also commonly spelled *trampó*) is simple but versatile, and cooks incorporate all manner of other ingredients into it: slices of tart apple or even apricots, a few capers to add zest, or, for substance, potatoes or chickpeas (garbanzo beans). *Trempó* can begin a meal, be served alongside grilled fish and meat, and be eaten as a snack or even as a breakfast. Here is the basic version; add to it at will. It should be juicy enough to need bread to soak up. Just be sure to dress it well with oil. The name derives from the verb *trempar*, 'to dress'.

✳ Stem the tomatoes and score an 'x' in the bottom of each one with the tip of a sharp knife.

✳ Bring a saucepan of water to a boil, add the tomatoes and blanch until the skin begins to split, about 30 seconds. Remove with a slotted spoon and put in a bowl of cold water to cool.

✳ Peel the tomatoes, finely chop and put in a mixing bowl. Add the peppers and onions and season with salt. Toss to blend. Dash with vinegar (if using). Add the olive oil and mix again. Divide among salad plates and serve.

Tomato Salad with Preserved Dried Fish from Formentera

Preparation time: 10 minutes,
   plus soaking time
Serves: 2

½ small onion, halved and thinly sliced,
   optional
2 large ripe tomatoes
50 g/2 oz (¼ cup) *peix sec* (dried fish,
   see page 24) in olive oil, or
   high-quality canned tuna and
   1–2 anchovies (see right)

DF ✳ GF ✳ 5 ✳ 30

During Formentera's summer, when tomatoes are plump and at peak flavour, and the desire for simple meals dominates one's appetite, this salad is both popular and perfect. It uses just three – or sometimes only two – of the island's most typical ingredients: tomatoes, sweet onions and *peix sec*, dried fish preserved in oil (see page 24). There is no need to add oil – the bit that clings to the dried fish is enough – or salt. As Formentera's *peix sec* is very hard to find off the island, use a generous amount of high-quality tuna instead and an anchovy or two. It won't have the same mild brininess or somewhat chewy texture as the original, but it still makes a perfect summer meal.

✳ Separate the onion segments (if using) and place in a bowl of iced water for 5–10 minutes.

✳ Core the tomatoes and slice crosswise. Arrange in overlapping layers on a large plate. Drain the onion and scatter over the tomatoes. Using 2 small spoons or forks, remove the dried fish from the jar, letting the oil drain back into the jar. (Press slightly with the forks to help.) Arrange the fish on top of the onion. Serve.

Formentera Country Salad

Preparation time: 20 minutes,
    plus cooling time
Cooking time: 30 minutes
Serves: 4

1 large red bell pepper
neutral oil, for brushing
3 medium white potatoes (about
    600 g/1 lb 5 oz total), cut into bite-size
    pieces
1 long sweet green pepper, stemmed,
    seeded and cut into thin slices
2 ripe tomatoes, cored and cut into
    wedges
2 tablespoons extra-virgin olive oil,
    plus extra for drizzling
200 g/7 oz *crostes* or large cubes of
    bread, well-toasted in the oven
100–150 g/3½–5 oz *peix sec* (dried
    fish, see page 24) in olive oil or
    high-quality tuna in olive oil
    (see right)
Salt

DF ✳

A fuller (and more popular) version of the tomato salad on the previous page with Formentera's *peix sec* (traditional dried fish preserved in oil, page 24), this is one of the tiny island's most iconic dishes. The contrasts in the bowl are exquisite. The *crostes*, or generous pieces of crispy, well-baked bread akin to large croutons, lend the salad its local name, and certainly add to its rustic feeling. While the dried fish is hard to find outside the island, the best substitute is using a generous amount of high-quality canned tuna or *bonito del norte* in olive oil. Add a couple of anchovies with the tuna for bolder flavours.

✳ Preheat the oven grill (broiler) to high. Line a baking sheet with aluminium foil for easier clean-up.

✳ Brush the red pepper with the neutral oil and set on the baking sheet. Grill (broil), turning as needed, until charred in places and tender, 20–30 minutes.

✳ Transfer to a large bowl, cover and let cool in the steam to make peeling easier. Once cool enough to handle, rub off the blackened skin and discard the stem and seeds. Tear or cut into generous pieces and set aside.

✳ Meanwhile, bring a pot of lightly salted water to a boil, add the potatoes and boil until tender, 10–12 minutes. Drain and let cool.

✳ In a salad bowl, combine the red peppers, potatoes, green pepper and tomatoes. Drizzle with the 2 tablespoons of olive oil and gently toss. Add the *crostes* and toss again. Using 2 small spoons or forks, remove the dried fish from the jar, letting the oil drain back down. Arrange the fish on top of the salad. Drizzle with more olive oil and scrve.

Farmer's Salad

Preparation time: 20 minutes,
    plus cooling time
Cooking time: 30 minutes
Serves: 4–5

1 large red bell pepper
3 medium white potatoes (about
    600 g/1 lb 5 oz), peeled and cut into
    2-cm/¾-inch pieces
1 sweet white onion, thinly sliced,
    segments separated
2 ripe tomatoes, cut into generous
    pieces
3–4 tablespoons extra-virgin olive oil
2 hard-boiled eggs, peeled and cut into
    generous pieces
Salt and pepper

VEG ✳ DF ✳ GF

This classic country salad from Ibiza and Formentera focuses on vegetables from the *hort* (garden) – potatoes, red bell peppers, onions, tomatoes. The raw onion and fresh tomatoes offer nice contrasts to the roasted peppers and boiled potatoes. Don't cut the pieces too small; they should be large enough that you need a knife to eat. It is excellent with some local dried fish, such as *peix sec* (see page 24), tossed in.

✳ Preheat the oven grill (broiler) to high. Line a baking sheet with aluminium foil for easier clean-up.

✳ Put the pepper on the prepared baking sheet and grill (broil), turning as needed, until charred in places and tender, 20–30 minutes.

✳ Transfer to a large bowl, cover and let cool in the steam to make peeling easier. Once cool enough to handle, rub off the blackened skin and remove the stem and seeds. Cut into generous pieces.

✳ Meanwhile, bring a pot of lightly salted water to the boil. Add the potatoes and gently boil until just tender, about 15 minutes. Drain in a colander and leave to cool.

✳ In a large salad bowl, combine the potatoes, peppers, onion and tomatoes. Season with salt and pepper and add the oil. Gently toss to mix well. Fold in the hard-boiled eggs. Serve at room temperature.

Menorcan-style Stuffed Aubergines

Preparation time: 30 minutes,
    plus cooling time
Cooking time: 1 hour 10 minutes
Serves: 4

4 smallish aubergines (eggplant)
    (about 1.4 kg/3 lb total)
3 tablespoons olive oil, plus extra for
    drizzling
1 yellow onion, finely chopped
1 small long sweet green pepper,
    stemmed, seeded and finely chopped
2 cloves of garlic, minced
5 ripe tomatoes, halved and grated
    (see page 25)
2 tablespoons minced flat-leaf parsley
1 large (US extra-large) egg, beaten
40 g/1½ oz (⅓ cup) fine dry
    breadcrumbs, for sprinkling
Salt and pepper

VEG ✳ DF

At the Thursday market in Es Mercadal, I always buy some of Menorca's smallish, flavourful aubergines (eggplant), which I love to stuff. The descriptive local name for the popular dish is 'little boats', as the aubergines are halved lengthwise, filled, given a good sprinkling of breadcrumbs and put into the oven. Versions of this are popular across the Balearic Islands. Prepared *a la mallorquina* (Mallorcan-style, page 87) means with minced (ground) meat in the filling mixture and frequently covered with tomato sauce. But *a la menorquina* (Menorcan-style) includes just vegetables (and usually a beaten egg as a binder). Menorcan home cooks also stuff other vegetables – onions, courgettes (zucchini) – but none is more classic than aubergines.

✳ Bring a large pot of lightly salted water to a boil. Halve the aubergines (eggplant) lengthwise and add to the water. Boil until they are becoming soft, 10–15 minutes. Carefully remove without breaking the skins and drain in a colander with the cut sides facing down.

✳ Once the aubergines are cool enough to handle, carefully scoop out the insides using a spoon, leaving the shells and shape intact; set the shells aside. Finely chop the aubergine pulp.

✳ Heat the oil in a large frying pan or sauté pan over medium heat. Add the onion and cook until soft, 8–10 minutes. Add the pepper and cook until aromatic and beginning to soften, 2–3 minutes. Stir in the garlic and then add the tomatoes. Cook until the mixture is pulpy and darker, about 10 minutes.

✳ Stir in the aubergine pulp and parsley, season with salt and pepper and cover the pan. Cook, frequently stirring and tapping with a wooden spoon to help break up the pieces, until pasty and very soft, 10–15 minutes. Add a couple of tablespoons of water, if needed. Spoon into a mixing bowl and let cool before stirring in the egg.

✳ Meanwhile, preheat the oven to 180°C/350°F/Gas Mark 4.

✳ Line a baking sheet with baking (parchment) paper for easier clean-up. Arrange the aubergine shells on the prepared sheet. Spoon the filling into the shells. Evenly sprinkle about 1 teaspoon of breadcrumbs across the top of each in an even layer. Drizzle the breadcrumbs with oil.

✳ Bake in the oven on an upper rack until the tops are golden, 10–15 minutes. Serve hot or let cool and serve at room temperature.

Mallorcan-style Stuffed Aubergines

Preparation time: 25 minutes,
    plus cooling time
Cooking time: 1 hour 10 minutes
Serves: 2–4

2 medium aubergines (eggplant)
3 tablespoons olive oil, plus extra
    for drizzling
1 yellow onion, finely chopped
200 g/7 oz minced (ground) meat,
    preferably an even mixture of beef
    and pork
1 clove of garlic, minced
2 ripe plum tomatoes, halved and
    grated (see page 25)
1 tablespoon minced flat-leaf parsley
1 teaspoon sweet paprika
1 egg, beaten
Fine dry breadcrumbs, for sprinkling
250–350 ml/8–12 fl oz (1–1½ cups)
    tomato sauce, preferably homemade
    (page 342), warmed, optional
Salt and pepper

DF *

Aubergines (eggplant) in Mallorca are typically stuffed with a combination of minced (ground) meat – an even blend of pork and beef – and the pulp of the aubergine. This is one of the island's most celebrated dishes. Before serving, it frequently gets topped with an aromatic tomato sauce. This recipe makes four stuffed halves, enough for four people as an appetizer or for two as a main dish.

* Bring a pot of lightly salted water to a boil. Halve the aubergines (eggplant) lengthwise and drop into the water. Boil for 5 minutes, remove with a slotted spoon and let drain in a colander with the cut sides facing down.

* Once cool enough to handle, carefully scoop out the insides using a spoon and knife, leaving the shells and shape intact; set the shells aside. Finely chop the aubergine pulp.

* Heat the oil in a large frying pan or sauté pan over medium heat. Add the onion and cook until soft, about 8 minutes. Add the minced (ground) meat and brown, about 5 minutes. Stir in the garlic and then add the tomatoes and cook for 2–3 minutes. Stir in the aubergine pulp and parsley, cover the pan and cook, stirring and tapping with a wooden spoon frequently, until pasty and soft, about 15 minutes. Add 2–3 tablespoons water during cooking to help soften. Stir in the paprika and season with salt and pepper. Transfer to a mixing bowl and let cool before stirring in the egg.

* Meanwhile, preheat the oven to 180°C/350°F/Gas Mark 4.

* In a rectangular baking dish, arrange the aubergine shells. Spoon the filling into the shells.

* Evenly sprinkle a thin layer of breadcrumbs across the top of each. Drizzle with oil.

* Bake in the hot oven until the aubergines are cooked through and golden on top, about 30 minutes.

* Arrange on plates. Cover with tomato sauce (if using). Serve hot or let cool and serve at room temperature.

Tomato & Potato Casserole

Preparation time: 20 minutes
Cooking time: 1 hour
Serves: 4–6

6 tablespoons olive oil
5–6 medium white potatoes (about
    1 kg/2¼ lb total), peeled and cut
    crosswise into 5-mm/¼-inch slices
5–6 large ripe but firm tomatoes (about
    1 kg/2¼ lb total), cored and cut
    crosswise into 1.5-cm/⅔-inch slices
1 tablespoon sugar
75 g/2⅔ oz (generous ½ cup) fine dry
    breadcrumbs
3 cloves of garlic, minced
2 heaped tablespoons finely chopped
    flat-leaf parsley
1 tablespoon sweet paprika
Salt and pepper

V ✳ VEG ✳ DF

This beloved Menorcan casserole takes its name from a *perol*, the deep terracotta casserole dish traditionally used to bake it. Layers of sliced potatoes are topped by tomatoes, which get a dusting of breadcrumbs, garlic and parsley. It makes a lovely side dish but, with a salad, the dish often becomes a meal of its own on my table. Very frequently, other ingredients are placed between the layers of potatoes and tomatoes – lamb, pieces of fish, slices of pork. See page 238 for *perol* with lamb shoulder. A generous amount of oil is key. Remove some of the excess with a large spoon before serving, if desired.

✳ Preheat the oven to 180°C/350°F/Gas Mark 4.

✳ Coat the bottom of a large perol or baking dish with 1 tablespoon of the oil. Rinse the potatoes and add overlapping slices. Season with salt and pepper and drizzle over 3 tablespoons of the oil. Cover with the tomato slices. Sprinkle the tomatoes with the sugar.

✳ In a small bowl, combine the breadcrumbs, garlic, parsley and paprika, and spread this mixture over the tomatoes. Drizzle the remaining 2 tablespoons of the oil over the breadcrumbs.

✳ Bake in the hot oven, uncovered, until a knife goes easily into the potatoes and the breadcrumbs are a touch golden, about 1 hour.

Menorcan Cheese

At the Thursday market in Es Mercadal, a handful of local cheesemakers set up stands to sell their *formatge*. At the top of the main street, from well before 7:00 p.m. when the market kicks off in summer, until 11:00 p.m. when it winds down, there is a line to buy cheese from Tirant Nou, one of thirty or so certified producers of Queso Mahón-Menorca.

Menorca has a long history of cheesemaking. Utensils dating back to 2000 BCE suggest it was being done here in prehistoric times; written records from the fifth century CE refer to cheese being consumed on the island; and documents in Arabic from around 1000 CE highlight Menorca's excellent cheese. Significant amounts were exported in the thirteenth century. The industry got a boost during the eighteenth century as the British who ruled the island shipped the cheese from Maó. The British also introduced black-and-white Friesian cows, which produce more milk than the native *vermella* (red) landrace breed. (The name comes from the cows' light brown coats that look reddish in the sunlight.) In 1985, the Spanish government awarded Menorca's cheese Denominación de Origen (DO) status. It is the only cheese in the Balearic Islands to have such designation, and one of the few in Spain that uses pure cow's milk.

The cheeses are hand-moulded, wrapped in a piece of white cotton cloth and hung by the four corners to drain. Manually pressed and tied off at the top, this process gives the cheeses their characteristic square shape with rounded edges and distinctive marks from the folds of cloth and top knot. The rinds vary in colours from orangish-yellow to brownish. The colour comes from rubbing a mixture of olive oil and paprika onto the surface before placing on wooden shelves, and it darkens as the cheeses mature. The rinds of the long-aged ones turn a rich, tobacco-brown colour. Finished cheeses weigh roughly 2.5 kg/5½ lb.

Under the DO's regulatory council specifications, there are three varieties of cheese according to levels of maturation. The mildest is *tendre* (soft). Matured for at least twenty-one days, it is elastic and soft, with milky, buttery notes and a light acidic touch. The popular *semi-curat*, matured for at least sixty days, has a nuttier flavour, a yellowish-ivory colour and easy-to-slice texture. The rind of *semi-curat* is an orangish-brown colour. *Curat* is further aged. Matured for at least 150 days, the rind is brownish and the cheese itself more yellow in colour. These longer-aged cheeses are flaky and brittle when cut, with complex flavours sometimes described as 'aged wood' and 'tanned leather.' Long on the palate, the taste can sometimes be a touch piquant.

While the Friesian breed remains Menorca's main dairy cow, there has been a recent resurgence of local *vermella* cows, which are well-adapted to not just the climate but also the hilly landscape of farms like Tirant Nou. The Friesians are better suited to barns and flat farms, and not to climbing up steep slopes to graze.

Tirant Nou's *lloc* (farmhouse), dating from the period of British rule in the eighteenth century and painted a deep red, sits prominently on the slopes of a hillside estate overlooking the Bay of Fornells in the north.

The husband-and-wife team behind Tirant Nou have seventy *vermella* cows. While they might give less milk – together, the herd can produce enough for about forty cheeses a day in winter – what they do produce is richer in buttermilk. But importantly, the cows can easily reach the upper pastures of the farm. The salty air and sweet grasses help give the cheese its distinctive aromatic notes.

For Tirant Nou's cheesemakers, such movement is key to the well-being of their cows, whose milk gets transformed into exquisite cheeses – cheeses that, each Thursday, I, along with many others, happily line up to buy and then enjoy over the following week.

Mallorcan Paprika

Inside Palma de Mallorca's two most iconic covered municipal food markets – Mercat d'Olivar and Mercat de Santa Catalina – is an Especias Crespí stall. In 1945, the Crespí family began selling their paprika around the island for people to use in sobrassada, Mallorca's famed cured pork sausage (see page 208). While the company has expanded and sells a wide range of spices and blends – their *quatre espècies* ('four spices,' a traditional Mallorcan blend of black pepper, cloves, cinnamon and nutmeg) is particularly good – paprika remains, without a doubt, Crespí's most important product. Their 30-gram/just over 1-ounce containers of paprika largely fill the shelves. Paprika continues to be Mallorca's most iconic spice.

Seeds to grow peppers arrived on Mallorca from the Americas in the sixteenth century, and by the seventeenth century paprika was appearing in recipes. The impact was profound, not just transforming sobrassada, but seasoning a wide range of dishes. The condiment is added to a host of preparations, from *coca* flatbreads to stewed cauliflower (page 102) and various rices. The most basic way to use it is drizzling a slice of warm, toasted bread with olive oil and giving it a generous dusting of paprika. In Mallorca this is called *sobrassada de pobre,* 'poor man's sobrassada'.

Mallorcan *pebre bord* (as paprika is called on the island) is a deep, uniform orangish-red colour, silky and powdery between the fingers and almost creamy on the tongue. The flavour is intense but not overwhelmingly so. Because of the production methods used, there are no roasted notes present nor smoky ones, as in the famed La Vera smoked paprika from Extremadura on the Spanish mainland. The popular version of *pebre bord dolç* is sweet rather than spicy.

There are a couple of things that make Mallorca's paprika unique. First is the type of pepper, which is the local *tap de cortí* variety of *Capsicum annuum*. Between February and April, seeds are sown in nurseries and then transplanted two months later to fields, where the peppers grow with their tips facing upwards in the intense summer sun. Harvesting when intensely red – that is, overripe – is staggered, usually done in three phases, from late August to October. The harvested peppers are first dried naturally in the sun on the farms themselves (this can take up to a week), and then head to an oven for a second drying process, which takes around six to twelve
hours. The dried peppers are then crushed, the stems are removed if they haven't already been, and then the peppers are finally ground in stone mills. One kilogram/2.2 lb of fresh peppers yields about 120 g/4¼ oz of finished paprika.

The distinctive product has official governing status and is sold under the 'Protected Designation of Origin Mallorcan Paprika' label. (In Catalan it is officially 'Pebre Bord de Mallorca', and in Spanish, 'Pimentón de Mallorca'.)

Mallorca has long exported its fine paprika. Customs records from Palma for 1884 show that 13,287 kg/29,293 lb of paprika headed to mainland Spain, 2,139 kg/4,716 lb to the Americas and 740 kg/1,631 lb to Europe and Africa. That would be enough of the spice for over a half million of those typical 30-gram Crespí *pebre bord* containers that fill the stall shelves in Mercat d'Olivar and Mercat de Santa Catalina.

Stuffed Artichokes

Preparation time: 20 minutes,
    plus cooling time
Cooking time: 1 hour 10 minutes
Serves: 3–4

½ lemon
8 artichokes, preferably smallish violet
    variety (about 1.25 kg/2¾ lb total)
75 g/2⅔ oz (generous ½ cup) fine dry
    breadcrumbs
2 cloves of garlic, minced
2 tablespoons minced flat-leaf parsley
1 teaspoon paprika
Olive oil, for drizzling
65 g/2¼ oz (⅔ cup) shredded cheese,
    preferably semi-cured Queso de
    Mahón-Menorca
Salt and pepper

VEG *

The popular local variety of artichokes in the Balearics is purplish-tinted. In spring, they are piled high in markets. The easiest way to prepare them is to first briefly boil to soften and then bake in the oven with olive oil and salt. This is a slightly more sophisticated method. While the artichokes in this recipe are filled with breadcrumbs and cured Menorcan cheese, some cooks prepare them with some sobrassada inside each instead. They are also delicious that way.

* Fill a pot with lightly salted water, squeeze in the juice from the lemon and drop it into the water. Bring the water to a boil over high heat.

* As the water is coming to a boil, working one at a time, pull away or cut the toughest leaves from the artichokes. Trim off the very top of the leaves with a serrated knife to reveal the centre. Roll gently under the hand to slightly loosen the remaining leaves. Trim the stem so that the artichokes will sit upright. Drop in to the water as you work, so they don't discolour.

* When the water reaches a boil, reduce the heat and gently boil the artichokes for 5 minutes. Remove with tongs and let drain and cool upside down in a colander for 5–10 minutes.

* Preheat the oven to 180°C/350°F/Gas Mark 4. In a bowl, mix together the breadcrumbs, garlic, parsley and paprika, and season with salt and pepper.

* Arrange the artichokes upright in a baking dish. With the help of a small spoon, slightly open the centre of each to make room for the filling. Season the inside of each with salt and pepper and drizzle with oil. For each artichoke, loosely pack in about 1 tablespoon of the cheese and then top with about 2 teaspoons of the breadcrumb mixture. Generously drizzle olive oil over the top of each.

* Pour 5 mm–1 cm/¼–½ inch water into the bottom of the baking dish. Cover with aluminium foil and bake for 45 minutes. Uncover and bake until tender, about 15 minutes. Test for doneness. The tip of a knife should slide easily into the base of an artichoke. Serve.

Roasted Red Peppers

Preparation time: 15 minutes,
    plus cooling time
Cooking time: 15 minutes–1 hour
Serves: 4

2 large red bell peppers
Olive oil, for covering and brushing
3 cloves of garlic, thinly sliced
Salt

V ✳ VEG ✳ DF ✳ GF ✳ 5

Roasted red bell peppers are enormously popular in the Balearic kitchen, and frequently top *coca* flatbread (*coca de pebrera*, page 42), go into salads (*enciam pagès*, page 82) and get spread across pieces of baked salt cod (page 184). But strips of peppers that have been steeped in olive oil with garlic, like in this recipe, are frequently eaten on their own with bread. They are also excellent served alongside grilled fish or meat, and with some olives and capers, can be turned into a perfect appetizer. The peppers can be roasted under the intense heat of a grill (broiler), in the oven wrapped in aluminium foil or, for lovely smoky notes, cooked outdoors on embers. Directions for all three methods follow. One important note: avoid all temptation of rinsing off the seeds that cling to ease the task of peeling – you certainly don't want to rinse away those lovely grilled flavours.

✳ To grill (broil) in the oven: preheat the oven grill (broiler) to high. Line a baking sheet with aluminium foil for easier clean-up. Brush the peppers with oil and set on the baking sheet. Grill, carefully turning as needed, until charred in places and tender, 20–30 minutes. Transfer to a large bowl, cover with cling film (plastic wrap) and let the peppers begin cooling in the steam for 15 minutes to make peeling easier. Uncover and allow to cool for 5–10 minutes more, or until cool enough to handle with the fingers.

✳ To roast in the oven: preheat the oven to 230°C/450°F/Gas Mark 8. Line a baking sheet with aluminium foil for easier clean-up. Brush the peppers with oil, individually wrap in aluminium foil and set on the baking sheet. Roast in the oven, turning a few times, until charred in places and tender, about 45 minutes. Remove from the oven and let cool in the foil for about 15 minutes to make peeling easier. Uncover and allow to cool for 5–10 minutes more, or until cool enough to handle with the fingers.

✳ To grill over embers: heat a barbecue. Grill the peppers on embers on the barbecue for 10–15 minutes, carefully turning as needed, being careful not to break them, until blackened. Transfer to a large bowl, cover with clingfilm and let the peppers begin cooling in the steam for 15 minutes to make peeling easier. Uncover and allow to cool for 5–10 minutes more, or until cool enough to handle with the fingers.

✳ Once cool enough to handle, rub off the skin and discard the stem and seeds. Do not rinse. Tear or cut into generous pieces.

✳ Lay the strips of peppers in a shallow bowl. Add the garlic, season with salt and cover with olive oil.

Swiss Chard with Raisins & Pine Nuts

Preparation time: 10 minutes
Cooking time: 10 minutes
Serves: 4

400 g/14 oz trimmed Swiss chard,
    thoroughly cleaned and chopped
40 g/1½ oz (¼ cup) seedless raisins
Warm water, for soaking
2 tablespoons olive oil
2 tablespoons pine nuts
salt and pepper

V ✳ VEG ✳ DF ✳ GF ✳ 5 ✳ 30

Bledes – Swiss chard in English, *acelgas* in Spanish – are a popular leafy green similar to spinach (which has smaller, softer leaves and thinner, greener stems). This rather straightforward way of preparing *bledes* is delicious. Add some minced garlic when cooking the pine nuts and raisins, or even some chopped bacon. A similar blending of savoury and sweet tops *coca* flatbreads (page 41) and fills savoury pastries (page 45).

✳ Bring a large pot of water to a boil, add the Swiss chard and boil until tender, 3–4 minutes. Transfer to a colander and drain well.

✳ Meanwhile, put the raisins in a small bowl, cover with warm water and soak for about 10 minutes to soften. Drain, then spread out on paper towels to dry.

✳ Heat the oil in a large frying pan or sauté pan over medium heat. Add the raisins and pine nuts, and cook, stirring frequently, until the raisins plump up and the pine nuts begin to turn golden brown, about 2 minutes. Add the Swiss chard, season with salt and pepper and sauté for 1 minute.

✳ Transfer to a serving bowl and serve immediately.

Escarole & Green Onion Fritters

Preparation time: 10 minutes,
    plus resting time
Cooking time: 15 minutes
Makes: 8–10 fritters

125 g/4¼ oz trimmed and cleaned
    escarole or curly endive (frisée), finely
    chopped
2 large (US extra-large) eggs
50 g/2 oz (⅓ cup) plain (all-purpose)
    flour
1 tablespoon finely chopped flat-leaf
    parsley
1 clove of garlic, minced
½ small onion, very thinly sliced
Neutral vegetable oil, for frying
Salt and pepper

VEG ✳ DF

Raoles are small fritters using all sorts of ingredients. While they are often prepared with leftovers like pieces of fish or seafood, some of the tastiest versions are quite simple and use leafy greens like escarole or chard. This Menorcan version with escarole uses very little batter – just enough so that the greens are lightly coated and, once in the oil and cooking, will hold together as a fritter. It shouldn't have too much batter (or oil), but rather be herby and green. Escarole is nice with the addition of finely chopped garlic and onions in the blend.

✳ Spread out the escarole on paper towels to dry if wet.

✳ In a mixing bowl, beat the eggs with salt and pepper. Beat in the flour and loosen with 1 tablespoon water. Fold in the parsley, garlic, onion and escarole. Let the batter rest for 15 minutes.

✳ Heat at least 2 cm/¾ inch of oil in a small frying pan over medium–high heat until the surface shimmers. Line a plate with absorbent paper towels.

✳ Working in batches that don't crowd the pan, carefully spoon about 1 generously heaped tablespoon of the batter into the oil for each fritter, pressing down to slightly flatten. Fry until golden brown on the outside and no longer raw on the inside, turning the fritters as needed, about 5 minutes per batch.

✳ Lift out with tongs, holding above the pan for a moment to let the oil drain back into the pan, then transfer to the absorbent towels to drain while you fry the rest. Serve hot.

Preparation time: 20 minutes
Cooking time: 1 hour
Serves: 4

4 tablespoons olive oil
250 g/9 oz boneless pork shoulder,
    cut into small pieces
1 yellow onion, halved and thinly sliced
4 cloves of garlic, minced
1 tomato, chopped
1 heaped tablespoon sweet paprika
½ head cabbage, cored and cut into
    strips (about 500 g/1 lb 2 oz)
50 g/2 oz fresh spinach leaves (about
    2 loosely packed cups)
¼ cauliflower, cut into small florets
    (about 150 g/5 oz)
3 heaped tablespoons minced flat-leaf
    parsley
200 g/7 oz thin slices of country-style
    bread (*pa de sopes*, see page 24)
Extra-virgin olive oil, for drizzling
Salt and pepper

DF ✳

'Mallorcan Soups' or 'Dry Soups'

There are two kinds of soup in Mallorca. There is *sopa*, in singular, that is like the global type that calls for a spoon. Then there is *sopes*, in plural, that is wholly unique to Mallorca and which you can almost eat with a fork. The name comes from the thin slices of bread called '*sopes*' that the simmered vegetables get served over and which absorb all of the liquid. While this gives the dish one of its common names (*sopes seques*, 'dry soups'), it is so identified with the island that it is usually called *sopes mallorquines* ('Mallorcan soups'). There are countless versions, both summer and winter, but cabbage is often at their heart, and there is usually a generous amount of paprika. You can serve it from a large casserole dish or on individual plates; directions for both ways are included.

✳ Heat the olive oil in a large pot or Dutch oven over medium heat. Add the pork and brown for about 5 minutes. Add the onion and cook until it is becoming tender, about 5 minutes. Stir in the garlic and then the tomato, and cook for 5 minutes more. Add the paprika and season generously with salt and pepper. Gradually add the cabbage, turning it over in the sauce. Pour in about 750 ml (25 fl oz/3 cups) water and bring to a boil. Add the spinach, cauliflower and parsley, and simmer until the cabbage is tender, 30–40 minutes.

✳ There are two ways to serve.

✳ To serve from a casserole pan: Cover the bottom of a large, flameproof casserole pan (see page 25) with a single layer of bread. Add about 500 ml (18 fl oz/2 cups) of the liquid from the pot. Gently push down the bread with the back of a slotted spoon. Add more liquid if the bread can absorb it. Once the liquid has been absorbed, scoop out the vegetables using a slotted spoon and place on top of the bread. Drizzle with extra-virgin olive oil, cover and let sit for 5 minutes before serving with wide bowls.

✳ To serve from wide, flat individual bowls: line the bottom of each bowl with pieces of bread in a single layer and ladle over about 120 ml (4 fl oz/½ cup) of the broth. Once it has been absorbed, add the vegetables with a slotted spoon. Drizzle with extra-virgin olive oil, cover and let sit for 5 minutes before serving.

Braised Cauliflower with Bacon, Pine Nuts & Raisins

Preparation time: 20 minutes
Cooking time: 50 minutes
Serves: 4

2 tablespoons olive oil
150 g/5 oz thick slices of lean bacon
    or salted and cured pork belly,
    trimmed and diced
1 yellow onion or 2 bulbous spring
    onions (scallions), finely chopped
2 cloves of garlic, minced
2 ripe tomatoes, halved and grated
    (see page 25)
60 ml/2 fl oz (¼ cup) brandy or cognac,
    or 120 ml/4 fl oz (½ cup) dry white
    wine
1 cauliflower (about 1 kg/2¼ lb), cut
    into florets
1 tablespoon sweet paprika
50 g/2 oz (⅓ cup) seedless raisins
Warm water, for soaking
2–3 heaped tablespoons pine nuts,
    dry-toasted (see page 25)
Salt and pepper

DF ✳ GF

One of the most common ways to prepare cauliflower in the Balearic Islands is to braise it – the dish is called *ofegada*, literally 'drowned'. This variation calls for the trio of bacon, paprika and brandy. Its earthiness gets a counterpoint of sweetness with the raisins and a nutty crunch from the pine nuts.

✳ Heat the oil in a large frying pan or sauté pan over medium heat. Add the bacon and cook until it begins to brown, about 3 minutes. Add the onion(s) and cook until soft, about 8 minutes. Stir in the garlic, add the tomatoes and cook until reduced, about 5 minutes. Stir in the brandy, cognac or wine, let the alcohol burn off for 1 minute, and then add the cauliflower. Season with salt and pepper, sprinkle in the paprika and add 175 ml (6 fl oz/¾ cup) water. Turn over the florets to coat with the sauce. Cover the pan snugly and cook over medium–low heat, turning the florets from time to time, until tender, about 30 minutes.

✳ Meanwhile, soak the raisins in a glass of warm water for 10 minutes to soften; drain.

✳ Add the raisins and pine nuts to the pan. Cook, uncovered, gently turning over a few times, until the cauliflower is tender but not breaking apart and the flavours are combined, 2–3 minutes. Transfer to a serving bowl and serve.

Layered Vegetables
with Tomato Sauce & Fried Egg

Preparation time: 30 minutes,
   plus salting time
Cooking time: 40 minutes
Serves: 4

2 aubergines (eggplant)
4 medium white potatoes (about
   800 g/1¾ lb total)
350 ml/12 fl oz (1½ cups) olive oil or
   a neutral oil, for frying
2 medium or 1 large courgette(s)
   (zucchini), trimmed and sliced
   crosswise into circles
1 red bell pepper, stemmed, seeded
   and cut into strips
4 cloves of garlic, skins on, lightly
   crushed under the palm
250 ml/8 fl oz (1 cup) tomato sauce,
   preferably homemade (page 342)
4 large (US extra-large) eggs, optional
Salt

V ✳ VEG ✳ DF ✳ GF

Another of Mallorca's emblematic dishes, *tumbet* is a medley of fried and neatly layered vegetables. A summer and autumn favourite, *tumbet* usually includes aubergines (eggplant), red bell peppers, potatoes and sometimes courgettes (zucchini). Served topped with tomato sauce (and often a fried egg), it makes a meal. After frying the vegetables, drain them for a moment on paper towels to avoid the final dish being excessively oily. Generally, the vegetables are fried in succession, layered into a terracotta casserole pan (*greixonera*, see page 25) and then heated in the oven for a few minutes before serving.

✳ Trim the ends of the aubergines (eggplant) and slice crosswise into 1-cm/½-inch-thick circles. Set the aubergines in a colander, liberally salt the slices and let sweat away some of their bitterness for about 30 minutes. (Dark beads will appear on the surface.) Rinse and pat dry with paper towels.

✳ Meanwhile, peel the potatoes and slice crosswise into 5-mm/¼-inch-thick circles. Soak in a large bowl of cold water. Drain and pat dry with paper towels.

✳ Preheat the oven to 150°C/300°F/Gas Mark 2. Line a platter with paper towels. Set out a large, shallow, flameproof casserole pan (see page 25) or baking dish.

✳ Heat the oil in a frying pan over high heat. Add the potatoes and fry until tender and becoming just golden, 8–10 minutes. Transfer with a slotted spoon to the paper towels to drain for a few minutes. Arrange on the bottom of the casserole.

✳ In the same pan over medium–high heat, fry the aubergines until tender and becoming just golden, 6–8 minutes. Transfer with a slotted spoon to the paper towels to drain for a couple of minutes. Arrange in a layer over the potatoes.

✳ In the same pan, fry the courgettes (zucchini) until tender and becoming just golden, 6–8 minutes. Transfer with a slotted spoon to the paper towels to drain for a couple of minutes. Season with salt and arrange in a layer over the aubergine.

✳ And finally, in the same pan, fry the pepper and garlic until the pepper is tender and the garlic aromatic but not scorched, 5–6 minutes. (Remove the garlic after about 3 minutes and set aside or discard). Transfer with a slotted spoon to the paper towels to drain for a couple of minutes. Arrange on top of the courgettes. Add the garlic if desired.

✳ Spread the tomato sauce evenly over the top of the vegetables. Put in the oven and warm for about 5 minutes.

✳ Spoon out a little of the oil from frying and heat in a small frying pan, then gently crack in the eggs (if using) and fry without turning until the yolks are runny and the whites opaque, about 2 minutes.

✳ Set the fried eggs on top of the vegetables and serve.

Braised Fresh Broad Beans

Preparation time: 20 minutes
Cooking time: 30 minutes
Serves: 4–6

2 tablespoons olive oil
1 generous bunch (about 250 g/9 oz)
    spring onions (scallions), trimmed
    and chopped
120 ml/4 fl oz (½ cup) dry white wine
800 g/1¾ lb fresh or thawed shelled
    broad (fava) beans (5–6 cups)
1 small dried chilli (chile) or cayenne
    pepper, optional
Small bunch of fresh herbs (fennel,
    thyme, marjoram, celery leaf, etc.),
    tied together
2 tablespoons minced fresh mint, plus
    leaves to garnish
Salt and pepper

V ✳ VEG ✳ GF ✳ 1 POT

This spring dish is best made using smaller, more tender fresh broad (fava) beans, sometimes called 'baby'. Along with a bouquet of herbs – fennel fronds, thyme, marjoram, celery leaf – one addition gives this dish its final distinctive touch: finely chopped fresh mint added at the end. The name *ofegats* literally means 'drowned' and refers to the beans being braised. This is the vegetarian version, but many cooks sauté some bacon and/or fresh sausage with the onions for bolder flavours. Note that it takes about 1 kg/2¼ lb of fresh pods to yield 250 g/9 oz of shucked beans.

✳ Heat the oil in a large, wide pot or Dutch oven over medium heat. Add the spring onions and cook until they begin to soften, about 5 minutes. Stir in the wine and let the alcohol burn off for 1 minute. Stir in the broad (fava) beans, add the chilli (chile) or cayenne, if using, and the herbs and season with salt and pepper. Cover the pot, reduce the heat to low and cook until the broad beans are tender, about 10–15 minutes, stirring from time to time. Add a touch of water if needed.

✳ Discard the tied herbs, fold in the fresh mint, spoon into bowls and serve with a few mint leaves scattered on top.

Pumpkin 'Frit' with Pork

Preparation time: 10 minutes
Cooking time: 50 minutes
Serves: 3–4

350 g/12 oz thick slices of boneless pork
     loin (preferably blade end), cut into
     larger than bite-size pieces
175 g/6 oz fresh pork belly, salted and
     cured pork belly (pancetta) or bacon,
     trimmed and chopped
4 tablespoons olive oil
6 cloves of garlic, skins on, lightly
     crushed under the palm
1 bay leaf
2 leeks, trimmed, white and tender
     green parts finely chopped
450 g/1 lb pumpkin or pumpkin squash,
     peeled, seeded and cut into 1.5-cm/
     ⅔-inch cubes
1 small dried chilli (chile) or 1 dried
     cayenne pepper, optional
Salt and pepper

DF ✳ GF ✳ 1 POT

Frit is the general name for a wide range of 'fried' dishes in Mallorca. While there are seafood versions (octopus, on page 217, is popular), many call for pork meat, especially in the central Es Pla region. The touch of earthy sweetness from the leeks and pumpkin are delightful with the pork. There are two cuts of pork here – loin (the blade end is preferable) and pork belly. While the latter is often fresh, using salt-cured pork belly (as Italian pancetta) or bacon is a lovely alternative. Towards the end of cooking, some cooks like to add pieces of a fresh local black sausage called *botifarró* (see page 23).

✳ Generously season the pork loin and pork belly with salt and pepper.

✳ Heat the oil in a large frying pan or sauté pan over medium–high heat. Add the pork loin and belly, and cook until the meat is browned, about 5 minutes. Add the garlic and bay leaf and cook until aromatic, about 1 minute. Stir in the leeks and pumpkin, reduce the heat to low and cook, mostly covered, until the pumpkin is tender, about 45 minutes. Towards the end, add the chilli (chile), if using.

✳ Serve immediately.

Baked Sweet Potatoes with Honey & Cinnamon

Preparation time: 5 minutes
Cooking time: 2 hours 30 minutes
Serves: 6

6 medium sweet potatoes (about
    1.5 kg/3¼ lb total)
Honey, for drizzling
Ground cinnamon, for dusting

VEG ✳ DF ✳ GF ✳ 5

Moniatos (sweet potatoes) are one of the many introductions from the Americas that feel so deeply traditional that it is hard to believe they haven't always been part of this ancient Balearic cuisine. One of the most popular ways to eat them is baked in the oven and served with honey and cinnamon, either for an afternoon snack or for dessert. In our house, we also serve them this way as a side dish. Use sweet potatoes that are roughly the same shape and size for more uniform baking. Ideally choose skinnier ones, which will cook a bit quicker.

✳ Preheat the oven to 150°C/300°F/Gas Mark 2. Line a baking sheet with baking (parchment) paper for easier clean-up.

✳ Arrange the sweet potatoes on the prepared baking sheet. Bake in the hot oven until tender – the skin will start to wrinkle and come away from the pulp, and the tip of a knife will easily enter, about 2½ hours.

✳ Remove from the oven and let cool until the sweet potatoes can be handled with the fingers. Either peel completely or open lengthwise. Drizzle generously with honey, dust with cinnamon and serve.

CHAPTER 4

EGGS

EGGS

Farmer's Egg Tortilla

Preparation time: 10 minutes
Cooking time: 35 minutes
Serves: 4

4 tablespoons olive oil, plus extra if
    needed
1 white potato, peeled and thinly sliced
1 yellow onion, thinly sliced
1 small or ½ large red bell pepper,
    stemmed, seeded and cut into
    generous pieces
1 tomato, cut into bite-size pieces
4 large (US extra-large) eggs
Salt

VEG ✳ DF ✳ GF

If an egg tortilla can absorb any of the season's flavours (from wild mushrooms
to skinny, foraged asparagus, page 117), then it can also incorporate whatever
is in the larder and turn a few vegetables into a delicious meal. In Formentera,
this *truita* often includes a quartet of produce that is always on hand – potatoes,
red bell peppers, onions and, unusually for tortillas, tomatoes.

✳ Heat the oil in a 23-cm/9-inch non-stick frying pan over high heat. Add the
potato and fry until tender, 8–10 minutes. Transfer with a slotted spoon to a
colander to drain off the excess oil and then transfer to a large bowl.

✳ In the same pan over medium–high heat, fry the onion and pepper until they
begin to soften, about 10 minutes. Add the tomato and cook for 2 minutes. Transfer
with a slotted spoon to the bowl, leaving as much oil in the pan as possible.
Remove the pan from the heat.

✳ In a separate bowl, beat the eggs, season with salt and pepper and pour over
the vegetables. Stir gently and let sit for a few minutes.

✳ The bottom of the pan should be lightly coated with oil; add a touch more
if needed, or scoop some out if there is too much in the pan. Heat over high heat.
Pour in the egg mixture and then immediately reduce the heat to low. Shake
the pan so that the tortilla doesn't stick. Cook until the eggs are nearly set and
the tortilla can be flipped, 6–8 minutes. With the help of a plate, flip the tortilla:
carefully flip onto the plate, then slide the tortilla back into the pan and cook until
cooked through but still a touch juicy, 5 minutes.

✳ Transfer to a serving plate. Let cool for a few minutes before cutting into wedges
and serving.

Egg Tortilla with Wild Asparagus

Preparation time: 5 minutes
Cooking time: 25 minutes
Serves: 2–3

150 g/5 oz tender wild asparagus
　　(about 30 stalks)
6 large (US extra-large) eggs
3 tablespoons olive oil
Salt and pepper

VEG ✳ DF ✳ GF ✳ 5 ✳ 30

Often found growing beside stone walls, *espàrrecs silvestres* – wild asparagus – are one of spring's tastiest offerings, and one of the things I most look forward to around Eastertime. The thin stalks have a bolder taste compared to their much fatter and shorter cultivated cousins. Sometimes their naturally pleasing bitterness can be too strong and overpower the eggs, so it is preferable to blanch the stalks in boiling water for a couple of minutes before cooking.

✳ Clean the asparagus, snapping off the hard, woody parts at the end of each stalk (it will naturally break where it becomes tender). Snap or cut each stalk into 2 or 3 pieces.

✳ Bring a pot of lightly salted water to a boil, add the asparagus and blanch for 1–2 minutes. Drain in a colander and let cool completely.

✳ In a bowl, beat the eggs with salt and pepper.

✳ Heat 1 tablespoon of the oil in a medium non-stick frying pan over medium heat. Add the asparagus and cook until tender and darker, about 8 minutes. Transfer to the bowl with the eggs.

✳ Carefully wipe out the pan. Heat the remaining 2 tablespoons of oil over high heat. Pour in the egg mixture and then immediately reduce the heat to low. Shake the pan so that the tortilla doesn't stick. Cook until the eggs are nearly set and the tortilla can be flipped, 6–8 minutes. With the help of a plate, flip the tortilla: carefully flip onto the plate, then slide the tortilla back into the pan. Cook until cooked through but still a touch juicy, 3–5 minutes.

✳ Transfer to a plate. Cut into wedges and serve.

Egg Tortilla with Fresh Broad Beans & Onions

Preparation time: 10 minutes,
    plus cooling time
Cooking time: 40 minutes
Serves: 3–4

5 tablespoons olive oil
2 medium yellow onions, thinly sliced
300 g/11 oz (2 cups) shucked tender
    broad (fava) beans or thawed frozen
    small broad beans
1 heaped tablespoon minced fresh herbs,
    such as marjoram and thyme
6 large (US extra-large) eggs
Salt and pepper

VEG ✳ DF ✳ GF ✳ 5

Fresh *faves* – broad (fava) beans – are a favourite on Ibiza and Formentera, where they appear over and over again on tables, including in egg tortillas. In early winter, when the smallish pods are very tender, they are cooked fresh in their shells without being shucked. (To do this, rinse the pods and trim into short sections.) As they grow and the pods become tougher, the beans are shucked before cooking. This dish uses plenty of onions and some fresh herbs. Fresh garlic shoots are also in the market around the same time and are delicious sautéed with the onions.

✳ Heat 3 tablespoons of the oil in a large frying pan over medium–high heat. Add the onions and cook until they become tender and take on some colour, about 12 minutes. Add the broad (fava) beans, reduce the heat to medium–low, cover the pan and cook, stirring frequently, until the broad beans are just tender, about 15 minutes. Stir in the herbs, remove the pan from the heat and let cool for 5 minutes.

✳ In a bowl, beat the eggs with salt and pepper. Fold in the beans and onions.

✳ Heat the remaining 2 tablespoons of oil in a 26-cm/10-inch non-stick frying pan over high heat. Pour in the egg mixture and then immediately reduce the heat to low. Shake the pan so that it doesn't stick. Cook until the eggs are nearly set and the tortilla can be turned, 6–8 minutes. With the help of a plate, flip the tortilla: carefully flip onto the plate, then slide the tortilla back into the pan and cook until cooked through but just a touch juicy, about 3 minutes.

✳ Transfer to a serving plate. Let cool for a few minutes before cutting into wedges and serving.

Omelette with Sobrassada & Fresh Mint

Preparation time: 10 minutes
Cooking time: 3 minutes
Serves: 1

2 extra-large (US jumbo) eggs
8–10 fresh mint leaves, minced
25 g/1 oz sobrassada (see page 208),
    casing removed and cut or pulled into
    small pieces
Olive oil, for greasing
Salt and pepper

DF ✳ GF ✳ 5 ✳ 30

Omelettes with sobrassada are often eaten inside a bun or bread roll for a late breakfast. But with a generous green salad, this *truita* makes an excellent (and quick) lunch or dinner. The fresh mint beaten with the eggs transforms the simple dish into something rather sublime. Because the omelette has sobrassada, the eggs require little, if any, salt.

✳ In a bowl, beat the eggs with the mint, add a pinch of salt and season with pepper. On a dish, set out the sobrassada, so it's ready to be added.

✳ Lightly oil a 25-cm/10-inch non-stick frying pan and heat over medium–high heat. Pour the egg mixture into the pan. As soon as the egg begins to set, arrange the pieces of sobrassada across the width of the centre. Once the egg is about fully set, fold over one third of the omelette towards the centre using a thin spatula, and then fold over the opposite third. Cook until the centre is set enough to turn over. Turn the omelette and cook until the egg in the centre is set, 2–3 minutes total cooking time. Slide onto a plate and serve immediately.

Eggs Scrambled with Summer Vegetables

Preparation time: 10 minutes
Cooking time: 16 minutes
Serves: 3–4

3 tablespoons olive oil
1 small long sweet green pepper or
   ½ green bell pepper, stemmed,
   seeded and finely chopped
2 cloves of garlic, skins on, lightly
   crushed under the palm
1 bay leaf
½ courgette (zucchini), trimmed, partly
   peeled, and cut into bite-size pieces
1 small or ½ large aubergine (eggplant),
   trimmed, partly peeled and cut into
   bite-size pieces
5 large (US extra-large) eggs
Salt and pepper

VEG ✳ DF ✳ GF ✳ 30

'Scrambled eggs' is an imperfect translation for *ous remenats*. The name means 'to stir'; once the vegetables have been sautéed and the beaten eggs poured into the pan, they are given a moment to begin to set before being stirred with just a handful of large sweeps of the wooden spoon around the wide pan. They should still be moist. The classic spring version calls for asparagus and tender garlic shoots (and sometimes shrimp), while in autumn it's made with wild mushrooms (page 124). Summertime in the Balearics means peppers, courgettes (zucchini) and aubergines (eggplant).

✳ Heat the oil in a large non-stick frying pan over medium–high heat. Add the green pepper, garlic and bay leaf and cook for 2 minutes. Add the courgette and aubergine and cook, stirring frequently, until tender, 10–12 minutes.

✳ Meanwhile, in a bowl, beat the eggs and season with salt and pepper.

✳ Pour the eggs into the pan and let set for 15 seconds. Stir, using large, slow, generous sweeps around the pan with a wooden spoon, until the eggs are done but still quite moist, 1–1½ minutes.

✳ Divide among plates, generously grind pepper over the top and serve.

Eggs Scrambled with Mushrooms, Garlic Shoots & Spring Onions

Preparation time: 10 minutes
Cooking time: 15 minutes
Serves: 4

6 large (US extra-large) eggs, beaten
2 tablespoons olive oil, or as needed
400 g/14 oz wild mushrooms, cleaned
    (see page 25) and halved or
    quartered if large
4 tender or sprouted garlic shoots,
    trimmed (white and pinkish-purple
    part only) and sliced crosswise in
    5-mm/¼-inch pieces
1 generous bunch (about 250 g/9 oz)
    spring onions (scallions), trimmed
    and sliced crosswise in 5-mm/
    ¼-inch pieces
2 tablespoons minced flat-leaf parsley
Salt and pepper

VEG ✳ DF ✳ GF ✳ 30

One of the best ways to fully appreciate the flavours of wild mushrooms is to cook them in the pan with scrambled eggs. Bloody milk caps (*esclata-sangs*) and chanterelles (*cames-seques*) are two favourite choices for fungi, though use what is in season and available. This dish is especially lovely when including *alls tendres* (tender garlic shoots) and spring onions (scallions). Similar in appearance to skinny spring onions, *alls tendres* have pinkish-white ends and heady garlic aromas. Don't crowd the pan when preparing this dish. Either use a large (30-cm/12-inch) frying pan or divide the ingredients in half and prepare in two batches.

✳ In a bowl, beat the eggs with salt and pepper.

✳ Heat the oil in a large non-stick frying pan over high heat. Add the mushrooms and cook until slightly golden on the edges, 5–10 minutes, depending on the mushroom. Transfer to a bowl.

✳ Reduce the heat to medium–low and add a touch more oil to the pan if needed. Add the garlic shoots and spring onions (scallions), and cook, stirring frequently, until tender, fragrant and a touch golden, about 2 minutes. Return the mushrooms to the pan, add the parsley and cook, stirring a few times, for 1 minute.

✳ Pour the eggs into the pan and let set for 15 seconds. Stir, using large, slow, generous sweeps around the pan with a wooden spoon, until the eggs are done but still quite moist, 1–1½ minutes.

✳ Divide among plates, generously grind pepper over the top and serve.

Sóller-style Eggs on Puréed Vegetables

Preparation time: 10 minutes
Cooking time: 20 minutes
Serves: 4

1 carrot, trimmed and roughly chopped
2 leeks, trimmed and the white and
    tender green parts roughly chopped
350 g/12 oz freshly shelled peas (about
    2 cups)
generous pinch of sugar
1 tablespoon olive oil
4 × 1-cm/½-inch-thick slices of
    sobrassada (about 200 g/7 oz total),
    casing removed
4 large (US extra-large) eggs
Salt and pepper

DF ✳ GF ✳ 30

Named for Sóller, the town on the southern slopes of the Serra de Tramuntana range, this dish is an interesting combination of fried eggs and sobrassada served on a bed of puréed vegetables that generally consist of fresh peas, leeks and carrots. The contrasts of flavours and textures is striking. A tasty if unorthodox substitution for the sobrassada here is using strips of fried bacon. Some add cream or stock (broth) to the vegetable purée, but it isn't necessary. The freshness of the vegetables makes for a nice contrast to the sobrassada and eggs. While ideally prepared in spring when peas are in season, it can be made anytime using thawed frozen peas.

✳ Bring a pot of 750 ml (25 fl oz/3 cups) water to a rolling boil, then add the carrot and boil for 5 minutes. Add the leeks and boil for 5 minutes. Add the peas and sugar and boil until all of the vegetables are tender, about 5 minutes. Strain, reserving at least 250 ml (8 fl oz/1 cup) of the liquid.

✳ Season the vegetables with salt and pepper, add 120 ml (4 fl oz/½ cup) of the reserved liquid and place in a blender or food processor, then purée until creamy, or pass through a food mill. Add a touch more of the reserved liquid if necessary. Cover and keep warm.

✳ Heat the oil in a small frying pan over medium–low heat. Add the sobrassada and cook until it turns a darker colour and begins to crumble, 30 seconds–1 minute. Transfer to a plate. In the same pan, gently crack in the eggs and fry without turning until the whites are opaque and the yolks still runny, about 2 minutes.

✳ Divide the purée among wide, shallow bowls, cover each with a slice of sobrassada and then top with an egg. Serve immediately.

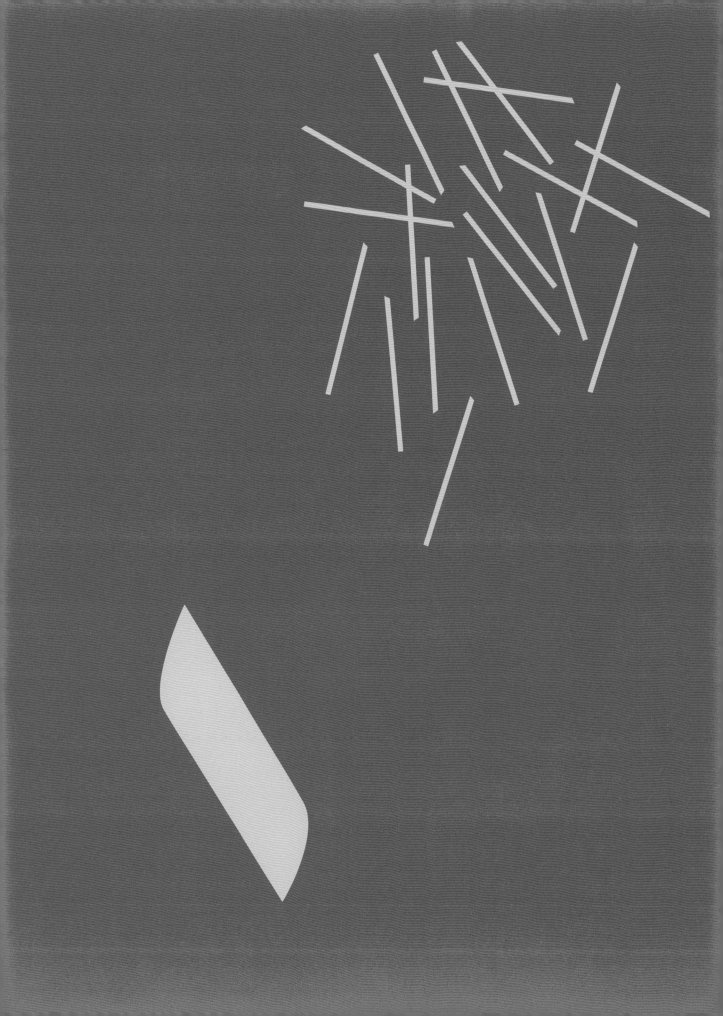

CHAPTER 5

RICE, PASTA & GRAINS

Fisherman's Rice 'On the Side'

Preparation time: 15 minutes,
    plus resting time
Cooking time: 50 minutes
Serves: 4

2 tablespoons olive oil
1 small, cleaned cuttlefish (see page 25),
    about 250 g/9 oz, cut into 1-cm/
    ½-inch pieces
2 cloves of garlic, minced
1 teaspoon finely chopped parsley
2 tomatoes, halved and grated
    (see page 25)
1 litre/34 fl oz (4¼ cups) broth from *bullit
    de peix* ('Boiled' Fish, page 160) or Fish
    Stock (page 338)
Pinch of saffron threads, crumbled,
    optional
200 g/7 oz (1 cup) short- or
    medium-grain white rice

DF ✳ GF

This is often served as the companion to Ibiza and Formentera's iconic *bullit de peix* (page 160). The broth from boiling fish and potatoes is used here to make a wide pan of rice, whose name means 'rice apart' or 'rice on the side'. While usually calling only for some cuttlefish, cooks occasionally also add a couple of prawns (shrimp) in the very beginning, frying them in the oil until they change colour, removing them from the pan and then laying them on the top of the rice for the last few minutes of cooking. If using broth from *bullit*, it will already have saffron, but if using fish stock (broth) add a pinch of saffron threads. Finally, restaurants usually serve the fish and potatoes first and then the rice, but in homes it's traditionally served in reverse order. It is hard to enjoy the fish while getting up and down from the table to prepare the rice. It is best to keep attention on the rice, serve it first and then follow it with the fish and potatoes. Note that the quantities for this are made to go with *bullit de peix*, so the rice amount is less as it will precede a platter of fish and potatoes. If you want to make this dish as a stand-alone one, use 300 g (10½ oz/1½ cups) of rice for 4 people and about 1.2 litres (40 fl oz/5 cups) of the stock.

✳ Heat the oil in a paella pan or very wide frying pan over medium–high heat. Add the cuttlefish and cook, stirring frequently, until golden, 8–10 minutes. Add the garlic, parsley and tomatoes and cook until the tomatoes are darker red, about 10 minutes, stirring frequently. Add 175 ml (6 fl oz/¾ cup) of the broth and simmer until reduced, 5–10 minutes.

✳ Meanwhile, in another pan, heat 750 ml (25 fl oz/3 cups) of the broth. (There will be a small amount left over; keep to use if needed.) Add the saffron (if needed).

✳ Stir the rice into the sauce and, once it is coated, pour over the hot broth. Bring to a boil. Cook, uncovered, over high heat for 10 minutes, stirring from time to time, checking that the rice is evenly distributed throughout the pan. Reduce the heat to low and cook without stirring until the rice is al dente, about 10 minutes. Add the remaining broth if the rice is not quite done and the pan too dry. Remove the pan from the heat and let rest, uncovered, for 5 minutes.

✳ Serve the rice in the pan in the middle of the table. Eat with spoons directly from the pan.

Fisherman's Brothy Rice

Preparation time: 10 minutes
Cooking time: 30 minutes
Serves: 4

2 tablespoons olive oil
1 small cleaned cuttlefish (see page 25),
    about 200–250 g/7–9 oz, cut into
    2-cm/¾-inch pieces
2 cloves of garlic, minced
1 tablespoon minced flat-leaf parsley,
    plus extra to serve
2 litres/2 quarts (8½ cups) broth from
    bullit de peix ('Boiled' Fish, page 160)
    and/or Fish Stock (page 338)
Pinch of saffron threads, crumbled,
    optional
200 g/7 oz (1 cup) short- or
    medium-grain white rice

DF ✳ GF ✳ 1 POT

This is another common way to prepare rice using the broth from *bullit de peix* (page 160). While a wide pan *arròs a banda* (page 131) might more dramatic, this is perhaps more comforting and, at home, more typical. Many fishermen in Formentera also say that it's the original way. (There is a similar version that calls for small pasta instead of rice on page 58.) If using broth from *bullit*, it will already have saffron. If not, add some in so that the soup has its characteristic golden-yellowish colour.

✳ Heat the oil in a soup pot over medium–high heat. Add the cuttlefish and cook until it is becoming tender and a touch golden, 5–8 minutes. Stir in the garlic and parsley and cook for 30 seconds. Pour in the broth and add the saffron (if using). Bring to a boil. Add the rice and cook until tender, about 20 minutes.

✳ Remove from the heat and let sit for a couple of minutes before serving in wide bowls, with more parsley, if desired.

Black Rice with Cuttlefish & Artichokes

Preparation time: 15 minutes,
  plus resting time
Cooking time: 1 hour
Serves: 4–5

4 medium artichokes (about 650 g/
  1½ lb total)
3 tablespoons olive oil
1 whole cuttlefish with ink sac (about
  650 g/1½ lb), cleaned (see page 25),
  ink sac reserved, cut into 2–3-cm/
  ¾–1-inch pieces
2 cloves of garlic, minced
1 long sweet green pepper, stemmed,
  seeded and chopped
4 ripe tomatoes, halved and grated
  (see page 25)
1.5 litres/50 fl oz (generous 6 cups)
  Fish Stock (page 338), warmed
  through
375 g/13 oz (1¾ cups) short-
  or medium-grain white rice
Pinch of saffron threads, crumbled
Salt
Allioli (page 339), for serving
Lemon wedges, to serve

DF ✳ GF

This showcases the pleasures of black rice. The ink of a cuttlefish or squid is incorporated into the dish and turns it a silvery-black. But the ink is there for more than colour. It adds a lovely flavour of the sea that, ultimately, slightly sweetens the dish, a combination that pairs perfectly with allioli. If the cuttlefish has already been cleaned and there is no ink sac, ink packets can be purchased separately. Two 4-gram/⅙-ounce packets are enough. See page 24 for more on ink. Shrimp make a lovely addition here, and I often pick up a few at the market when buying the cuttlefish. Cook them in the pan at the beginning, remove and return at the end of cooking. (See Rice with Pork Ribs, Cuttlefish and Artichokes on page 138 for details on how to incorporate shrimp in this dish.)

✳ Trim the artichokes and cut into eighths following the directions on page 25.

✳ Heat the oil in a shallow, flameproof casserole pan (see page 25), sauté pan or Dutch oven over medium heat. Add the cuttlefish and cook, stirring frequently, until becoming tender and a touch golden, about 10 minutes. Add the artichokes and cook for 5 minutes, stirring frequently. Stir in the garlic and green pepper and cook until aromatic, 1–2 minutes. Stir in the tomatoes. Season with salt and cook over low heat until pasty, about 15 minutes.

✳ Add the hot stock to the pot. When it reaches a boil, stir in the ink, and then add the rice and saffron. Cook, stirring from time to time to keep the rice from sticking, until the rice is al dente, about 18 minutes. It should be a bit loose at the end; add more stock or hot water if needed.

✳ Remove the pan from the heat, loosely cover with paper towels and let rest for 5 minutes for the starches in the rice to firm up. Serve with lemon wedges, and allioli to dollop generously on the rice.

Seafood Rice

Preparation time: 45 minutes
Cooking time: 1 hour
Serves: 4

250 g/9 oz small or medium mussels, cleaned
4 tablespoons olive oil
2 cloves of garlic, peeled
8 whole large shrimp or prawns, with heads and shells
1 cuttlefish (about 450 g/1 lb), cleaned (see page 25) and cut into 1–2-cm/ ½–¾-inch pieces
½ bunch spring onions (scallions) or 1 small onion, finely chopped
3 ripe tomatoes, halved and grated (see page 25)
1.75 litres/60 fl oz (7 ½ cups) Fish Stock (page 338), warmed
Pinch of saffron threads, crumbled
1 tablespoon finely chopped flat-leaf parsley
300 g/11 oz (1 ½ cups) short- or medium-grain white rice
Salt

DF ✳ GF

There are three basic levels of moistness to rice in the Balearics. On one end is *arròs sec*, literally 'dry rice' and often now generally called 'paella', where the rice, cooked in a wide pan, is separate and without any liquid remaining. On the other end is *caldós* or *brouós*, which is brothy or soupy with at least enough liquid at the end that you need a spoon to eat it. Many, though, fall in the middle and are called *melós*, *encallat* or *encalladet*, which means the rice is moist. This seafood rice is one of these 'in the middle' dishes. To make it soupier, increase the amount of stock (broth). It's as simple as that. Everything else remains the same.

✳ Put the mussels in a saucepan, cover with 60 ml (2 fl oz/¼ cup) water and bring to a boil over high heat. Lower the heat, cover the pot and simmer, shaking the pot from time to time, until the mussels have opened, about 2 minutes. Strain and set aside to cool. Discard any mussels that didn't open. Twist off and discard the 'empty' shell of each. Set the others aside.

✳ Heat the oil in a shallow, flameproof casserole pan (see page 25), Dutch oven or heavy sauté pan over medium–high heat. Add the garlic and cook until it begins to soften and become aromatic, 30 seconds–1 minute. Remove from the pan and reserve. Add the shrimp or prawns and cook until they change colour, about 2 minutes. Transfer to a plate. Remove any stray legs or tentacles from the pan.

✳ In the same pan over medium–high heat, cook the cuttlefish for 5 minutes. Add the spring onions or onion, reduce the heat and to medium cook until they start to soften, 3–5 minutes. Add the tomatoes and cook until darker and pasty, about 10 minutes. Stir in 120 ml (4 fl oz/½ cup) of the stock and simmer to reduce for 10 minutes, stirring from time to time. Add a touch more of the stock if it threatens to dry out. Sprinkle in the saffron and add the remaining stock. Bring to a boil.

✳ Meanwhile, in a mortar, make a simple picada by pounding the reserved garlic and the parsley with 1 or 2 tablespoons of liquid from the pan to form a paste. Set aside.

✳ Add the rice to the pan and boil for 10 minutes. Stir in the picada, add the reserved shrimp and mussels and season with salt. Cook, stirring from time to time to keep from sticking, for 8–10 minutes or until the rice is tender.

✳ Remove from the heat and let rest for a few minutes. Ladle into bowls and serve.

Rice with Pork Ribs, Cuttlefish & Prawns

Preparation time: 30 minutes,
   plus resting time
Cooking time: 1 hour 30 minutes
Serves: 4–5

12–16 mussels, cleaned
4 tablespoons olive oil
8–12 prawns (shrimp), with shells
   and heads
500 g/1 lb 2 oz pork ribs,
   cut into 2-cm/¾-inch pieces
1 yellow onion, finely chopped
1 long sweet green pepper
   or ½ green bell pepper, stemmed,
   seeded and finely chopped
3 cloves of garlic, minced
500 g/1 lb 2 oz cuttlefish or squid,
   cleaned (see page 25) and cut
   into 2-cm/¾-inch pieces
3 ripe tomatoes, halved and grated
   (see page 25)
2 litres/68 fl oz (8½ cups) Fish Stock
   (page 338)
1 teaspoon sweet paprika
Pinch of saffron threads, crumbled
375 g/13 oz (1¾ cups) short-
   or medium-grain white rice

DF ✳ GF

A classic mixing of seafood and pork (generally known as *mar i muntanya*, 'sea and mountain'), with rice sucking up all the flavours of the pan, this rich dish has a final consistency that is quite moist, but it can easily be made 'soupy' by simply adding more stock (broth). In autumn, add a handful of chopped mushrooms just before adding the rice. It is excellent served with allioli – see page 339 for a quick way to prepare this fundamental garlic and olive oil emulsion. We have eaten enough versions of this rice dish on weekends over the years that it has become a family comfort food.

✳ Put the mussels in a saucepan, cover with 60 ml (2 fl oz/¼ cup) water and bring to a boil over high heat. Lower the heat, cover the pot and simmer, shaking the pot from time to time, until the mussels have opened, about 2 minutes. Strain and set aside to cool. Discard any mussels that didn't open. Twist off and discard the 'empty' shell of each. Set the others aside.

✳ Heat the oil in a shallow, flameproof casserole pan (see page 25), Dutch oven or heavy sauté pan over medium heat. Add the prawns (shrimp) and cook until they change colour, 2–3 minutes. Remove from the pan and set aside. Remove any stray legs or tentacles from the pan.

✳ Add the pork and cook, stirring frequently, until it takes on a lovely brownish colour, about 6 minutes. Add the onion, green pepper and garlic, and cook until the onion softens, about 5 minutes. Add the cuttlefish and cook for 10 minutes. Finally, add the tomatoes and cook, stirring frequently, until they darken and lose their acidity, 10–15 minutes. Add a few tablespoons of the stock if it looks like it's drying out.

✳ Stir in 250 ml (8 fl oz/1 cup) of the stock, reduce the heat to low–medium and simmer for 20–30 minutes, stirring frequently. Add in a touch of water if needed to keep it from drying out at the end. The pork should be quite tender.

✳ Stir in the paprika and saffron. Pour 1.5 litres (50 fl oz/generous 6 cups) of the stock into the pan and bring to a boil. (There will be some stock remaining. Keep to add later if needed.) When it reaches a strong boil, sprinkle in the rice. Cook for 10 minutes, stirring from time to time, and then return the shrimp to the pan, along with the mussels. Reduce the heat to medium–low and cook, stirring from time to time to keep from sticking, until the rice is al dente, about 8 minutes. It should be a bit loose at the end; add more stock or hot water if needed.

✳ Remove the pan from the heat, loosely cover with paper towels and let rest for 5 minutes for the starches in the rice to firm up before serving.

'Dirty' Rice

Preparation time: 20 minutes
Cooking time: 1 hour 30 minutes
Serves: 4

750 g/1⅔ lb mixed meat (rabbit,
    chicken, partridge or quail, pork ribs,
    etc.), cut into bite-size pieces
2 tablespoons olive oil
1 yellow onion or 2 bulbous spring
    onions (scallions), finely chopped
1 small long sweet green pepper,
    stemmed and seeded, half finely
    chopped
2 cloves of garlic, minced
2 ripe tomatoes, halved and grated
    (see page 25)
265 g/9 oz (1⅓ cups) short- or medium-
    grain white rice
50 g/2 oz (⅓ cup) shelled peas
100 g/3½ oz mushrooms, halved
    or quartered lengthwise
    depending on size
2 heaped tablespoons minced flat-leaf
    parsley
2 teaspoons *quatre espècies* (four
    spices) seasoning (see page 23)
Small pinch of saffron threads,
    crumbled
1 small dried chilli (chile) or 1 dried
    cayenne pepper, optional
Salt and pepper
Lemon wedges, for serving

DF ✳ GF ✳ 1 POT

This Mallorcan classic was once largely associated with *caça* (hunting) and usually included game birds such as partridge as well as some of their blood, which gave the rice its 'dirty' name (and colour). Today, *arròs brut* usually incorporates rabbit, chicken, pork and, in better versions, farm-raised game birds, and omits the blood. As for vegetables, cooks can add a wide range, from wild mushrooms to artichokes, green beans and peas. Key to the dish is the spicing, namely using *quatre espècies* (a 'four spices' blend of black pepper with clove, cinnamon and nutmeg), plus saffron and a small dried red chilli (chile). Especially in the interior of the island, it is common to serve this with strips of fresh (raw) green peppers to eat on the side and lemon wedges to juice into the bowl.

✳ Generously season the meats with salt and pepper. Heat the oil in a large, flameproof casserole pan (see page 25), Dutch oven or heavy sauté pan over medium heat. Add the meat and cook, turning as needed, until browned, about 5 minutes. Reduce the heat to medium–low. Add the onion(s) and chopped green pepper and cook for 5 minutes. Stir in the garlic, then add the tomatoes and cook for 10 minutes.

✳ Pour in 2 litres (68 fl oz/8½ cups) water, bring to a low boil and gently boil, partly covered, until the meats are tender, about 40 minutes, depending on the type of meats used.

✳ Add the rice, peas, mushrooms, parsley, spices, saffron and chilli (chile), if using, and cook, uncovered, until the rice is tender, about 20 minutes. It should be very loose and soupy. Add a touch of water while cooking if needed.

✳ Meanwhile, cut the remaining ½ green pepper into strips. Put on a plate with the lemon wedges.

✳ Ladle the rice into bowls. Serve with the lemon wedges and green peppers on the side.

Butchering-day Rice

Preparation time: 20 minutes
Cooking time: 1 hour 20 minutes
Serves: 6

200 g/7 oz lean pork, cut into small
   pieces
200 g/7 oz pork ribs, cut into 2-cm/
   ¾-inch pieces
1 bone-in chicken leg (drumstick and
   thigh, about 350 g/12 oz), cut into
   pieces with a cleaver
1 chicken liver (about 50 g/2 oz)
3 tablespoons olive oil or lard
1 yellow onion, finely chopped
1 long sweet green pepper or ½ smallish
   green or red bell pepper, stemmed,
   seeded and cut into small pieces
2 cloves of garlic, skins on
2 tomatoes, halved and grated
   (see page 25)
1.75 litres/60 fl oz (7½ cups) Chicken
   Stock (page 338) or Vegetable Stock
   (page 339)
2 tablespoons minced flat-leaf parsley
1 tablespoon sweet paprika
150 g/7 oz mushrooms, preferably wild,
   cleaned (see page 25) and cut
   if needed
300 g/11 oz (1½ cups) short-
   or medium-grain white rice
Small pinch of saffron threads,
   crumbled
150 g/5 oz (¾ cup) cooked white beans,
   rinsed, optional
Salt and pepper

DF ✳ GF

As with every other popular, traditional dish, there are numerous versions of *arròs de matances*, a hearty rice prepared around the time of butchering pigs (*matances*, see page 229). Most versions call for pork and chicken, and some also include small white beans (not many; you find just a couple of beans in each spoonful), pieces of blood sausage (*botifarró*, see page 23), sobrassada or mushrooms. As with Seafood Rice (page 137), simply add more stock (broth) to give this dish a soupier final consistency.

✳ Season the pork, pork ribs, chicken and chicken liver with salt and pepper.

✳ Heat the oil in a large, flameproof casserole pan (see page 25), Dutch oven or heavy sauté pan over medium heat. Add the meats and cook until nicely browned, about 7 minutes, but remove the liver from the pan when cooked through (2–3 minutes) and reserve.

✳ Add the onion, pepper and garlic and cook for 5 minutes, stirring frequently. Add the tomatoes and cook until they are reduced, about 8 minutes. Stir in 250 ml (8 fl oz/1 cup) of the stock, partly cover the pan and simmer for 30 minutes. The ribs should be quite tender. Remove the garlic, peel and reserve.

✳ Meanwhile, in a mortar with a pestle, combine the reserved chicken liver with the reserved peeled cloves of garlic, parsley and paprika, then pound to a paste with about 2 tablespoons of liquid from the pan.

✳ Pour the remaining 1.5 litres (50 fl oz/generous 6 cups) of the stock into the pan and bring to a boil. Stir in the pounded paste. Add the mushrooms, rice and saffron and cook, stirring from time to time to keep from sticking, until the rice is al dente, about 18 minutes. Add the beans (if using) towards the end to warm through. The texture should be a bit loose at the end, so add more stock or hot water if needed.

✳ Remove from the heat and let rest for 5 minutes. Serve at the table from the casserole pan.

Rice with Rabbit, Green Beans & Leeks

Preparation time: 15 minutes,
    plus resting time
Cooking time: 1 hour 30 minutes
Serves: 6

1 cleaned rabbit (about 1 kg/2¼ lb),
    cut into 12 pieces
4 tablespoons olive oil
2 leeks, trimmed and the white and
    tender green parts finely chopped
250 g/9 oz tender green beans, trimmed
    and cut into 4–5-cm/1½–2-inch
    lengths
4 cloves of garlic, minced
3 tomatoes, halved and grated
    (see page 25)
120 ml/4 fl oz (½ cup) dry white wine
pinch of saffron threads, crumbled
500 g/1 lb 2 oz (2½ cups) short-
    or medium-grain white rice
Parsley leaves, to garnish, optional
Salt and pepper

DF ✳ GF ✳ 1 POT

Perhaps because rice dishes are never prepared for one and rarely even for two at home, they tend to be festive on the islands. That is even the case when the ingredients are deeply rustic, like this *arròs* with rabbit, green beans and leeks. Bone-in chicken drumsticks and/or thighs make an easy substitution for rabbit. This *arròs* dish is *melós* or *encallat*, falling somewhere between dry and soupy. For a particularly exquisite – and festive – version of this, prepare it over a wood fire, allowing the aromatic smoke to help flavour the rice.

✳ Generously season the rabbit with salt and pepper.

✳ Heat the oil in a large, shallow, flameproof casserole pan (see page 25), Dutch oven or heavy sauté pan over high heat. Add the rabbit and generously brown, about 10 minutes. Transfer to a large platter.

✳ Add the leeks to the pan and cook over medium heat until they begin to soften, about 5 minutes. Add the green beans and cook for 5 minutes, stirring from time to time. Stir in the garlic and then add the tomatoes. Cook, stirring frequently, until the tomatoes darken, about 5 minutes. Add the wine and let the alcohol cook off for 2 minutes. Sprinkle in the saffron and return the rabbit to the pan. Pour over 1.75 litres (60 fl oz/7½ cups) water and bring to a boil. Reduce the heat and simmer for 30 minutes. The rabbit and beans should be tender.

✳ Add the rice and cook over high heat for 10 minutes. Taste for seasoning and add more salt if needed. Reduce the heat to low and cook until the rice is *al punto*, with just a hint of bite to it, about 7 minutes.

✳ Remove from the heat, cover the pot with a clean dish towel and let sit for about 5 minutes before serving with parsley, if using.

Lenten Rice with Salt Cod, Cauliflower & Peas

Preparation time: 20 minutes,
    plus soaking and desalting time
Cooking time: 40 minutes
Serves: 4

250 g/9 oz salt cod
3 tablespoons olive oil
2 cloves of garlic, peeled
1 leek, trimmed and finely chopped
1 small long sweet green pepper
    or ½ green bell pepper, stemmed,
    seeded and finely chopped
2 tomatoes, halved and grated
    (see page 25)
1 tablespoon minced fresh mint leaves
1 tablespoon minced flat-leaf parsley
pinch of saffron threads, crumbled
1.75 litres/60 fl oz (7 cups) Vegetable
    Stock (page 339) or Fish Stock
    (page 338)
300 g/11 oz cauliflower, cut into
    bite-size florets
300 g/11 oz (1½ cups) short-
    or medium-grain white rice
120 g/4 oz (about 1 cup) shelled peas
Lemon wedges, optional
Salt, if needed

DF ✳ GF

Until not so long ago, a number of *bacallà* (salt cod) dishes were frequently served around the islands on Fridays and during the period of Lent. While *bacallà* has become less common (and more expensive), many traditional favourites still appear in springtime, including rice with salt cod, cauliflower and other seasonal vegetables (leeks, peas, green beans). This delicious and comforting dish has become part of my repertoire of March and April favourites. While you can use water here, vegetable or fish stock (broth) will impart more flavour. It shouldn't require any salt, but taste towards the end of cooking to be certain.

✳ Beginning 2 or 3 days ahead, desalt the cod following the directions on page 25. If using a skin-on piece (or pieces), do not remove the skin.

✳ Drain in a colander, skin-side up, for at least 1–2 hours. Pat dry with paper towels.

✳ Heat a non-stick frying pan over medium heat. Lay the salt cod on the pan and cook until the segments begin to separate, about 4 minutes, depending on the thickness of the piece. Transfer to a plate. Once cool enough to handle, remove the skin and gently flake apart, removing any bones. Set aside.

✳ Heat the oil in a shallow, flameproof casserole pan (see page 25), Dutch oven or heavy sauté pan over medium–high heat. Add the garlic and cook until it begins to soften and become aromatic, 30 seconds–1 minute. Remove from the pan and reserve. Add the leek and green pepper and cook until soft, about 5 minutes. Add the tomatoes and cook until darker and pasty, 8–10 minutes, stirring frequently. Add the reserved flaked salt cod and turn to coat in the sauce.

✳ Meanwhile, prepare a picada. In a large mortar with a pestle, combine the reserved garlic with the mint, parsley and saffron, then pound to a paste with a few tablespoons of water. (See page 175 for more on making a picada.)

✳ Add the stock to the casserole pan and bring to a boil. When it reaches a strong boil, add the cauliflower and rice. Cook for 10 minutes, stirring from time to time. Stir in the picada and add the peas. Reduce the heat to medium–low and cook, stirring from time to time to keep from sticking, until the rice is al dente, about 8 minutes.

✳ It should be a bit loose at the end, so add more stock or hot water if needed. Taste for salt and add if needed. Serve hot, with a lemon wedge on the side, if using.

Baked Gratin Pasta

Preparation time: 15 minutes
Cooking time: 45 minutes
Serves: 6

3 tablespoons olive oil
1 yellow onion, finely chopped
1 small long sweet green pepper,
    stemmed, seeded and finely chopped
2 cloves of garlic, minced
200 g/7 oz minced (ground) beef
200 g/7 oz minced (ground) pork
5 tomatoes, halved and grated
    (see page 25) or peeled
    and finely chopped
1 teaspoon minced thyme or marjoram
500 g/1 lb 2 oz dried penne pasta,
    preferably ridged
Butter, for greasing
75 g/2⅔ oz (¾ cup) shredded cured or
    semi-cured cheese, preferably Queso
    Mahón-Menorca
2 eggs, well beaten
Salt

When words have the suffix -*ada* in Catalan, it is usually in noun form, signifying a collective or large quantity of something. And when that word refers to food, there is usually a festive (and often seasonal) element involved: a *sardinada*, *caracolada* or *botifarrada* (a barbecue with, respectively, lots of sardines, snails or fresh pork sausages). In Menorca, there is a beloved dish that gets this suffix, too: *macarronada*. This means lots of *macarrons,* the name for penne pasta. The classic penne pasta shape here is a rather narrow one, but some prefer larger ones, closer to square-cut and ridged rigatoni, which work particularly well for this dish. Note that there is a tomato *sofregit*, not tomato *salsa*, so while there is some tomato, it is not saucy. It is key to use local cured Menorca cheese if possible. Also, somewhat uniquely, a layer of beaten egg gets poured over the top. The eggs are an original island touch, adding a richness to the dish and giving the topping an even more lovely gratin.

✳ Heat the oil in a Dutch oven or large frying pan or sauté pan over medium heat. Add the onion and green pepper and cook until soft, about 10 minutes. Stir in the garlic and then the minced (ground) meat. Brown the meat for 4–5 minutes. Add the tomatoes and thyme and cook for 10 minutes. Add 120 ml (4 fl oz/½ cup) water and cook, stirring frequently, for 10 minutes.

✳ Meanwhile, bring a large pot of salted water to a boil. Add the pasta and boil until al dente, or firm but not brittle, using the timing on the package for guidance. Drain the pasta, reserving 120 ml (4 fl oz/½ cup) of the pasta water.

✳ At the same time, preheat the oven grill (broiler) to high. Grease a large oval or rectangular baking dish with butter.

✳ When the sauce is ready, add the pasta to the pan and stir in 60–120 ml (2–4 fl oz/ ¼–½ cup) of the reserved pasta water to moisten, and turn over until the pasta is well coated with the sauce. Spoon into the baking dish. Sprinkle the cheese across the top. Spoon the beaten eggs over the cheese.

✳ Place under the hot grill until a nice gratin has formed, about 5 minutes.

Mallorcan-style Pasta

Preparation time: 10 minutes
Cooking time: 45 minutes
Serves: 4–5

2 tablespoons olive oil
1 small red or yellow onion,
   finely chopped
2 cloves of garlic, minced
175 g/6 oz minced (ground) beef
   or a blend of beef and pork
120 g/4 oz sobrassada (see page 208),
   casing removed
400 g/14 oz can whole peeled tomatoes,
   all juices reserved
Sprigs fresh aromatic herbs, such
   as marjoram or thyme
400 g/14 oz dried macaroni
   or penne pasta
Shredded hard cheese, for topping
Salt

If the classic Menorca pasta dish on page 149 has plenty of the island's local cured cow's milk cheese, then in Mallorca many cooks add to this family favourite some of its celebrated cured paprika-rich sobrassada. Such pasta dishes are far from recent additions to the Mallorcan kitchen. Pasta has been on the island since the days of Arab rule a thousand years ago, and dishes with tubular pasta (both smooth and ridged) have been known here as *macarrons* since the nineteenth century thanks to influence from Italy. This version is particularly nice using canned tomatoes in winter.

* Heat the oil in a large, shallow, flameproof casserole pan (see page 25), Dutch oven or sauté pan oven over medium heat. Add the onion and cook until soft, about 8 minutes. Stir in the garlic and then the minced (ground) meat and brown, 3–4 minutes. Stir in the sobrassada and cook until it separates, 3–4 minutes. Add the tomatoes and cook, breaking them up with the back of a wooden spoon, for 5 minutes. Add the herbs and 120 ml (4 fl oz/½ cup) water, bring to a boil and simmer for 15 minutes, stirring frequently.

* Meanwhile, bring a large pot of salted water to a rolling boil, add the pasta and boil for 9–12 minutes until al dente, or firm but not brittle, using the timing on the package for guidance. Drain the pasta, reserving about 120 ml (4 fl oz/½ cup) of the pasta water.

* When the sauce is ready, remove the sprigs of herbs. Add the pasta to the pan with some of the reserved pasta water if needed to moisten, and turn over until the pasta is coated with the sauce. Spoon into wide bowls, sprinkle with cheese and serve.

Wine Harvest Fideos with Lamb

Preparation time: 15 minutes,
   plus resting time
Cooking time: 1 hour 50 minutes
Serves: 4

4 tablespoons olive oil
1 yellow onion, finely chopped
1 leek, trimmed and finely chopped
3 cloves of garlic, skins on, lightly
   crushed under the palm
500 g/1 lb 2 oz stewing lamb,
   cut into bite-size pieces
3 tomatoes, halved and grated
   (see page 25)
100 ml/3½ fl oz (⅓ cup) red wine
Pinch of ground cinnamon
Pinch of allspice (Jamaica pepper)
Pinch of ground spice cloves
Pinch of ground nutmeg
1 small dried chilli (chile) or 1 dried
   cayenne pepper, optional
1.5 litres/50 fl oz (generous 6 cups) meat
   or Chicken Stock (page 338), or more
   if needed, warmed through
150 g/5 oz fideos pasta or thin spaghetti,
   broken into 2–4-cm/¾–1½-inch
   lengths
Chopped parsley, to garnish, optional
Salt and pepper

DF ✳ 1 POT

The Mallorcan town of Binissalem, located at the seam where the plains meet the Serra de Tramuntana mountains, is at the centre of the island's wine industry. During the *vermar* (harvest), this brothy dish with thin pasta noodles (*fideus*) remains a festive favourite. In Binissalem, the classic *fideus* are like thin spaghetti but a couple of times longer. The pasta comes doubled over in a bag, and cooks simply crush them in the bag before adding to the broth. (This means that there tends to be a range of lengths of pasta in the bowl.) The quartet of spices – cinnamon, nutmeg, allspice and cloves – helps give this dish its signature flavour. In the past, it was made using mutton, an older animal that took longer to stew.

✳ Heat the oil in a deep, flameproof casserole pan or Dutch oven over medium heat. Add the onion, leek and garlic and cook until tender, about 10 minutes. Season the lamb with salt and pepper, add to the pan and cook until browned, about 3 minutes. Add the tomatoes and cook until darker and pasty, about 10 minutes. Pour in the wine and cook for 5 minutes, stirring frequently. Stir in the cinnamon, allspice, cloves, nutmeg and chilli (chile), if using.

✳ Add the hot stock to the pan and bring to a boil, then reduce the heat to low–medium and simmer, partly covered, until the meat is very tender, about 45 minutes–1 hour.

✳ Add the pasta and boil until tender, 8–13 minutes, though follow the time on the package for guidance. Add more stock (or water) if needed to keep it quite soupy.

✳ Remove the pot from the heat and let rest for 5 minutes before ladling into wide soup bowls and serving with chopped parsley, if using.

Fideos with Fish & Clams

Preparation time: 20 minutes,
    plus soaking time
Cooking time: 1 hour
Serves: 4

250 g/9 oz small fresh clams, purged
    of sand
4 fish steaks (about 500 g/1 lb 2 oz total)
    or 400 g/14 oz cleaned and peeled
    skate wings, cut into 4 pieces
1 lemon wedge
3 tablespoons olive oil
1 yellow onion, finely chopped
2 cloves of garlic, minced
3 ripe tomatoes, halved and grated
    (see page 25)
1 litre/34 fl oz (4½ cups) Fish Stock
    (page 338)
1 teaspoon sweet paprika
200 g/7 oz thick fideos pasta or
    spaghetti, broken into 2-cm/¾-inch
    lengths
Salt and pepper

DF *

In this dish, the short, skinny noodles – *fideus* or *fideos* in Spanish – are not boiled and then sauced, but instead are cooked in the pan to absorb all of the flavours. In the sea version, a favourite choice is to use *rajada* (skate), a gelatinous fish that adds a silkiness to the broth. Steaks of other fish will work perfectly, too – just avoid using excessively bony varieties. Monkfish makes a good choice. The final consistency of the dish should be at least moist enough that you need a spoon to eat it. Be sure the clams have been purged of sand. To do this, soak in a bowl of cold water with a very generous pinch of salt for about an hour, then drain and rinse.

* Put the clams in a medium saucepan, cover with 500 ml (18 fl oz/2 cups) water and add a pinch of salt. Cover the pan, bring to a boil over high heat and cook until the clams have opened, about 1 minute after the water reaches a boil. Strain the liquid and reserve. Discard any clams that did not open. Set the clams aside.

* Put the fish in a bowl and squeeze the lemon wedge over the top. Set aside.

* Heat the oil in a shallow, flameproof casserole pan (see page 25), Dutch oven or sauté pan over medium heat. Add the onion and cook until soft, about 8 minutes. Stir in the garlic, then add the tomatoes and cook until darker and pasty, about 10 minutes, stirring in 3–4 tablespoons of the reserved clam liquid as it cooks. Add a touch more liquid if it threatens to scorch. Season with salt and pepper.

* Meanwhile, bring the fish stock and 250 ml (8 fl oz/1 cup) of the reserved clam liquid to a boil in a large saucepan. Reduce the heat to low, cover the pan and keep hot.

* When the tomato base is ready, add the paprika and fideos to the casserole pan and cook for 2 minutes. Pour in the hot stock, bring to a boil and boil for 5 minutes. Arrange the pieces of fish and the reserved clams around the pan, and cook, shaking the pan from time to time, until the fish is done and the fideos tender, about 12 minutes.

* Remove from the heat and let sit, uncovered, for 5 minutes. Serve at the table from the casserole pan into wide bowls.

Rice from the Land

Preparation time: 10 minutes
Cooking time: 1 hour
Serves: 4–5

400 g/14 oz (2 cups) coarse bulgur
2 tablespoons olive oil
2 tomatoes, halved and grated
   (see page 25) or peeled and chopped
500 g/1 lb 2 oz assorted pieces of
   pork ribs, pork belly, black sausage
   (*botifarró*), sobrassada and so on, cut
   into pieces a bit larger than bite-size
1 sweet potato or white potato, peeled
   and cut into bite-size pieces
1 whole bulb of garlic
Salt

DF ✳

While this ancient Menorcan winter dish is called *arròs de la terra* – literally 'rice from the earth' (or land) – it is made with dried and crushed grains of wheat instead of rice. There is only a single producer of this wheat left on the island, and even in Menorca it is extremely difficult to find. Nowadays it is mostly prepared using the similar and widely available coarse bulgur (cracked wheat berries). The dish is simple to prepare, with everything added raw, including the pork ribs and pieces of sweet potato, and baked in the oven. The ribs can be browned in a sauté pan before adding for deeper flavours – if so, don't toss that oil, but use it when coating the bulgur grains.

✳ Preheat the oven to 180°C/350°F/Gas Mark 4.

✳ In a bowl, generously season the bulgur with salt, then add the oil and tomatoes and toss together. Spread out in a terracotta baking dish around 30 cm/12 inches in diameter. The bulgur should be about 2 cm/¾ inch deep. Arrange the pieces of meat and sweet potato around the pan. Peel away the flaky outer layers of the garlic while leaving the bulb intact, and set in the centre of the pan. Add 500 ml (18 fl oz/2 cups) water.

✳ Bake in the oven until the water has been absorbed, the texture is 'dry' and a golden crust has formed on the surface, about 1 hour. Serve at the table straight from the pan.

CHAPTER 6

FISH

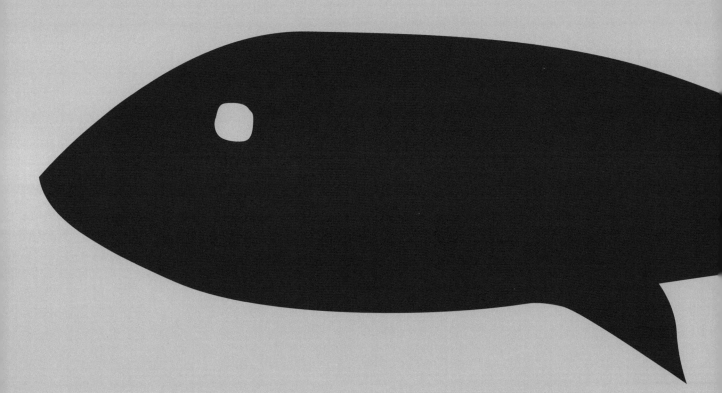

'Boiled' Fish

Preparation time: 20 minutes
Cooking time: 45 minutes
Serves: 4

1–1.5 kg/2¼–3¼ lb white-fleshed
    fish, such as scorpion fish, grouper,
    sea bream or monkfish, scaled and
    cleaned
2 tablespoons olive oil
1 yellow onion, roughly chopped
1 long sweet green pepper or ½ green
    bell pepper, stemmed, seeded and
    cut into large pieces
4 cloves of garlic, roughly chopped
1 tomato, cored and cut into wedges
4 medium white potatoes (about
    800 g/1¾ lb total), peeled and
    quartered lengthwise
Generous pinch of saffron threads,
    crumbled
Allioli (page 339) or Homemade
    Mayonnaise (page 340), optional
Lemon wedges, optional
Salt and pepper

DF ✳ GF

Bullit de peix is one of the most emblematic dishes in Ibiza and Formentera.
The name translates to 'boiled fish'. It is the first step in a two-part dish, with
the (boiled) fish and potatoes served as one course and the broth used to make
another course. The most famous of those is a wide pan of 'dry rice' called *arròs
a banda* (page 131), but there are other traditional brothy versions as well made,
with either rice (page 132) or pasta (page 58). While restaurants tend to serve the
fish first then the rice, in homes it is generally the other way around, opening with
a wide pan of rice and finishing with a platter of fish. Locally, scorpion fish, John
Dory, grouper and sea bream are the top choices, but any fresh fish will work.
It is best to use large pieces that won't break up. Allioli is typically served with
the fish and potatoes, but homemade mayonnaise is also excellent.

✳ If whole, remove and reserve the heads and tails of the fish. Cut the fish into
generous steaks. Season with salt and pepper and set aside.

✳ Heat the oil in a large pot over medium heat. Add the onion and green pepper
and cook until soft, about 8 minutes. Stir in the garlic, then add the tomato and
cook for 10 minutes until pasty. Add the potatoes and fish heads and tails, if you
have them, and turn to coat in the sauce. Add 1.5 litres (50 fl oz/generous 6 cups)
water, bring to a boil and boil for 5 minutes. Set the fish steaks in the pot, add the
saffron and return the liquid to a boil. Cover the pot, reduce the heat to low and
gently boil until the potatoes are tender and the fish cooked through, 10–15 minutes.

✳ Remove and discard the heads and tails. With a slotted spoon, carefully remove
the fish and potatoes without breaking them and arrange on a platter. Cover with
aluminium foil to keep warm until ready to serve.

✳ Strain the broth and reserve, pressing to get all of the liquid. There should be
about 1.25 litres (42 fl oz/5¼ cups) of broth. Use for one of the dishes listed above,
or store for another use.

✳ Serve the fish and potatoes with allioli or mayonnaise on the side, and
lemon wedges.

Baked Fish with Spinach & Swiss Chard

Preparation time: 45 minutes
Cooking time: 1 hour
Serves: 4–5

350 ml/12 fl oz (1½ cups) neutral oil,
	for frying
4–5 medium white potatoes, peeled
	and sliced crosswise
1 whole large fish (about 800 g–1 kg/
	1¾–2¼ lb), such as red porgy
	(common sea bream), gilthead sea
	bream or sea bass, cleaned
juice of ½ lemon
2 teaspoons sweet paprika
4 cloves of garlic, skins on, lightly
	crushed under the palm
200 g/7 oz trimmed spinach leaves,
	chopped
200 g/7 oz trimmed Swiss chard leaves,
	chopped
2 ripe tomatoes, halved and grated
	(see page 25)
1 tablespoon olive oil
50 g/2 oz (scant ½ cup) fine dry
	breadcrumbs
Salt and pepper

DF ✳

One of the most common ways to bake fish in Mallorca is under a bed of greens – namely Swiss chard and spinach. Some cooks like to toss these with spring onions (scallions) (called *sofrit* on the island) and flat-leaf parsley. As for fish, use whatever looks good in the market. This recipe is timed for a whole fish that weighs 800 g– 1 kg/1¾–2¼ lb, such as a large sea bass, sea bream or *pagre* (*Pagrus pagrus*), a wide- ranging fish with an oblong body known in English as red porgy or common sea bream, and it will serve four people. If desired, add a tablespoon each of pine nuts and raisins when tossing the greens. It is an impressive dish that I love to serve to guests for a later summer dinner on the terrace. It never fails to please.

✳ Preheat the oven to 180°C/350°F/Gas Mark 4.

✳ Heat the oil in a large frying pan over medium–high heat. Add the potatoes and fry until just tender but not breaking, 12–15 minutes, turning as needed to keep from getting browned. Transfer with a slotted spoon to a colander to drain for a few minutes. Spread evenly across the bottom of an oven tray, large baking dish or baking sheet to make a bed for the fish.

✳ Season the fish with salt and pepper, juice the lemon over the top and sprinkle over 1 teaspoon of the paprika. Put the cloves of garlic in the cavity. Lay the fish on top of the potatoes. Bake in the oven for 10 minutes.

✳ Meanwhile, in a mixing bowl, toss the spinach, chard and grated tomatoes with the olive oil and remaining 1 teaspoon of paprika. Season with salt and pepper.

✳ Remove the fish from the oven and spread the spinach mixture across the top. The fish should be completely covered. Sprinkle over the breadcrumbs in an even layer.

✳ Cover with aluminium foil and bake in the oven until the greens are tender and wilted, about 20 minutes. Remove the foil, move the tray to a higher position and turn on the grill (broiler) element of the oven. Grill (broil) until the breadcrumbs are dark golden and crunchy, 5–10 minutes. Serve whole at the table.

Baked Red Mullet
on a Bed of Vegetables

Preparation time: 15 minutes
Cooking time: 1 hour
Serves: 4

4 medium white potatoes (about
    800 g/1¾ lb total), peeled and cut
    crosswise into thin slices about
    3 mm/⅛ inch thick
1 yellow onion, halved and thinly sliced
1 red bell pepper, stemmed, seeded
    and cut into strips
2 cloves of garlic, minced
1 tablespoon finely chopped flat-leaf
    parsley
1 teaspoon finely chopped marjoram
2 tablespoons olive oil, plus extra for
    drizzling
60 ml/2 fl oz (¼ cup) white wine
4–6 large red mullet (23–25 cm/9–10
    inches long; about 200 g/6 oz each),
    cleaned and scaled
3 tablespoons fine dry breadcrumbs
1 heaped teaspoon sweet paprika
2 tablespoons pine nuts, optional
Salt and pepper

DF ✳

Molls (red mullet) can often be found in a variety of sizes in the islands' fish markets. While small ones are best fried or grilled, larger ones – around 23–25 cm/9–10 inches in length and weighing 175–200 g/6–7 oz – are perfect for the oven. As the fish take much less time to bake than the vegetables, they are added later, when the potatoes are nearly done. Plan around 15 minutes of baking time for this size of red mullet.

✳ Preheat the oven to 180°C/350°F/Gas Mark 4.

✳ In a large mixing bowl, toss the potatoes, onion, pepper, garlic, parsley, marjoram and oil, and season with salt and pepper. Spread out on an oven tray or edged baking sheet. Drizzle over the wine. Cover snugly with aluminium foil and bake in the hot oven until the potatoes are nearly done, about 45 minutes.

✳ Pat the fish dry. In a bowl, blend the breadcrumbs and paprika.

✳ Lay the mullet on top of the vegetables. Sprinkle each fish with some of the breadcrumb mixture and drizzle with oil. Scatter the pine nuts (if using) around the top. Bake, uncovered, until the fish are cooked through, 10–15 minutes.

✳ Serve immediately.

Sea Bream in a Salt Crust with Allioli

Preparation time: 30 minutes
Cooking time: 15 minutes
Serves: 4

2 (450-g/1-lb) or 3 (280-g/10-ounce)
    whole sea bream with head and tail,
    or sea bass, red snapper, rockfish or
    another non-oily white fish
2 kg/4½ lb coarse sea salt, or as needed
3 large (US extra-large) egg whites
Chopped parsley, to serve, optional
Allioli (page 339)

DF ✳ GF ✳ 5

What could be more fitting for these islands than baking a fish under a bed of sea salt harvested in local saltpans and serving it with a garlic-and-olive allioli emulsion? While cooks today make this popular dish in the oven, it originated with fishermen, who placed a whole fish on a slab of marble, covered it with slightly moistened salt and cooked it over a small fire, essentially creating a single-use biodegradable oven with the salt. It was simple, ingenious and practical. It also perfectly adheres to the goal of heightening – rather than disguising – the natural flavours of the freshest products. The best way to achieve that is under a mound of sea salt. In Ibiza, fish *a la sal* is always served with allioli.

✳ Preheat the oven to 220°C/425°F/Gas Mark 7.

✳ Trim the fish's gills, but do not slice open the cavity along the stomach. Rather, pull out the intestines through the gills (or ask your fish supplier to do it). If the fish has already been cleaned in the standard way with its stomach open, tuck a small piece of aluminium foil around the outside of the belly to keep salt from entering the cavity. Leave on the head and tail.

✳ In a large bowl, mix the salt with the egg whites until the salt feels slightly damp.

✳ Line a rimmed baking sheet or roasting pan that can accommodate the fish with baking (parchment) paper for easier clean-up. Spread enough of the salt to form a base about 1.25 cm/½ inch thick. Gently pat down. Lay the fish on top, and then cover completely with the remaining salt in an even, 1.25-cm/½-inch-thick layer, gently patting down. Be sure the fish is completely covered.

✳ Carefully set in the hot oven without shifting the salt. Bake for about 15 minutes. (Calculate about 15 minutes per 450 g/1 lb of whole fish.) The shell will turn a touch brown and often begin to slightly crack towards the end of baking. Do not pry open the shell to check doneness.

✳ Using a wooden kitchen mallet or hammer, gently tap the shell to crack open. Pull away larger chunks of salt, and brush away loose grains. Gently lift out the fish and set on a platter. Working quickly, remove the skin, then lift the fillets off and place on a clean plate. Scatter with parsley and serve immediately with the allioli on the side.

Fish with Parsley Allioli

Preparation time: 15 minutes
Cooking time: 25 minutes
Serves: 5

1 litre/34 fl oz (4½ cups) Fish Stock
    (page 338) or water
pinch of saffron threads, crumbled
4 medium white potatoes (about
    800 g/1¾ lb total), peeled and cut
    into generous pieces
4 large fish steaks from a firm,
    white-fleshed variety (about 225 g/
    8 oz each)
180 ml/¾ cup Allioli (page 339)
3 packed tablespoons minced flat-leaf
    parsley
½ teaspoon sweet paprika, optional
Salt and pepper

DF ＊ GF

Straightforward and tasty, this classic of the Formentera kitchen boils fish and potatoes and then serves them covered in a thin 'green sauce', made by whisking allioli and finely chopped flat-leaf parsley with broth from boiling the fish. Some in Formentera also refer to this version more specifically as *salsa de julivert* ('parsley sauce'). While this recipe can be prepared with water, boiling the fish and potatoes in fish stock (broth) heightens their taste.

＊ Put the stock and saffron in a large pot and bring to a boil. Taste for seasoning and add salt if needed. Scoop out a small glass of the stock and set aside to cool. Add the potatoes to the pot and boil until they are becoming tender, about 10 minutes. Season the fish with salt and pepper and set into the pot. Reduce the heat and gently boil for about 10 minutes, or until the fish is done but not falling apart. With a slotted spoon, gently lift out the fish and potatoes – holding them above the pot for a moment to drain – and transfer to a serving platter.

＊ While the fish is cooking, put the allioli, parsley and paprika (if using) in a mixing bowl and slowly whisk in 3–5 tablespoons of the reserved stock until you have a runny (but not watery) sauce that coats the back of a spoon.

＊ Spoon the sauce all over the fish and potatoes and serve immediately.

John Dory with Fried Onions

Preparation time: 20 minutes
Cooking time: 30 minutes
Serves: 3–4

1 kg/2 ¼ lb John Dory or another
    firm-fleshed white fish, cleaned
neutral oil, for frying
250 g/9 oz (1⅔ cups) plain (all-purpose)
    flour, for dredging
3 medium yellow or white onions
    (about 600 g/1 lb 5 oz total),
    cut crosswise as thinly as possible
Lemon wedges, to serve, optional
Salt

DF ✳ 5

In the Balearic Islands, John Dory is known as *gall de Sant Pere*, or Saint Peter's rooster. There are two parts to that meaning: the rooster for the long spines on the dorsal fin and Saint Peter for the dark spot on each side of the tall, skinny fish. This refers to the Biblical story of when Saint Peter had to pay Caesar's taxes, and he caught a fish and plucked a gold coin from its mouth. Those spots are said to be marks from the apostle's fingers. That etymology gives little indication of the incredible deliciousness of this fish. One of the classic ways to cook John Dory in Mallorca is fried and served under a big mound of thinly sliced fried onions.

✳ Cut the fish into finger-thick steaks. Season with salt.

✳ Heat at least 2 cm/¾ inch of oil in a large frying pan over medium–high heat until the surface shimmers. Put the flour in a large bowl. Line a platter with paper towels.

✳ Working in batches that don't crowd the pan, dip the fish pieces into the flour until lightly coated all over, then shake off the excess. Carefully set in the hot oil and fry until golden and cooked through, 3–5 minutes per batch, depending on the thickness of the piece and if it has bones. Transfer to the paper towels to briefly drain the excess oil. Fry the remaining fish pieces in the same manner and briefly drain. Arrange on a serving platter.

✳ In the same pan, working in batches that don't crowd the pan, lightly flour the onions, shaking off the excess flour in a large sieve or strainer. Fry in the hot oil until golden and a touch crunchy, 6–8 minutes per batch. Briefly drain in a strainer and scatter on top of the fish. Repeat with the remaining onions.

✳ Serve immediately with lemon wedges, if you like.

Skate & Potatoes with Crushed Almonds & Saffron

Preparation time: 15 minutes
Cooking time: 30 minutes
Serves: 4–6

6 medium white potatoes, peeled
  and sliced crosswise
1 kg/2¼ lb skinned skate wings,
  trimmed into 6 or so pieces, or
  monkfish steaks
100 g/3½ oz (⅔ cup) toasted almonds,
  roughly chopped
2 hard-boiled eggs, peeled and roughly
  chopped
1 small slice day-old or toasted bread,
  roughly chopped
2 cloves of garlic, peeled
1 heaped tablespoon finely chopped
  flat-leaf parsley, plus extra to serve
Generous pinch of saffron threads,
  crumbled
2 tablespoons olive oil
Lemon wedges, to serve, optional
Salt and pepper

DF ✳

One of the many fish dishes that showcase the often original combinations of ingredients in the Balearic kitchen is this baroque one of skate stewed with potatoes, saffron and almonds. Pounding almonds with hard-boiled eggs, saffron and some bread into a *picada* flavours the dish but also thickens the sauce. The popular technique goes back to the Middle Ages and is used here with one of the most popular fish in the Balearics, *rajada* (skate). Some home cooks like to prepare the dish in the oven, others in a shallow terracotta casserole pan on the stove. This is the stovetop version – the way that I always prepare it.

✳ Bring a pot of lightly salted water to a boil, add the potatoes and gently boil until becoming tender, 10–12 minutes. Drain, reserving about 500 ml (18 fl oz/ 2 cups) of the liquid.

✳ Bring another pot of lightly salted water to a boil, add the skate and gently boil for 4 minutes. Transfer with a slotted spoon to a platter.

✳ Prepare a picada: in a large mortar with a pestle, pound the almonds, hard-boiled eggs, bread, garlic, parsley and saffron. Stir in a few tablespoons of the reserved liquid, and season with salt and pepper. Or blend, in brief pulses, in a food processor, adding a touch of the reserved liquid as needed. (See page 175 for more on making a picada.)

✳ Coat the bottom of a shallow, flameproof casserole pan (see page 25), Dutch oven or sauté pan with the oil and arrange the potatoes over it in an even layer. Arrange the skate in a single layer on top. Loosen the picada with about 250 ml (8 fl oz/1 cup) of the reserved liquid and pour over the top. Cook, uncovered, over medium–low heat until the fish is cooked through and the sauce thickened, about 10 minutes.

✳ Add a touch more of the reserved liquid, if needed, to keep it moist. Serve with a parsley leaf and lemon wedges, if desired.

Sofregit or Sofrit:

Home-cooked stews, soups and rice dishes usually begin with a base and build up from there. For many dishes in the Balearics, that base is called *sofregit* or *sofrit* (*sofrito* in Spanish), a slowly sautéed medley of onions and tomatoes, usually garlic, often sweet green pepper and frequently some minced flat-leaf parsley in olive oil. Depending on the dish itself, it might also include some chopped cuttlefish or pork. In Mallorca, the onions of choice are usually skinny spring onions (scallions), so identified with this preparation they are locally called *sofrit*.

The first rule to a good *sofregit* is that it cannot be rushed. The sweetness of the onions must be slowly drawn out without scorching – this takes around 10 minutes – before the tomatoes are added. Tomatoes can be peeled and chopped, but halving and then grating them is not just easier but also gets at that prime part just under the skin (see page 25 for notes on grating tomatoes). As the tomatoes cook, their water evaporates, their acidity dissipates and their colour darkens, a process that usually takes 10–15 minutes. A couple of tablespoons of water or stock (broth) can be added towards the end to keep them from drying out, and a generous pinch of sugar can help sweeten the tomatoes. The *sofregit* is done when the tomatoes have evaporated all of their water, at which point it takes on a darker red colour and brilliant tone and has a pasty texture. Beyond this point there is a risk of sticking and scorching.

Incorporating garlic into the *sofregit* can be done in various ways. I like to stir minced garlic into the pan once the onions are done and let them cook for only 30 seconds or so while stirring, just long enough for them to become aromatic but not to scorch, before immediately adding the tomatoes. Sometimes whole cloves lightly crushed and left in their skins are be added with the onions and sautéed together. Especially when a recipe calls for a *picada* (a pounded paste of nuts, garlic and maybe parsley that gets stirred in at the end of a dish, see opposite), whole cloves of peeled garlic can go into the pan first with the oil before the onions and cook alone for 30 seconds or so, just enough to begin to soften and become aromatic, before being removed and reserved for the *picada*. This cuts that raw bite of the garlic when it gets eventually incorporated into the dish. It also flavours the oil in which the *sofregit* will be prepared.

Picada

If a *sofregit* (or *sofrit*, see opposite) begins many dishes and acts as a base on which to build, then a *picada* often ends it.

Derived from the verb *picar*, meaning 'to pound' (also to hit, crush, bite, smack, sting and itch), a *picada* is made by pounding almonds (or hazelnuts), garlic, a pinch of salt and usually some minced flat-leaf parsley to a paste in a mortar with a pestle. A tablespoon or two of liquid helps turn it into a compact paste. You don't want to find pieces of nuts. The almonds or hazelnuts need to be well pounded. Slip off the papery skin of the nuts before pounding.

Sometimes there is a small amount of dried (or fried) bread or savoury biscuit to give it more body, while some recipes call for a hard-boiled egg yolk. Saffron threads are also occasionally pounded with the *picada*. Nuts are omitted in certain dishes, such as in many fisherman's rices, where the picada often includes just garlic, parsley and maybe some saffron threads.

The *picada* gets stirred into a range of dishes – braised meats, soups and stews, rices, stewed legumes – at the end of their cooking. The *picada* thickens the sauce, gives it some backbone and adds a deepening layer of nutty flavour. One of the unique elements of the Catalan kitchen, it was introduced to the Balearic kitchen in the Middle Ages.

Pounding in a mortar with a pestle gives the best control over the texture of the *picada*. That said, it can also be quickly whirred in a food processor. This, though, usually requires a touch of liquid. Use brief pulses and scrape down the bowl with a rubber spatula in between to keep the pasty mixture within the blade's reach.

The *picada* is generally integrated into a dish during the last 5–10 minutes of cooking. When adding, it is easiest to loosen it with a bit of liquid before stirring in, as you don't want to find any clumps of *picada*.

Amounts called for might seem almost non-consequential – maybe just a dozen toasted almonds – but the difference to the final dish is striking. The *picada* alters the final flavour, colour and texture of the dish.

Fried Skate with Garlic & Parsley

Preparation time: 5 minutes,
  plus marinating time
Cooking time: 15 minutes
Serves: 4

1 kg/2¼ lb skinned skate wings
6 lemon wedges
neutral oil, for frying
4–6 heaped tablespoons plain
  (all-purpose) flour
4 cloves of garlic, minced
2 heaped tablespoons minced flat-leaf
  parsley
Salt and pepper

DF ✳ 30

Rajada (skate) remains a deeply popular fish in the Balearic Islands, and kitchens continue to prepare it in a host of traditional ways. In Ibiza, it is stewed with potatoes, crushed almonds, hard-boiled eggs and saffron (page 172), in Menorca it is frequently baked between a layer of sliced potatoes and a layer of sliced tomatoes, and in Mallorca cooking the fish with tomato sauce is a favourite. But while each of those is delicious, a much more straightforward way is frequently used in order to fully appreciate the flavour and texture of this flat, gelatinous fish: it is lightly floured and fried, and topped with a pinch of chopped garlic and parsley before being served. Simplicity at its tastiest.

✳ Cut the skate into generous pieces. Put in a large bowl, season with salt and pepper and squeeze over 1 or 2 of the lemon wedges. Turn to coat and let marinate for 10 minutes.

✳ Put the flour in a wide bowl. Line a platter with paper towels. In a small bowl, mix the garlic and parsley with some drops of lemon juice and set aside.

✳ Heat 1–2 cm/½–¾ inch of oil in a frying pan over medium–high heat until the surface shimmers. Working in batches that don't crowd the pan, dip the fish into the flour until lightly coated all over, then shake off the excess. Carefully set in the hot oil and fry until golden and cooked through, 6–8 minutes per batch, depending on the thickness of the piece. Transfer to the paper towels to briefly drain any excess oil. Fry the remaining fish and briefly drain.

✳ Spread some of the garlic-parsley mixture on each piece of fish and serve immediately with the remaining lemon wedges.

Ibizan-style Tuna with Raisins & Pine Nuts

Preparation time: 15 minutes
Cooking time: 40 minutes
Serves: 4

3 tablespoons olive oil
2 medium yellow onions, finely chopped
1 long sweet green pepper or ½ green
    bell pepper, stemmed, seeded and
    chopped
2 cloves of garlic, minced
3 medium tomatoes, halved and grated
    (see page 25)
1 teaspoon sweet paprika
120 ml/4 fl oz (½ cup) dry white wine
4 tuna steaks, about 2 cm/¾ inch thick
    (175–200 g/6–7 oz each)
1 small cinnamon stick
2 heaped tablespoons pine nuts,
    dry-toasted (see page 25)
2 heaped tablespoons seedless raisins
Salt and pepper

DF ✳ GF ✳ 1 POT

Known as *tonyina a l'eivissenca* – Ibizan-style tuna – this dish is a treat and offers a melody of sweet and savoury flavours. Watch that they don't overcook, as tuna can easily become dried out. The recipe is a true delight and celebration of the treasures of Ibiza's gastronomy that captures the unique flavours of the island.

✳ Heat the oil in a large frying pan over medium heat. Add the onions and green pepper and cook until soft, 10–15 minutes. Stir in the garlic, add the tomatoes and cook until darker and pasty, about 10 minutes, stirring in 3–4 tablespoons water as it cooks. Stir in the paprika and then the wine, letting it cook for 1 minute.

✳ Season the tuna steaks with salt and pepper and lay into the pan without overlapping. Cook for 2 minutes, then gently turn the steaks. Add the cinnamon stick, pine nuts and raisins. Reduce the heat to low and cook until the tuna is cooked through, about 10 minutes, gently shaking the pan from time to time to help the sauce thicken. Serve.

Sardines in Escabeche Marinade

Preparation time: 15 minutes,
    plus marinating time
Cooking time: 25 minutes
Serves: 4

500 g/1 lb 2 oz fresh whole sardines
    or another small blue fish
50 g/2 oz (⅓ cup) plain (all-purpose)
    flour, for dusting
250 ml/1 cup, plus 3 tablespoons, olive
    oil, plus extra for covering if needed
8 cloves of garlic, skins on, lightly
    crushed under the palm
1 yellow onion, halved lengthwise and
    thinly sliced crosswise
1 carrot, cut crosswise into 5-mm/
    ¼-inch-thick pieces
3 bay leaves
10 black peppercorns
120 ml/4 fl oz (½ cup) white wine
    vinegar
Salt

DF ✳

This herb-laden marinade with olive oil and vinegar is an ancient short-term preservative. *Escabetx*, with its origins during the Muslim rule of the islands, is popular along the western end of the Mediterranean. The choice of which fish to use for *escabetx* in the Balearics varies from island to island. *Gerret* (a small, local picarel) are often preferred in Ibiza, while skate or a dogfish called *gató* in Mallorca and mullet in Formentera are more common. In Formentera, *llampuga* (*dorado* in Spanish and known in English as dolphinfish or mahi-mahi), which appears in local waters in late summer and early autumn, is another traditional choice. Sardines, though, are for me the best: the size of the fish is perfect; they are widely available and inexpensive; and, most importantly, their flavour combines perfectly well with the herby tartness of *escabetx*. Along with the herbs, carrots are essential here, but some small florets of cauliflower would be a lovely touch. The fish should fit snugly in the dish in order to be covered with the marinade. For medium sardines, a 15 × 25-cm/6 × 10-inch rectangular dish is ideal. Over the years, this has moved beyond being a favourite of ours to enjoy in Menorca to being a household speciality.

✳ Beginning at least 2 days ahead: clean and remove the heads and entrails of the sardines. Pat dry with paper towels. Season with salt.

✳ Place the flour on a plate or in a shallow bowl. Dip the fish into the flour until lightly coated all over, then shake off the excess.

✳ Heat the 3 tablespoons of oil in a small frying pan over medium heat. Working in batches as needed, fry the fish until they are just cooked through and the skin is golden, turning once using 2 wide spatulas, 3–5 minutes total per batch, depending on the size of the fish. Transfer to a rectangular ceramic or glass dish. Lay the fish side by side, alternating head–tail so they fit snugly together.

✳ Heat the 250 ml (8 fl oz/1 cup) oil in a frying pan, sauté pan or saucepan over medium heat. Add the garlic, onion, carrot, bay leaves and peppercorns, and cook until the onion begins to become tender, about 8 minutes. Very carefully pour in the vinegar and bring to a boil. Remove from the heat and let cool for a few minutes.

✳ Pour the mixture over the fish to completely cover. If the marinade does not cover them, top up with more oil as needed. Let cool to room temperature. Cover with clingfilm (plastic wrap) and refrigerate for at least 2 days to allow the sardines to take on the escabeche's characteristic flavours. Store in the refrigerator for up to 1 week.

✳ Remove about 1 hour before serving and serve at room temperature, or a little cool, with some of the marinade spooned over the top.

Fried Sardines with Sweet Tomato & Onion Sofregit

Preparation time: 30 minutes
Cooking time: 50 minutes
Serves: 4

FOR THE SOFREGIT
4 tablespoons olive oil
2 yellow onions, finely chopped
4 cloves of garlic, skins on, lightly
   crushed under the palm
4 or 5 ripe tomatoes (about 700 g/
   1½ lb total), halved and grated
   (see page 25)
1 bay leaf
1 heaped tablespoon finely chopped
   flat-leaf parsley
½ teaspoon sweet paprika
1 teaspoon sugar

FOR THE SARDINES
1 kg/2¼ lb fresh whole sardines or
   another small 'blue fish'
65 g/2¼ oz (½ cup) plain (all-purpose)
   flour, for dusting
Neutral oil, for frying
Salt and pepper

DF *

While *sofregit* (or *sofrit*) – a slow-cooked medley of onions and tomatoes – usually acts as a base to stews and rice dishes (see page 174), it can, on occasion, be a relish-like stand-alone topping. Spooned over fried sardines it is, simply, perfect. Other types of 'blue fish' are also excellent, as are sea bass and sea bream. While many cooks say it is best to leave the fish with *sofregit* for an hour or two before serving to let the flavours deepen, in our house we like the fish just-fried and still a touch hot under that bed of *sofregit*. Calculate five or so medium sardines per person. I like to use ones that weigh about 50 g/2 oz each. (Note that Mediterranean sardines tend to be a touch smaller than their Atlantic Ocean counterparts.)

* Prepare the sofregit: heat the olive oil in a shallow, flameproof casserole pan (see page 25), frying pan or sauté pan over medium–high heat. Add the onions and garlic and cook until soft, 10–12 minutes. Add the tomatoes, bay leaf, parsley, paprika and sugar, then reduce the heat to medium–low and cook, stirring frequently, until dark red and pasty, 20–30 minutes. Towards the end, add a few tablespoons of water to keep it from scorching.

* Meanwhile, prepare the sardines: Scale, clean and remove the heads and entrails. Pat dry with paper towels. Season with salt and pepper. Put the flour in a bowl. Line a plate with absorbent paper towels.

* Heat at least 2 cm/¾ inch of oil for frying in a small frying pan over high heat until the surface shimmers. Working in batches as needed, lightly flour the fish and fry until cooked through and the skin is golden and a touch crispy, turning just once using 2 wide spatulas, 2–4 minutes total depending on the size of the fish. Remove with tongs and set on the paper towels to soak up some of the excess oil. Repeat with the remaining fish.

* Arrange the fish on a platter. Spoon the over the sofregit and serve.

Salt Cod with Roasted Red Peppers, Tomatoes & Garlic

Preparation time: 30 minutes, plus
    soaking, desalting and cooling time
Cooking time: 45 minutes
Serves: 4

800 g/1¾ lb thick boneless salt cod
    fillets, cut into 4–8 pieces
2 red bell peppers (about 600 g/
    1 lb 5 oz total)
4 ripe tomatoes (about 500 g/
    1 lb 2 oz total)
4 tablespoons olive oil, plus extra
    for brushing and as needed
2 heaped tablespoons plain
    (all-purpose) flour, for dusting
4 cloves of garlic, thinly sliced crosswise
1 sprig thyme
1 sprig marjoram
1 bay leaf
1 teaspoon sugar
½ teaspoon sweet paprika
Minced flat-leaf parsley, to garnish,
    optional

DF ✳

Once it has been soaked for a few days, salt cod has a silky texture unique among fish, and its mild, almost sweet flavours pair perfectly with the roasted red bell peppers and tomatoes served here. The final dish is a glorious combination of flavours. Scatter some toasted pine nuts over the top to add yet another interesting layer of texture and taste.

✳ Beginning 2 or 3 days ahead, desalt the cod following the directions on page 25. Do not remove the skin. Drain in a colander, skin-side up, for at least 1 hour. Pat dry with paper towels.

✳ Preheat the oven grill (broiler) to high. Line a baking sheet with aluminium foil for easier clean-up.

✳ Brush the peppers and tomatoes with oil and set on the baking sheet. Grill (broil), turning as needed, until charred in places and tender, about 15 minutes. Transfer to a large bowl, cover and let cool in the steam for about 20 minutes to make peeling easier.

✳ Once the peppers are cool enough to handle, rub off the blackened skin and discard the stem and seeds. Tear or cut into long strips and set aside. Peel, core and roughly chop the tomatoes, reserving all juices.

✳ Preheat the oven to 180°C/350°F/Gas Mark 4. Put the flour in a wide bowl.

✳ Heat the 4 tablespoons of oil in a large frying pan over medium–high heat. Dip the cod into the flour until lightly coated all over, then shake off the excess. Place in the pan and fry, turning once, until golden and not yet flaking apart, about 4 minutes total. Remove the pan from the heat. Transfer the pieces of cod to absorbent paper towels to briefly drain. In a baking dish, carefully arrange the pieces skin-side down.

✳ To the same pan, add the pepper strips and garlic, season with salt and cook over medium heat until soft and aromatic without allowing the garlic to scorch, about 5 minutes. Remove with a slotted spoon and spread over the cod.

✳ Still in the same pan, adding a touch more oil if needed, combine the tomatoes, thyme, marjoram, bay leaf, sugar and paprika. Season with salt and cook, stirring frequently, until darker and pasty, about 10 minutes. Remove and discard the herbs. Spoon the sauce in a layer over the peppers.

✳ Put the baking dish in the oven and bake for 5–10 minutes until the cod pieces are warmed throughout.

✳ Scatter some parsley (if using) over the top and serve.

Mallorcan-style Salt Cod

Preparation time: 45 minutes,
  plus soaking and desalting time
Cooking time: 1 hour 10 minutes
Serves: 4

4 thick boneless salt cod fillets,
  150–200 g/5–7 oz each
250 g/9 oz trimmed Swiss chard,
  roughly chopped
10 g/½ unpacked cup finely chopped
  flat-leaf parsley
1 bunch (about 200 g/7 oz) spring
  onions (scallions), trimmed, white
  and tender green parts cut
  lengthwise then crosswise into
  1-cm/½-inch pieces
1 heaped tablespoon pine nuts, optional
1 heaped tablespoon seedless raisins,
  optional
1 heaped tablespoon sweet paprika
3 tablespoons olive oil
2 heaped tablespoons plain
  (all-purpose) flour, for dusting
250 ml/8 fl oz (1 cup) neutral oil,
  for frying
4 medium white potatoes (about
  800 g/1¾ lb total), peeled and cut
  crosswise into 5-mm/¼-inch-thick
  circles
2 plum tomatoes, cut crosswise into
  1-cm/½-inch-thick slices
Salt and pepper

DF ✳

Salt cod is more than an essential ingredient during Lent and in times of penance. An entire gastronomic culture developed around it over the centuries. Many of the old regional cookbooks might have a recipe or two for chicken, but there will be dozens for salt cod. This is one of the most popular ways to prepare salt cold on Mallorca. Baked in the oven on a bed of potatoes and under a blanket of Swiss chard and spring onions (scallions), it's so popular in Mallorca that the dish often goes by the name *a la mallorquina*, Mallorcan-style.

✳ Beginning 2 or 3 days ahead, desalt the cod following the directions on page 25. Do not remove the skin. Drain in a colander, skin-side up, for at least 1 hour. Pat dry with paper towels.

✳ Put the Swiss chard and parsley in a large mixing bowl. Add the spring onions (scallions) to the bowl. Add the pine nuts and raisins (if using), along with the paprika and olive oil. Season with salt and pepper and toss to blend well.

✳ Preheat the oven to 180°C/350°F/Gas Mark 4. Put the flour in a wide bowl.

✳ Heat the oil for frying in a large frying pan over medium–high heat. Working in 2 batches, fry the potatoes, turning as needed, until just tender, about 10 minutes per batch. Transfer with a slotted spoon to a colander to drain for a few minutes, then spread evenly across the bottom of a baking dish.

✳ Dip the cod into the flour until lightly coated all over, then shake off the excess. Fry in the same pan until beginning to turn golden but not yet flaking apart, about 4 minutes total, beginning with the skin-side facing up and turning only once. Transfer the cod with the skin-side up to a plate to drain. Arrange skin-side down on top of the potatoes.

✳ Spread the vegetable mixture over the top of the cod. Arrange the tomato slices on top.

✳ Bake in the hot oven until the greens have wilted and are tender, about 30–40 minutes. Serve.

Salt Cod with Allioli Gratin

Preparation time: 15 minutes,
    plus soaking and desalting time
Cooking time: 40 minutes
Serves: 4

4 thick boneless salt cod fillets,
    about 200 g/7 oz each
250 ml/8 fl oz (1 cup) neutral oil,
    for frying
5 medium white potatoes, peeled
    and cut crosswise into 5-mm/
    ¼-inch-thick circles
2 heaped tablespoons plain
    (all-purpose) flour, for dusting
120–175 ml/4–6 fl oz (½–¾ cup) Allioli
    (page 339)

DF ✳ 5

This classic salt cod dish might be quite straightforward to prepare, but it always feels highly original and sophisticated at the table when serving. The layer of potatoes here are needed to help balance the flavours and make it a full meal. Watch the gratin, as it turns brown quickly – don't let it scorch. Scattering some capers around the cod will make a lovely addition.

✳ Beginning 2 or 3 days ahead, desalt the cod following the directions on page 25. Do not remove the skin. Drain in a colander, skin-side up, for at least 1 hour. Pat dry with paper towels.

✳ Heat the oil in a frying pan over medium–high heat. Working in 2 batches, fry the potatoes until just tender, about 10 minutes per batch. Transfer with a slotted spoon to a colander to drain. Remove the pan of oil from the heat.

✳ Preheat the oven to 180°C/350°F/Gas Mark 4. Put the flour in a wide bowl.

✳ Reheat the pan of oil over medium heat. Dip the cod into the flour until lightly coated all over, then shake off the excess. Fry until the pieces begin to turn golden but are not yet flaking apart, beginning with the skin-side facing up and turning only once, about 4 minutes total. Transfer the cod with the skin-side up to a plate to drain.

✳ Spread the potatoes evenly across the bottom of a shallow baking dish. Arrange the cod skin-side down on top of the potatoes. Spoon the allioli in a generous layer over the fish.

✳ Bake in the hot oven for 5 minutes to reheat the potatoes. Move the dish to a higher rack and change the oven setting to medium grill (broil). Cook until the allioli is golden on top, about 5 minutes, watching very carefully so as not to let it scorch. Serve from the baking dish.

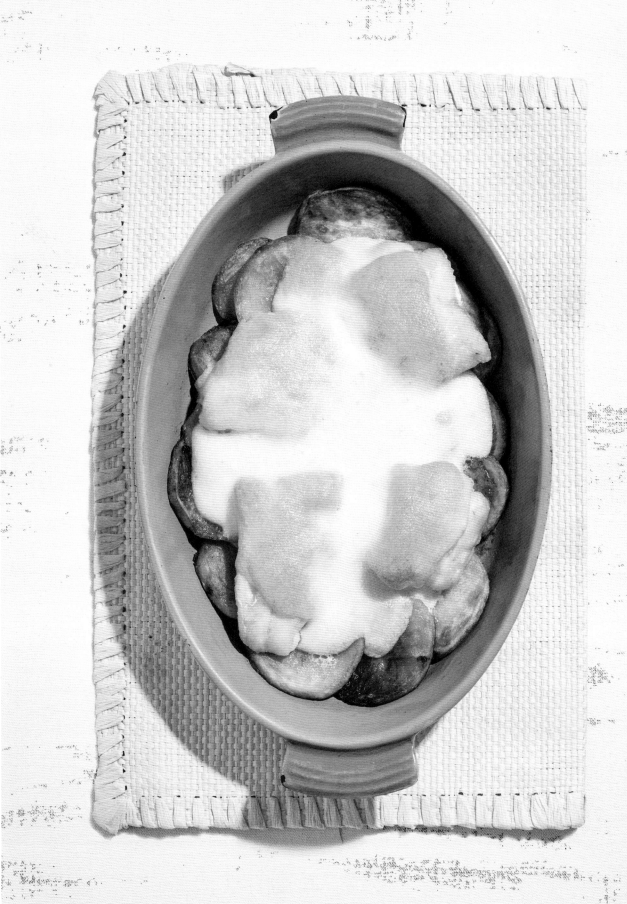

CHAPTER 7

SEAFOOD

Seafood 'Frit' with Potatoes & Red Peppers

Preparation time: 30 minutes
Cooking time: 1 hour
Serves: 4–6

15–20 mussels, cleaned
175 ml/6 fl oz (¾ cup) neutral oil,
    for frying
4 medium white potatoes (about 800 g/
    1¾ lb total), peeled, halved crosswise,
    then each half quartered
1 red bell pepper, stemmed, seeded
    and cut into 2.5-cm/1-inch pieces
3 tablespoons olive oil
350 g/12 oz cleaned cuttlefish (see
    page 25) or squid (calamari), cut into
    2-cm/¾-inch pieces
350 g/12 oz cleaned monkfish or
    another firm, white-fleshed fish,
    cut into 2-cm/¾-inch cubes
350 g/12 oz peeled prawns (shrimp),
    thawed if frozen
2 cloves of garlic, minced
2 yellow onions, finely chopped
2 heaped tablespoons finely chopped
    fresh fennel fronds

DF ✳ GF

Although many of Mallorca's numerous *frit* ('fried') dishes have pork, there are some based on seafood as well, including *Frit de pop* (page 217) with octopus, *frit mariner* (page 194) based on squid (calamari) and this one with a mixture of seafood. As with other *frits*, the ingredients are fried separately in succession and then passed into a large terracotta casserole pan (in Mallorca known as a *greixonera*), given a substantial seasoning of chopped fennel fronds and cooked for a few minutes together to warm and to blend flavours.

✳ Put the mussels in a small saucepan, and pour over 120 ml (4 fl oz/½ cup) water. Bring to a boil over high heat. Lower the heat, cover the pot and simmer, shaking the pot from time to time, until the mussels have opened, 3–4 minutes. Strain. Discard any mussels that did not open. Once cool enough to handle, remove the mussels from their shells, discarding the shells. Set aside.

✳ Heat the oil for frying in a frying pan over medium–high heat. Add the potatoes and fry, turning as needed, until golden and tender, about 12–15 minutes. Transfer with a slotted spoon to absorbent paper towels to briefly drain. Transfer to a large, shallow, flameproof casserole pan (see page 25).

✳ In the same frying pan, fry the red pepper until tender, about 5 minutes. Transfer with a slotted spoon to absorbent paper towels to briefly drain and then put in the casserole pan with the potatoes.

✳ In a clean frying pan, heat the olive oil over medium–high heat. Add the cuttlefish and cook until golden and tender, about 15 minutes. Add the monkfish and cook, turning as needed, for 5 minutes or until just cooked through. Add the prawns (shrimp) and cook until they have turned opaque throughout, about 2 minutes. Transfer everything to the casserole pan using a slotted spoon.

✳ To the same frying pan, add the garlic, followed by the onions. Cook over medium heat until soft, 6–8 minutes. Stir in the fennel and reserved mussels, and cook for 2 minutes, stirring frequently. Transfer to the casserole pan.

✳ Place the casserole pan over low heat and cook, gently stirring the mixture to allow the flavours blend, for 5 minutes. Serve.

'Frit' with Squid, Potatoes, Spring Onions & Red Peppers

Preparation time: 20 minutes
Cooking time: 40 minutes
Serves: 4–6

120 ml/4 fl oz (½ cup) neutral oil,
    for frying
3 medium white potatoes (about
    600 g/1 lb 5 oz total), peeled and cut
    into 1-cm/½-inch dice
3 tablespoons olive oil
500 g/1 lb 2 oz squid (calamari) or
    cuttlefish, cleaned (see page 25;
    300 g/11 oz cleaned), cut into 1-cm/
    ½-inch square pieces
1 generous bunch (about 250 g/9 oz)
    spring onions (scallions), trimmed
    and cut into 1-cm/½-inch pieces
3 cloves of garlic, skins on, lightly
    crushed under the palm
2 small whole dried red chillies (chiles)
1 red bell pepper, stemmed, seeded and
    cut into 1-cm/½-inch squares
3 heaped tablespoons finely chopped
    fresh fennel fronds
Salt and pepper

DF ✳ GF

Particularly popular in the interior part of Mallorca, this somewhat streamlined version of seafood *frit* (page 192) keeps the focus on squid (calamari). And while it is streamlined, the chopping can feel somewhat laborious. It's important, though, as the dice need to be small. The fresh fennel fronds give it a characteristic flavour.

✳ Heat the oil for frying in a frying pan over medium–high heat. Add the potatoes and fry until tender but not yet browned, 10–12 minutes. Transfer with a slotted spoon to a colander to drain.

✳ Meanwhile, heat the olive oil in a separate frying pan or sauté pan over medium–high heat. Add the squid (calamari) or cuttlefish and cook until the water that it releases has evaporated, about 4 minutes. Add the spring onions (scallions), garlic and chillies (chiles) and cook until they begin to soften, 3–4 minutes. Add the red pepper and cook for 3–4 minutes more. Cover the pan and cook over low heat until all the ingredients are soft, about 10 minutes.

✳ Transfer the potatoes and all the ingredients in the frying pan to a large, flameproof casserole pan (see page 25) and season with salt and pepper. Add the fennel and cook over low heat, gently stirring the mixture to allow the flavours blend for 3–5 minutes.

✳ Serve hot.

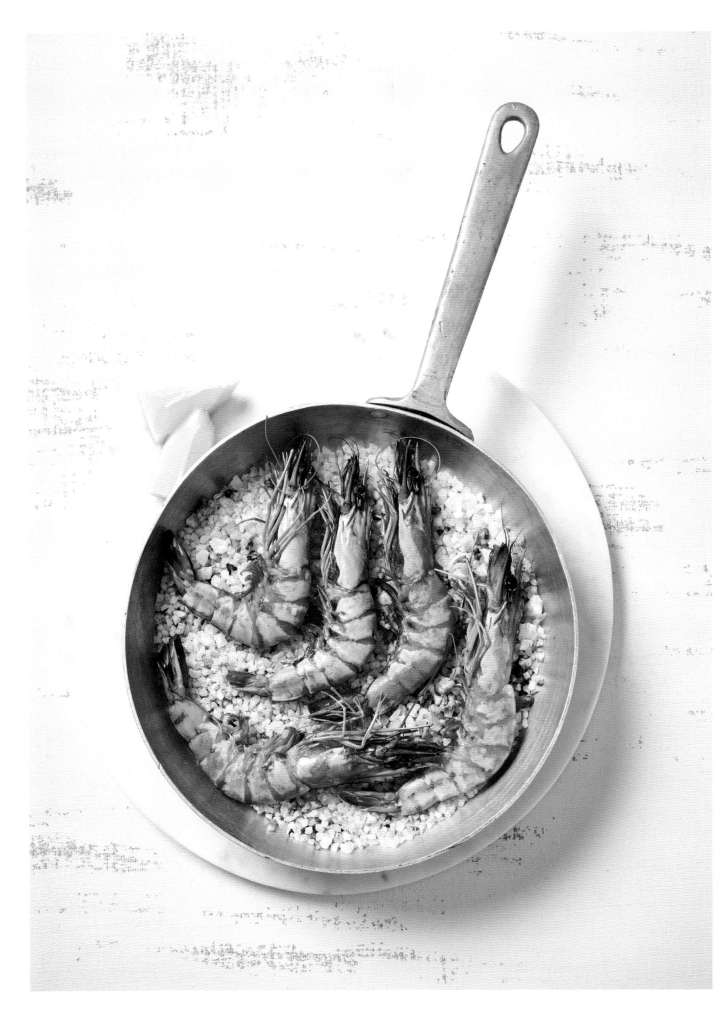

Red Prawns Cooked
on a Bed of Salt

Preparation time: 5 minutes
Cooking time: 10 minutes
Serves: 4

Coarse sea salt
12–20 prawns (shrimp) with heads
  and shells

DF ✳ GF ✳ 5 ✳ 30

Prized red Sóller prawns are always cooked in the most straightforward manner to fully capture their vibrant flavours and fine texture. While that often means on a griddle (grill) pan, many locals prefer to cook them on a bed of hot salt. One of the pleasures when eating the prawns is removing the head – where the flavours are the most concentrated – and, while gently squeezing, sucking out the juices. Then you peel and eat the rest. Sóller prawns can be large – over 20 cm/8 inches in length. Cooking time depends on size. Do not overcook. They should be just done and still juicy.

✳ Cover the bottom of a griddle or large frying pan with about 1 cm/½ inch of salt.

✳ Heat over medium–high heat until the salt is hot. Carefully lay the prawns (shrimp) on top of the salt, reduce the heat to medium–low and cook until the prawns begin to turn white, about 5 minutes. Turn with tongs and cook for 3–5 minutes until they have just turned fully white.

✳ Remove the pan from the heat, transfer the prawns to a platter and serve immediately.

Fisherman's Shrimp
with Onions & Brandy

Preparation time: 5 minutes
Cooking time: 20 minutes
Serves: 2–4

3 tablespoons olive oil
1 yellow onion, finely chopped
6 cloves of garlic, skins on, lightly
   crushed under the palm
12–20 large shrimp with heads and shells
60 ml/2 fl oz (¼ cup) brandy or cognac
Parsley leaves, to garnish, optional
Salt and pepper

DF * GF * 5 * 30 * 1 POT

The sweetness of slow-cooked onions and the earthiness of the brandy are perfect complements to shrimp in this simple dish. It makes a lovely appetizer. It is hard to gauge serving sizes here, as the shrimp are so tasty that they are hard to stop eating, certainly in my house. I always serve with plenty of bread.

* Heat the oil in a large, shallow, flameproof casserole pan (see page 25), frying pan or sauté pan over medium heat. Add the onion and garlic and patiently cook until tender and just beginning to turn golden, 12–15 minutes. Season with salt and pepper. Lay the shrimp on the onions and pour over the brandy or cognac. Cook until the shrimp are cooked through, turning a few times, 3–5 minutes. Serve at the table from the casserole pan, scattered with parsley, if using.

Lobster with Fried Potatoes & Fried Eggs

Preparation time: 10 minutes,
    plus cooling time
Cooking time: 20 minutes
Serves: 2

1 whole fresh or thawed frozen lobster
    (700 g–1 kg/1½–2¼ lb)
6 tablespoons olive oil
3 medium white potatoes (about
    600 g/1 lb 5 oz total), peeled and
    thinly sliced crosswise
1 long sweet green pepper or ½ green
    bell pepper, stemmed, seeded and
    cut into pieces
2–4 large (US extra-large) eggs
Salt and pepper

DF ✳ GF ✳ 5 ✳ 30

A perfect combination of simplicity and decadence: lobster with fried potatoes and sweet green peppers, served with eggs fried in the same oil. In the last decade, this has become the most popular way for restaurants to prepare lobster in summer on Ibiza and Formentera. While some traditionalists may scorn it as fast food, it combines the ingredients to perfection. If anything, call it fast very good food. Add a small dried chilli (chile) or some cloves of garlic crushed in their skins for added bumps of flavour.

✳ If using fresh lobster, place the lobster in the freezer for 15 minutes (this numbs the lobster). Remove the lobster from the freezer, then lay it, stomach-side down, on a chopping (cutting) board. Find the cross on the back of its head. Insert the tip of a large, heavy knife into the head and firmly plunge it through the shell with a sharp blow, right through to the chopping board.

✳ Turn the lobster over on its back and split in half lengthwise, cutting along the belly. Remove the dark green matter. Cut the lobster tail crosswise into 2 or 3 pieces with a heavy knife or kitchen scissors, leaving the meat attached to the shell. Cut the large claws in half. Season with salt and pepper and set aside.

✳ Heat the oil in a large frying pan or sauté pan over medium–high heat. Add the potatoes and fry, turning as needed, until tender, 6–8 minutes. Transfer to a platter with a slotted spoon. In the same pan, fry the green pepper until tender, about 2 minutes. Transfer with a slotted spoon to the platter. Reserve 2–3 tablespoons of the oil.

✳ In a clean frying pan or sauté pan, heat the reserved oil over high heat and add the lobster pieces. Cook until the colour of the meat changes from pearl to white throughout, about 5 minutes. Transfer to the serving platter with a slotted spoon. Keep the same pan on the heat and gently crack in the eggs. Fry without turning until the whites are opaque and the yolks still runny, about 2 minutes. Arrange the eggs across the top of the lobster and serve immediately.

'Dirty' Squid Stewed with its Ink

Preparation time: 20 minutes
Cooking time: 1 hour 5 minutes
Serves: 3–4

700 g/1½ lb medium whole squid
    (calamari), cleaned (see page 25), ink
    sac reserved or with 2 (7 gram/⅓ oz)
    packets of squid ink (see page 24)
2 tablespoons olive oil
2 cloves of garlic, minced
2 tomatoes, halved and grated
    (see page 25)
1–2 bay leaves
175 ml/6 fl oz (¾ cup) white wine
120 ml (4 fl oz/½ cup) warm water
Salt

DF ✳ GF

This is a relatively fuss-free recipe for one of Formentera's most popular squid (calamari) dishes. While some versions include two types of sausage – blood sausage (*botifarró*, see page 23) and sobrassada (see page 208) – the focus here remains on the squid, with its ink playing a key supporting role. See the note on page 24 about squid ink, which can be purchased separately in tiny packets.

✳ Open the squid (calamari) tubes and cut lengthwise into 2.5-cm/1-inch-thick strips. Set aside.

✳ Heat the oil in a large, shallow, flameproof casserole pan (see page 25), Dutch oven or heavy sauté pan with a lid over medium heat. Add the garlic and tomatoes and cook until the tomatoes begin to darken, about 5 minutes. Add the squid and bay leaf, season with salt and cook for 5 minutes, stirring frequently as it releases its moisture. Pour over the wine, partly cover the pan and simmer for 45 minutes. Add a touch of water, if needed, towards the end to keep it from drying out.

✳ Meanwhile, in a bowl, snip open the ink sacs and add the warm water to dissolve.

✳ Stir the diluted ink into the pan and cook until the squid is very tender and the sauce reduces, about 10 minutes. Serve.

Fish-stuffed Squid

Preparation time: 30 minutes
Cooking time: 1 hour 20 minutes
Serves: 2–4

4 medium whole squid (calamari), with
    tubes about 15 cm/6 inches in length
120 g/4 oz boneless fish fillets, finely
    chopped
2 cloves of garlic, minced
2 tablespoons minced flat-leaf parsley
4 tablespoons olive oil
2 medium yellow onions, finely chopped
2 tomatoes, halved and grated
    (see page 25)
1 teaspoon sugar
3 tablespoons brandy
Salt and pepper

DF ✳ GF

Just about everything gets stuffed into squid (calamari) tubes, it seems, from sobrassada (page 208) to hard-boiled eggs, pine nuts and raisins and even minced (ground) meat. This version from Formentera calls for something else: fish. It's simple and devilishly tasty when topped with a sweet onion-and-tomato *sofregit*. There's a hint of brandy here because, after all, it's a fisherman's dish.

✳ Clean the squid (calamari) or ask your fish supplier to do so: trim off the tentacles and set aside. Remove the hard, clear quill from inside the tubes and any innards that remain. Wash the tubes well and set aside whole. Finely chop the legs.

✳ Place the legs in a bowl with the chopped fish fillets, garlic and parsley. Generously season with salt and pepper and combine to make a stuffing paste. Stuff the reserved tubes with the mixture and secure the end of each with a cocktail stick or toothpick to close. Set aside.

✳ Heat the oil in a medium frying pan or sauté pan over medium heat. Add the onions and cook until soft, about 8 minutes. Add the tomatoes and sugar and cook until thick and pasty, about 10 minutes. Set the stuffed tubes in the pan. Pour over the brandy and cook for 1 minute. Drizzle in about 120 ml (4 fl oz/½ cup) water, reduce the heat, partly cover the pan and cook, turning from time to time, until the squid are tender (a cocktail stick will go in easily), 45 minutes–1 hour. Add a touch more water if needed.

✳ Remove the cocktail sticks. Arrange the squid on a serving plate and spoon the sauce over the top. Serve.

Grilled Squid Stuffed with Sobrassada

Preparation time: 5 minutes
Cooking time: 12 minutes
Serves: 4

4 whole medium squid (calamari) (about
    175–200 g/6–8 oz each) with tubes
    about 15–18 cm/6–8 inches in length
100 g/4 oz sobrassada (see page 208),
    casing removed
4 teaspoons honey
1 tablespoon olive oil

DF ✳ GF ✳ 5 ✳ 30

Squid (calamari) and sobrassada – the iconic paprika-rich cured pork sausage –
are often paired together in the Balearic kitchen. While many versions involve
a complicated process of stuffing, I like the simplicity of this one from Mallorca,
and certainly prepare it more frequently: sticking a piece of sobrassada into the
tube, adding some honey and cooking it hot and fast on a griddle. It takes all of
five minutes to prepare and little more than ten minutes to cook. It's simple but
extremely tasty. Some honey here is key to drawing together the flavours.

✳ Clean the squid (calamari) or ask your fish supplier to do so (see page 25). Trim
off the tentacles and set aside. Remove the hard, clear quill from inside the tubes
and any innards that remain. Wash the tubes well and set aside.

✳ Put the sobrassada into a bowl, drizzle over the honey and mix well. Divide into
quarters and push into each squid tube. Secure the end of each tube with a cocktail
stick or toothpick to close.

✳ Heat the oil in a heavy griddle or frying pan over high heat. Add the squid and
cook, turning just a few times, until golden and tender (a cocktail stick will easily
enter), 10–12 minutes.

✳ Transfer to plates and serve immediately.

Sobrassada

Nothing in the Balearic pantry is more unique to or distinctive of the islands' gastronomic identity than sobrassada. The raw, cured pork sausage is omnipresent. It is not just eaten as charcuterie, but is also frequently used as an ingredient, including with seafood and even in some sweet dishes.

Dating back to the Romans, popular since the Middle Ages and originally pale in colour, it found its current form with the arrival of peppers (for paprika) from the New World, which gave sobrassada its instantly recognizable deep red colour. Aromas and flavours of paprika are clear and very present in sobrassada. Paprika accounts for around 5 per cent of the total weight of the stuffing. That's a highly significant amount – around 50 g/2 oz of the ground spice (about ½ cup) for every 1 kg/2¼ lb of filling. Apart from some technological advances in industrial production (better machines for mincing the pork, perfect control of the temperature and humidity while curing and some changes in the casing), little has changed over the years.

Sobrassada is traditionally the most important product of the *matança* (pig butchering, see page 229). In our house in Menorca, the previous owners prepared hundreds of sobrassades every year and hung them from the beams of the attic.

With an irregular cylindrical shape, the smooth outside has an intensely darkish red colour. Cut open, the marbled red stuffing is well blended, somewhat sticky, softish and quite spreadable. It can be pulled apart with the fingers (unlike cured chorizo, which needs to be chopped with a knife). Made from a blend of minced pork meat and fat, it is seasoned with sweet paprika (and sometimes a bit of picante paprika, too), along with salt and other spices such as black pepper, rosemary, thyme and oregano. The raw mixture gets inserted into the casing and cured in drying rooms for up to six months, or even longer for the largest pieces. During the drying process, the sobrassada takes on its characteristic properties.

Among the various sizes and shapes, the most common is called *rissada*, club-shaped pieces that weigh around 800 g/1¾ lb and get cured for 6–12 weeks. Other common shapes include: *llonganissa*, long and thinnish, often cured in a bow, weighing just 200–300 g/7–10½ oz; *semirissada,* which weighs about 500–800 g/ 1 lb 2 oz–1¾ lb; *bufeta*, with a semi-spherical shape and weight of up to 8 kg/18 lb, but usually around 1.5 kg/3¼ lb; and the largest, *bisbe*, which uses the pig's stomach as a casing and can vary greatly in weight from 4 to 30 kg/9 to 66 lb.

While sobrassada is eaten on bread – preferably with some honey (page 30) – it is a surprisingly frequent ingredient in the kitchen. Across the Balearics, sobrassada fills squid (page 207) and brioche-like buns (page 46), gives a boost to meatballs (page 249) and tomato sauce for pasta (page 150) and transforms a simple egg omelette into something ravishing (with fresh mint, page 120). It even gets used in sweet pastries, namely ensaïmades.

A bit of sobrassada can give anything some flavour. Or rather, it can give it *more* flavour.

Mayonnaise

While the French might have popularized mayonnaise, it originated in Menorca. *Mahonesa* (or *maionesa*) is named for Menorca's capital Mahón (or Maó).

The story goes something like this: during the eighteenth-century occupation of the island by the British, there was a seven-year interlude of French rule. In 1756, the Duke of Richelieu – Louis François Armand de Vignerot du Plessis – expelled the British from the port of Mahón and the rest of the island. (The British would get control back from a treaty in 1763.) One evening, the duke dined out and the host served meat accompanied by a typical emulsion of olive oil and egg yolk. The duke was impressed, and when he returned to France, he carried home the recipe for what he christened *mahonnaise* after the city of Mahón. Over time, the spelling evolved to mayonnaise (in both French and English).

As culinary historians point out, there is no mention of this emulsion in French cookery books before the Menorca venture. Except in Provence, cooking with olive oil wasn't that common in France at the time.

It's a very different tale in Menorca, where it frequently appears in the island's earliest cookery book, *Art de la cuina* (*Art of Cooking*) by the Menorcan friar Fra Francesc Roger (1706–1764/67). And it is not an obscure reference. The olive oil-and-egg emulsion wasn't named mayonnaise yet, and Fra Roger called it the 'good' (*bo*) version of garlic-and-olive oil allioli. Mayonnaise was the transformation of the bolder and more rustic allioli into something subtler and more refined, something richer, and for the higher classes, using what was good in the egg: the yolk.

The recipes that Fra Roger included in his work were indeed aimed at a higher class: *llagosta al forn amb allioli bo* (baked lobster with good allioli), *pilotes de llagosta amb formatge, espícies i allioli bo* (lobster balls with cheese, spices and good allioli), *aranyes amb salsa de tomàtigues, allioli bo i alls escalivats* (rockfish with tomato sauce, good allioli and roasted garlic) and so on. And while he gives instructions on preparing these exquisite dishes, nowhere in his ample tome does Fra Roger explain how to make the popular emulsion that accompanies many of them. It was just too obvious, simple and well-known to bother explaining.

The traditional way to make mayonnaise is in a mortar, mashing the yolk and then adding oil drop by drop while moving the wooden pestle in the same direction without stopping until the emulsion is fully formed. Nowadays, that laborious process has been simplified and greatly sped up with the use of an immersion hand blender. Using the whole egg, a bit more oil and a dash of vinegar to help with the emulsion, it takes just 30 seconds. (See page 340 for directions on preparing both versions.)

Served with locally-harvested mussels (page 218), added to steamed vegetables and dolloped on fish, mayonnaise remains nearly as widespread in Menorca today as it was in the days of Fra Roger. Certainly, there is no need for something fancy like the friar's baked lobster to enjoy it. It is highly delightful simply slathered on a slice of bread.

Slow-cooked Squid with Sobrassada & Honey

Preparation time: 10 minutes
Cooking time: 1 hour
Serves: 3–4

3 tablespoons olive oil
500 g/1 lb 2 oz cleaned medium squid
 (calamari) (see page 25), cut into
 1-cm/½-inch-thick pieces
1 yellow onion, halved and thinly sliced
75 g/2⅔ oz sobrassada (see page 208),
 casing removed
1 tablespoon honey
2 tablespoons pine nuts, dry-toasted
 (see page 25)

DF ✳ GF ✳ 1 POT

Grilled Squid Stuffed with Sobrassada (page 207) is the quick version of a Mallorcan classic combination of flavours. This is its slow-cooked cousin: the squid (calamari) gets patiently cooked with onions, sobrassada and honey until exceedingly tender. It's bold and makes a great tapa or appetizer. Serve with bread. A treat.

✳ Heat the oil in a shallow, flameproof casserole pan (see page 25), Dutch oven or heavy sauté pan over medium heat. Add the squid (calamari) and onion and cook, stirring frequently, until the liquid released by the squid has evaporated, about 15 minutes. Add the sobrassada and honey, mostly cover the pan and cook over very low heat until the squid is very tender, about 40 minutes. Stir in a few tablespoons of water from time to time to keep it from scorching.

✳ Scatter with the toasted pine nuts and serve at the table from the casserole.

Small Squid Stewed with Onions & White Wine

Preparation time: 10 minutes
Cooking time: 35 minutes
Serves: 3–4

4 tablespoons olive oil
3 medium yellow onions (about 600 g/
    1 lb 5 oz total), thinly sliced
6–8 cloves of garlic, skins on, lightly
    crushed under the palm
500 g/1 lb 2 oz cleaned small squid
    (calamari) (see page 25), cut
    crosswise into 2 or 3 pieces, about
    4 cm/1½ inches in length
2 small bay leaves
120 ml/4 fl oz (½ cup) white wine

DF ✳ GF ✳ 1 POT

One of the tastier ways to prepare squid (calamari) is to slowly cook them with white wine and an abundance of onions. This recipe works well with small whole *calamarsets* (their tubes measure about 7.5 cm/3 inches in length before cooking). If using larger ones, cut the tubes crosswise into generous pieces. The white wine offers a fresh, slightly acidic note that nicely complements the squid. I like to add a couple of sprigs of fresh thyme from my garden.

✳ Heat the oil in a large, shallow, flameproof casserole pan (see page 25), Dutch oven or heavy sauté pan over medium–high heat. Add the onions and garlic and cook until the onions are soft, about 10 minutes. Add the squid (calamari) and bay leaves and cook, stirring frequently, until the squid turns white, about 3 minutes. Stir in the wine. Reduce the heat to low and cook, uncovered, until the squid and onions are tender, about 20 minutes.

✳ Serve in the casserole at the table.

Cuttlefish Pica-Pica

Preparation time: 15 minutes
Cooking time: 1 hour
Serves: 4

4 tablespoons olive oil
1 kg/2¼ lb cuttlefish or squid (calamari),
    cleaned (see page 25) and cut into
    2-cm/¾-inch pieces or strips
2 cloves of garlic, minced
2 yellow onions, finely chopped
120 ml/4 fl oz (½ cup) dry white wine
6 tomatoes, halved and grated
    (see page 25)
1 teaspoon sweet paprika
Pinch of sugar
1 small dried chilli (chile) or 1 dried
    cayenne pepper
Salt and pepper

DF ✳ GF ✳ 1 POT

This beloved Mallorcan bar tapa is usually made using cuttlefish rather than squid (calamari), but it is excellent with the latter as well. If using squid, the cooking time is a tad shorter. Many bars add a dried chilli (chile), which offers a pleasing heat in contrast to the sweetness of the dish.

✳ Heat the oil in a large, shallow, flameproof casserole pan (see page 25), Dutch oven or heavy sauté pan over medium heat. Add the cuttlefish and cook until it has released its moisture and takes on some colour, about 12 minutes.

✳ Stir in the garlic and then add the onions. Cook, stirring frequently, until the onions begin to turn translucent, about 12 minutes. Stir in the wine and let cook for 2 minutes. Add the tomatoes, paprika, sugar and chilli (chile), and season with salt and pepper. Cook until the cuttlefish is tender and the sauce sweet and pasty, about 30 minutes.

✳ Add a touch of water at the end if it looks like it will dry out. Serve.

Octopus 'Frit' with Fried Potatoes, Onions & Red Peppers

Preparation time: 20 minutes
Cooking time: 1 hour
Serves: 4–6

500 g/1 lb 2 oz fresh octopus, cleaned (see page 25)
6 tablespoons mild olive oil
3 medium white potatoes (about 600 g/1 lb 5 oz total), peeled, halved lengthwise and sliced crosswise
1 yellow onion, finely chopped
½ large red bell pepper, stemmed, seeded and diced
1 long sweet green pepper, stemmed, seeded and diced
6 cloves of garlic, skins on, lightly crushed under the palm
1 teaspoon sweet paprika
Chopped parsley, to garnish, optional
Salt and pepper

DF ✳ GF

The classic fisherman's breakfast on Formentera (and Ibiza) is a plate of *frit de pop*, octopus with fried potatoes, onions and peppers, served with plenty of bread and a hearty glass of wine, and followed with a strong coffee. It remains beloved and is eaten any time of day. In Spain, many fish suppliers now sell high-quality pre-cooked legs of octopus, making this dish a much quicker meal to prepare.

✳ Fill a large pot with water, bring to a rolling boil and add a generous pinch of salt. Submerge the octopus in the water, cover the pot and cook at a rolling boil over high heat until tender, about 20 minutes. It's done when a cocktail stick, toothpick or tip of a knife pricked quite deeply into the upper part of a leg enters with little resistance. Transfer to a platter and let cool. Cut into bite-size pieces and set aside.

✳ Heat the oil in a large, flameproof casserole pan (see page 25) or Dutch oven over high heat. Add the potatoes and fry, turning as needed, until tender, 12–15 minutes. Transfer with a slotted spoon to a plate.

✳ In the same pan, fry the onion until becoming soft, 6–8 minutes. Add the peppers and garlic, and cook until the peppers are tender, 6–8 minutes.

✳ Add the reserved octopus and potatoes to the casserole pan, add the paprika, season with salt and pepper and cook for 5 minutes over low heat to combine the flavours. Serve with parsley, if using.

Steamed Mussels
with Homemade Mayonnaise

Preparation time: 15 minutes
Cooking time: 5 minutes
Serves: 3–4

freshly made Homemade Mayonnaise
    (page 340)
2 bay leaves
2 lemon slices
1 kg/2¼ lb small to medium mussels,
    cleaned

DF ✳ GF ✳ 5 ✳ 30

Sometimes the best dishes are the simplest ones. And while this one is indeed simple, it's also pure Maó (Mahón): small mussels cultivated on the floating *muscleres* in the city's clear and deep port (one of the longest natural harbours in the world), served with a just-made bowl of the island's own iconic *salsa* named for the city, mayonnaise. (See page 209 for more on the history of mayonnaise.) It's about the flavours of the bivalves themselves, which pair so nicely with homemade mayonnaise.

✳ When you have prepared the mayonnaise, spoon into a small serving bowl, cover and refrigerate until ready to serve.

✳ In a large pot, combine the bay leaves, lemon slices and 120 ml (4 fl oz/½ cup) water. Add the mussels, cover the pot and bring to a boil. Steam until the mussels have opened, shaking the pot from time to time, 3–5 minutes. Transfer with a slotted spoon to a large serving bowl, discarding any that did not open.

✳ Serve immediately with the mayonnaise.

CHAPTER 8

PORK, LAMB & BEEF

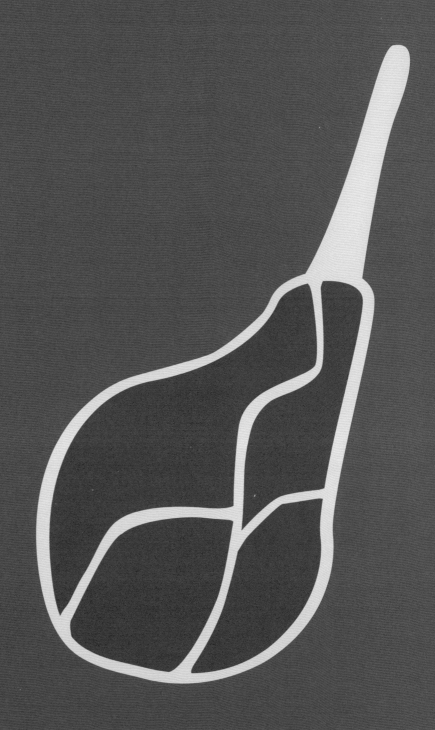

Pork Loin with Cabbage

Preparation time: 15 minutes
Cooking time: 1 hour
Serves: 4

500 g/1 lb 2 oz boneless pork loin
    (preferably blade end), cut crosswise
    into 1-cm/½-inch-thick fillets
4 tablespoons olive oil
1 yellow onion, finely chopped
4 cloves of garlic, minced
3 tomatoes, halved and grated
    (see page 25)
100 ml/3½ fl oz (⅓ cup) dry white wine
1 tablespoon sweet paprika
1 carrot, cut crosswise into thin circles
1 bay leaf
1 sprig thyme
1 small head green cabbage
    (about 1 kg/2¼ lb), trimmed,
    halved and cored, tough mid-rib
    veins removed, cut into strips
Salt and pepper

DF ✳ GF ✳ 1 POT

Pork and cabbage are a popular combination in the Balearic kitchen. In Mallorca, *llom amb col* can be an elaborate preparation of loin rolled into cabbage leaves and braised. But there are simpler versions found as well, like this Menorcan one. Use the blade end of the loin (known as *dues colores*, 'two colours'), which has a near-s-shaped division of leaner white meat and darker, fattier meat, which remains moister and more tender as it cooks.

✳ Season the slices of pork with salt and pepper.

✳ Heat the oil in a large, shallow, flameproof casserole pan (see page 25), Dutch oven or heavy sauté pan over medium–high heat. Add the pork and sear on both sides until golden brown, 30 seconds–1 minute per side. Transfer to a plate.

✳ In the same pan, fry the onion over medium heat until it begins to soften, about 8 minutes. Stir in the garlic and then add the tomatoes and cook until darker and rich, about 10 minutes. Stir in the wine and let the alcohol burn off for 1 minute. Stir in the paprika, add the carrot, bay leaf and thyme, and season with salt.

✳ Progressively add the cabbage, as the pan allows, adding more as it begins to wilt down. Add 120 ml (4 fl oz/½ cup) water, cover the pan and cook until the cabbage is tender, about 30 minutes in total, adding another 120 ml (4 fl oz/½ cup) water or more as needed during cooking to keep it moist.

✳ Return the reserved pork to the pan and cook, uncovered, turning from time to time in the cabbage, until the pork is done and the flavours combined, 5–10 minutes. Serve immediately.

Roasted Pork Loin with Onions & Pomegranate Syrup

Preparation time: 15 minutes
Cooking time: 1 hour 15 minutes
Serves: 4

1–1.25 kg/2¼–2½ lb boneless pork loin
   (preferably blade-end), in 1 piece
2 tablespoons olive oil
4 medium yellow onions (about 800 g/
   1¾ lb total), thinly sliced
4 cloves of garlic, skins on, lightly
   crushed under the palm
2 sprigs thyme, optional
60 ml/2 fl oz (¼ cup) white wine
Pomegranate Syrup (page 344)
Salt and pepper

DF ✳ GF

While roasting a whole pork loin with plenty of onions is enough for a delicious meal, serving the slices with some sweet and fruity (but slightly tangy pomegranate syrup to drizzle over the top turns it into something spectacular. Ask your butcher to give you the blade end of the loin, which will remain tender during cooking.

✳ If desired, tie, or have your butcher tie, the loin with cotton string so that it retains its shape. Season with salt and pepper.

✳ Preheat the oven to 200°C/400°F/Gas Mark 6. Set out a roasting pan or large baking dish.

✳ Heat the oil in a large frying pan or sauté pan over high heat. Add the loin and generously brown on all sides, turning as needed, for 5–7 minutes. Transfer to the roasting pan.

✳ In the same frying pan, fry the onions until they lose their rawness and begin to brown on the edges, about 8 minutes. Stir in the garlic and cook for 30 seconds. Spoon everything over the loin, including all the oil from the pan. Add the thyme (if using) and drizzle over the wine.

✳ Roast, uncovered, in the hot oven for 50–60 minutes, depending on the thickness of the loin, until the pork is still pink in the middle and an instant-read thermometer probed to the centre of the loin reads at least 63°C/145°F.

✳ Transfer the loin to a chopping (cutting) board and let rest for 3 minutes. Remove the string if it has been tied. Slice and arrange on a serving platter, drizzle over some pomegranate syrup and scatter the onions from the pan around the sides. Serve with extra syrup on the side to add as desired.

Pork Loin with Wild Mushrooms

Preparation time: 15 minutes
Cooking time: 25 minutes
Serves: 4–5

700 g/1½ lb thinly sliced boneless
    pork loin
3 tablespoons olive oil
1 yellow onion, thinly sliced
6 cloves of garlic, skins on, lightly
    crushed under the palm
700 g/1½ lb mushrooms, preferably
    wild, cleaned (page 25) and larger
    ones halved or quartered
60 ml/2 fl oz (¼ cup) white wine
    or brandy
1 heaped tablespoon minced flat-leaf
    parsley
Salt and pepper

DF ✳ GF

The tradition of foraging for wild mushrooms is deeply ingrained in Balearic culture. So is the love of eating the rewards of that search. The mushrooms tend to be prepared in relatively straightforward manners that highlight, or at least don't disguise, the luscious, earthy flavours of the fungi themselves. They combine well with other ingredients, including slices of pork loin. Sear the slices very quickly in the pan first to flavour the oil, but also to give them a lovely golden colour. This recipe is the type of unfussy preparation found in homes but also in bar-restaurants inside the islands' covered food markets.

✳ Generously season the pork with salt and pepper.

✳ Heat the oil in a large frying pan or sauté pan over high heat. Working in batches, sear the slices of pork for 15–30 seconds on each side and transfer to a platter. Add the onion and garlic to the same pan and cook until the onion begins to soften, 3–5 minutes. Add the mushrooms, reduce the heat to medium, and cook until they start to become tender, about 5 minutes. Pour over the wine or brandy, stir in the parsley and cook for 5 minutes, stirring frequently. Return the meat to the pan, turning over in the sauce to coat. Reduce the heat to low and cook until the flavours are combined and the pork cooked through, about 5 minutes.

✳ Transfer to a large serving platter and serve immediately.

Wild Mushrooms

The parking lot of Cala Pilar is crowded on this autumn weekend morning. It's a thirty-minute walk through a pine and oak forest to a bluff on the northern coast, and then down a trail to one of the most stunning beaches in Menorca: a wide curve of turquoise water bordered by golden sand and backed on one end by a steep red stone cliff.

But there are few signs of people on the trail, and the beach remains virtually empty. People have not come for the beach, although the day is sunny and the sea remains (just!) pleasant enough for a quick swim. They've come for the wild mushrooms.

There is a strong tradition of foraging in the Balearic Islands – wild asparagus, herbs, blackberries, snails ('Mallorcan truffles'), figs from roadside trees. But more than anything else, it is foraging for mushrooms that has remained a deeply popular tradition.

In Menorca alone, some 900 varieties of fungi have been identified. Around 150 of those are edible – which does not always mean tasty and non-toxic.

One variety is so beloved and sought-after in Menorca that it gives its name to the generic phrase to look for mushrooms, *anar a cercar esclata-sangs*. In Catalan, the name *esclata-sangs* – *Lactarius sanguifluus* – translates to 'bursts of blood' because of the distinctive reddish liquid that oozes from the fungi when it is cut. Commonly known as bloody or bleeding milk caps in English and *rovellons* in Spanish, it is more rusty-red than the orange of *Lactarius deliciosus*, saffron milk caps.

Esclata-sangs begin to emerge from the ground after the late-summer rains at the end of September and early October, and generally last through December. The main season begins around All Saints' Day (1 November) and peaks in November.

While *esclata-sangs* reign supreme for Menorcans, two other varieties of fungi come closely behind in terms of prized finds for the basket (and the frying pan): *cames-seques* (*Cantharellus cibarius*, or golden chanterelles) and a type of *gírgoles* (oyster mushrooms). *Cama-seques* are among the first species found, right after the late-summer rains, hidden under the oak leaves. *Gírgoles* are also an autumn mushroom, but depending on the weather, they can be found in clearings and along hedges into spring.

Few secrets are kept on how to prepare wild mushrooms. Ask anyone with a basket of mushrooms in the parking lot at the end of the day, and you'll receive a plethora of strongly opiniated advice. But ask where they found them, and most people fall silent. Good luck getting any clues to favourite spots from strangers, or even friends. If someone does offer ideas on where to look, assume it's wrong, and it was given as a way to throw off any competition for the glorious fungi that grows up through the loam.

Every Pig Has Its Saint Martin's Day

It is impossible to overestimate the importance of the annual *matança* that took place across the Balearics. It is so deeply embedded in popular culture – and on the plate.

La matança del porc is the butchering of a pig and preparing of sobrassada and other charcuterie, and the festive activities that surround it. (The term is often used in plural, *ses matances*.) This took place when the weather finally turned cold in late autumn. The first pigs were butchered and their meat ground, seasoned and stuffed into casings to be hung following long-standing traditions. It wasn't done alone but with the help of friends and family. Hard work but festive, it took a full day, sometimes two. But there would be sobrassada and other charcuterie to enjoy for the year ahead. A pig might yield hundreds of sobrassades and other types of cured sausages.

This did not only take place on farmsteads. In the back garden of our Menorca house, in the centre of the village, the family of the previous owners would gather with friends and family to butcher a pig that had been raised on the outskirts of town. They prepared sobrassada and other cured charcuterie from the animal, and hung them to cure from high wood beams in the attic.

Modern government regulations have left the act of butchering to professionals, and very few make their own sobrassada any longer. But even if the *matança* no longer happens so widely across the islands, it remains a cultural and culinary touchstone. Various traditional dishes were prepared around the occasion, converting the *matança* into something of a gastronomic festival. Numerous dishes today continue to reference it in their names. Two popular examples from Mallorca are *frit de matances* (page 232) and *sopa de matances*.

A cada porc li arriba el seu Sant Martí, goes the popular refrain: 'Every pig has its St Martin's Day.' That day – 11 November– marks the beginning of the *matances*. The saying means everyone will eventually have to pay the price or compensate for their transgressions, or that every sinner will have his penance. While pigs might not sin, they certainly reach their inevitable end in the Balearics, and eventually end up on tables across the islands.

Roast Suckling Pig Quarter

Preparation time: 20 minutes,
    plus marinating time
Cooking time: 2 hours
Serves: 4

Juice of 1 lemon
2 tablespoons olive oil
2 tablespoons brandy or wine
1 suckling pig quarter (about 1.5 kg/3¼ lb)
2 tablespoons lard or butter
2 sprigs rosemary
2 sprigs thyme
2 sprigs marjoram, optional
1 bay leaf
Salt and pepper

DF ✳ GF

Porcella (suckling pig) is very popular on Mallorcan tables around Christmas (and in many rustic-style restaurants nearly all year). It is a highly festive dish. A typical whole *porcella* weighs about 6 kg/13 lb. Around Christmas, New Year's and Kings' Day (6 January), butchers sell quarters (about 1.5 kg/3¼ lb) that feed four (and will fit easily into the oven). It is a simple but remarkable dish. Cooking time is about two hours. While it is excellent with some fried potatoes, an even tastier option is to scatter 500 g/1 lb 2 oz of small new potatoes around the base of the pork about halfway through the cooking time. They take about an hour or so.

✳ The night before, prepare the marinade. Whisk together the lemon juice, oil and brandy or wine, and season generously with salt and pepper. In a baking dish, brush the pork with the marinade and lay skin-side down. Pour the remaining marinade over the top. Cover and refrigerate overnight.

✳ Remove the pork from the refrigerator about an hour before roasting to let it return to room temperature.

✳ Preheat the oven to 220°C/425°F/Gas Mark 7.

✳ Remove the pork from the marinade (reserve the marinade) and set it in a baking dish so that the skin-side is facing up. Rub with the lard. Pour over the reserved marinade, along with 120 ml (4 fl oz/½ cup) water. Add the herbs. Bake in the hot oven for 20 minutes. The skin should be beginning to brown.

✳ Turn the piece skin-side down, reduce the oven temperature to 180°C/350°F/Gas Mark 4, and bake for 1 hour, basting from time to time.

✳ Turn the pork skin-side up. Bake until the meat is very tender and the skin is crispy and has a lovely dark golden-brown colour, about 30 minutes. Add more water to the dish if it threatens to dry out during roasting.

✳ If needed at the end, change the oven to grill (broil) mode and move the baking dish up to a higher rack to achieve the golden crispiness. Serve with your chosen potatoes.

Butchering-day 'Frit'

Preparation time: 20 minutes
Cooking time: 30 minutes
Serves: 4

500 g/1 lb 2 oz thick slices of fresh pork belly, trimmed and cut into generous bite-size pieces

500 g/1 lb 2 oz slices of boneless pork loin (preferably blade end), cut into generous bite-size pieces

200 g/7 oz slices of pork or beef liver, cut into generous bite-size pieces, optional

250 ml/8 fl oz (1 cup) mild olive oil, for frying

3 medium white potatoes (about 600 g/1 lb 5 oz total), peeled and cut crosswise into 5-mm/¼-inch-thick circles

1 red bell pepper, stemmed, seeded and cut into 2.5-cm/1-inch pieces

8 cloves of garlic, skins on, lightly crushed under the palm

4 small bay leaves

Salt and pepper

DF ✳ GF

Mallorca is the land of traditional *frits*, literally 'fried' dishes. *Frit mallorquí* is made with lamb while this one calls for pork. Eaten during the time of the *matança* (winter butchering of a pig, see page 229), and made using pieces of loin, fresh pork belly, sometimes ribs and occasionally liver, it remains a favourite. As with the other *frits*, the series of ingredients are fried separately, placed into a large terracotta casserole dish and then mixed and reheated together before serving. The time of the *matança* overlaps with that of wild mushrooms, which make a delicious and not uncommon addition to this *frit*.

✳ Generously season the pork belly, loin and liver (if using) with salt and pepper. Set each aside separately. Have a large casserole pan (see page 25) or serving bowl ready.

✳ Heat the oil in a large frying pan or sauté pan over medium–high heat. Add the potatoes and fry until just tender, 8–10 minutes. Remove from the pan with a slotted spoon, holding for a moment above the pan for the oil to drain, then transfer to the casserole or bowl.

✳ In the same pan, fry the pepper until tender, 4–5 minutes, then transfer to the casserole with the slotted spoon. Reduce the heat to medium–high. Add the garlic and bay leaves to the pan and fry, stirring almost continually, until aromatic, about 1 minute. Do not let them scorch. Transfer with the slotted spoon to the casserole. Add the pork belly to the pan and fry until golden, about 4 minutes, then transfer to the casserole. Add the loin to the pan and fry until just cooked through, 3–4 minutes, then transfer to the casserole. Reduce the heat to medium, add the liver to the pan (if using) and fry, using a splatter guard, until cooked through, 2–3 minutes, then transfer to the casserole.

✳ Using large spoons, gently toss the ingredients in the casserole to blend. If the casserole is flameproof, do this over low heat to also warm it slightly. Serve immediately.

Pork Tongue with Capers

Preparation time: 30 minutes
Cooking time: 1 hour 45 minutes
Serves: 4–6

3 pork tongues (1 kg/2¼ lb total)
2 cloves of garlic, skins on
1 bay leaf
8 black peppercorns
35 g/1¼ oz (¼ cup) drained
    and rinsed capers
Salt and pepper

FOR THE SAUCE
3 tablespoons olive oil
1 yellow onion, finely chopped
2 cloves of garlic, minced
1 carrot, cut crosswise into thin circles
4 medium tomatoes, halved and grated
    (see page 25)
60 ml/2 fl oz (¼ cup) dry white wine
¼ teaspoon sweet paprika

DF ✳ GF

Capers (*tàperes*) are common in the Balearic pantry. The most famous dish featuring them is stewed tongue. On Menorca, cooks generally use smallish beef tongues (these weigh about 1 kg/2¼ lb each), but on Mallorca, smaller pork tongues (about 250 g/9 oz or a bit larger each) are often used. When stewed, pork tongue becomes exceedingly tender. I now always make this dish using pork tongue, as its milder flavour allows the herbs and capers to show off more. You can use beef tongue for this recipe, just allow more time for it to initially boil. The final sauce is often quite loose, but there are some cooks who like to stir in a touch of flour at the end with the capers to thicken it up a touch. Capers come stored in vinegar. Be sure to drain and rinse before adding.

✳ Rinse the tongues well and trim the root end. Put in a large pot with the whole cloves of garlic, bay leaf and peppercorns. Cover with abundant water and bring to a boil. Reduce the heat, cover the pot and gently boil until the tines of a fork can pierce the tongues easily, about 1½ hours. Transfer with a slotted spoon to a plate to cool. Reserve about 250 ml (8 fl oz/1 cup) of the liquid.

✳ As the tongues cook, begin making the sauce: Heat the oil in a shallow, flameproof casserole pan (see page 25), Dutch oven or heavy sauté pan over medium heat. Add the onion and cook until soft, about 8 minutes. Add the minced garlic and then the carrot and tomatoes, and cook until pulpy, about 15 minutes, adding a few tablespoons of water during cooking to keep it moist. Now add 120 ml (4 fl oz/½ cup) water and gently cook until the carrots are tender, about 5–10 minutes. Add the wine and cook for 1 minute to burn off the alcohol before stirring in the paprika.

✳ Scrape the skin off the tongues with a blunt knife and discard. Trim away the fat, gristle and any remaining tough sections at the root end. Transfer the tongue to a chopping (cutting) board and cut crosswise into thinnish slices about 7.5 mm/⅓ inch thick. Season with salt and pepper.

✳ Lay the sliced tongue in the sauce and turn over to coat. Add the capers and moisten with the 250 ml (8 fl oz/1 cup) of reserved liquid, then cover the pan and gently cook for 10 minutes. Serve.

Liver in Garlicky Sauce

Preparation time: 20 minutes
Cooking time: 40 minutes
Serves: 4

500 g/1 lb 2 oz pork or beef liver
3 cloves of garlic, minced
1 heaped tablespoon flat-leaf parsley
60 ml/2 fl oz (¼ cup) brandy or cognac
3 tablespoons olive oil
1 yellow onion, thinly sliced
3 ripe tomatoes, halved and grated
    (see page 25)
1 small whole dried or fresh chilli (chile),
    optional
2 tablespoons pine nuts, dry-toasted
    (see page 25)
Salt and pepper

DF ✳ GF

This dish is sometimes called *fetge amb salsa* (liver with sauce), and at other times something slightly more specific, *fetge amb allet*, which refers to the garlic (*all*) included. The sauce can be passed through a food mill to make it smoother and more refined, or left chunky. It's popular during the *matança*, the winter butchering of a pig (see page 229). Pork liver is softer than its beef counterpart and doesn't get as firm and dry when cooked, but it can be more difficult to find. If using beef liver, note that it can quickly overcook.

✳ Cut the liver at an angle into strips about 1 cm/½ inch thick, 2.5 cm/1 inch wide and 6 cm/2½ inches in length. Season with salt and pepper.

✳ In a mortar, pound the garlic and parsley to a paste with some drops of the brandy and set aside.

✳ Heat the oil in a frying pan or sauté pan over medium–high heat. Working in 2 batches, add the liver and cook for about 30 seconds per side, turning with tongs. Transfer the liver to a plate using the tongs.

✳ In the same pan, fry the onion until soft, about 8 minutes. Spoon in the garlic-parsley paste and cook until aromatic, 1–2 minutes. Pour over the remaining brandy and cook for 2 minutes. Add the tomatoes and cook until thicker and pulpy, 10–12 minutes. Stir in 250 ml (8 fl oz/1 cup) water, bring to a simmer and cook for 5 minutes. It should be saucy. If desired, let cool for a moment and pass it through a food mill, then return it to the pan. Add the chilli (chile) (if using).

✳ Return the liver to the sauce in the pan, turn to coat, cover with a lid and cook over low heat until the liver is cooked through, about 5 minutes. Transfer to a large serving platter, scatter over the pine nuts and serve immediately.

Potato & Tomato Casserole with Lamb Shoulder

Preparation time: 15 minutes
Cooking time: 1 hour 20 minutes
Serves: 2

4 medium white potatoes (about
    800 g/1¾ lb total), peeled and cut
    crosswise into 5-mm/¼-inch slices
1 yellow onion, halved and cut crosswise
    into 5-mm/¼-inch slices
5 tablespoons olive oil
1 lamb shoulder with shank (about
    800 g/1¾ lb), cut into 2 portions
3 large ripe but firm tomatoes, cored
    and cut crosswise into 2-cm/¾-inch
    slices
3 cloves of garlic, minced
2 heaped tablespoons finely chopped
    flat-leaf parsley
3 tablespoons fine dry breadcrumbs
Salt and pepper

DF ✳ 1 POT

One popular way to prepare lamb on Menorca is baking it between a layer of sliced potatoes and onions and a layer of tomatoes topped with breadcrumbs. This recipe calls for a lamb shoulder, but lamb chops are also popular. Have your butcher cut the lamb shoulder into two portions for easier serving, as this recipe generously serves two people. See page 88 for the basic version that's just potatoes and tomatoes, with nothing between them.

✳ Preheat the oven to 180°C/350°F/Gas Mark 4.

✳ In a large, deep baking dish, add the potatoes and onion in layers. Season with salt and pepper, drizzle with 2 tablespoons of the oil and moisten with about 60 ml (2 fl oz/¼ cup) water. Put the lamb on top. Cover with the tomato slices. Spread the garlic and parsley atop the tomatoes and then sprinkle over the breadcrumbs. Drizzle the remaining 3 tablespoons of oil over the top.

✳ Bake in the oven, uncovered, until a knife goes easily into the potatoes and the lamb is tender, about 1 hour 20 minutes. Serve.

Country-style Sauté of Meats, Sausages & Vegetables

Preparation time: 20 minutes
Cooking time: 1 hour 40 minutes
Serves: 4–5

700 g/1½ lb bone-in chicken pieces,
    skin removed
250 g/9 oz bone-in lamb pieces
250 g/9 oz pork ribs
1 bay leaf
4 tablespoons olive oil
4 medium white potatoes (about
    800 g/1¾ lb total), peeled and
    quartered lengthwise, or 12 whole
    small white potatoes
1 bulb of garlic
2 tablespoons minced flat-leaf parsley
¼ teaspoon ground cinnamon
Pinch of saffron threads, crumbled
2 small blood sausages, preferably
    botifarró (see page 23)
100 g/3½ oz sobrassada (see page 208),
    with casing, in a single piece
Salt and pepper

DF ✳ GF

One of Ibiza's most iconic non-seafood dishes, *sofrit pagès*, uniquely includes chicken, lamb and pork, plus some cured pork sausage: black *botifarró*, similar to black pudding (blood sausage), which has fennel notes, and paprika-rich sobrassada. It's a heady dish, once traditional for Christmas, Easter and other important festive occasions but now eaten throughout the winter. It is also typical on Formentera, some say from the 1950s when it was brought by people coming from Ibiza to work in Formentera's saltworks. Note that it is served 'dry'. A stock (broth) is made in the beginning, added to the pan of meats and potatoes and cooked down until it evaporates.

✳ In a soup pot or large saucepan, combine the chicken, lamb, pork ribs and bay leaf, cover with 1 litre (34 fl oz/4¼ cups) water and bring to a boil. Skim off any foam. Reduce the heat to low, cover the pot and simmer until tender but not falling apart, 45–60 minutes, removing the chicken when it's done, after 30–45 minutes. Strain the meats well, reserving the stock (broth).

✳ Heat the oil in a large, shallow, flameproof casserole pan (see page 25), Dutch oven, sauté pan or frying pan over medium heat. Add the strained meat and brown for about 5 minutes. Add the potatoes and cook for 5 minutes, turning from time to time. Add the bulb of garlic, parsley and 500 ml (18 fl oz/2 cups) of the reserved stock. Gently cook for 15 minutes.

✳ Stir in the cinnamon and saffron, season with salt and pepper and set the black sausages and sobrassada in the pan. Cook until the potatoes are tender and the liquid has evaporated, about 15 minutes. Add more of the reserved liquid while cooking, if needed, to keep it from drying out. Serve in the casserole pan at the table.

Lamb Chops with Red Peppers & Potatoes

Preparation time: 10 minutes
Cooking time: 20 minutes
Serves: 2–3

175 ml/6 fl oz (¾ cup) neutral oil, for frying
3 medium white potatoes (about 600 g/1 lb 5 oz total), thinly sliced crosswise
600 g/1 lb 5 oz lamb rib and loin chops
4 tablespoons olive oil
1 small red bell pepper, stemmed, seeded and cut into 2.5-cm/1-inch pieces
6 cloves of garlic, skins on, lightly crushed under the palm
1 small bay leaf
Salt and pepper

DF ✳ GF ✳ 30

A dish that is a guaranteed success, this Formentera recipe bursts with rustic flavours. It serves two to three people. Increase amounts to serve more – but be careful not to overcrowd the pan. Use both rib and loin chops.

✳ Heat the oil for frying in a frying pan over high heat. Add the potatoes and fry, turning as needed, until just tender, about 8 minutes. Transfer with a slotted spoon to a colander to drain excess oil.

✳ Cut each of the lamb chops into 2 or 3 pieces. Generously season with salt and pepper.

✳ Heat the olive oil in a large frying pan or sauté pan over high heat. Add the lamb and brown on each side, about 2 minutes total. Add the red pepper, garlic and bay leaf, and cook, stirring and turning the pieces as needed, until the lamb is done and the pepper is becoming tender, about 4 minutes. Add the reserved fried potatoes and cook until they are hot, about 2 minutes, turning gently to combine flavours but avoid breaking the potato slices. Serve immediately.

Fried Lamb Rib Chops with Garlic

Preparation time: 10 minutes
Cooking time: 25 minutes
Serves: 2

10 lamb rib chops (about 400 g/14 oz
    total)
350 ml/12 fl oz (1½ cups) mild olive oil
    or a neutral oil, for frying
10 cloves of garlic in the skin
3 bay leaves
2 dried red chillies (chiles)
3 medium white potatoes (about
    600 g/1 lb 5 oz total), cut into 1-cm/
    ½-inch-thick frites
Salt and pepper
Coarse salt, to serve

DF ✳ GF

This Mallorcan classic comes from the agricultural flatlands of Es Pla around the towns of Sineu and Petra. It is preferable to use rib chops that are on the smallish size. Figure around five chops per person. Garlic is key to the recipe – use one whole clove (with its skin) per chop. To make this for four people, prepare in two batches rather than crowding the pan. We always serve with a big green salad to make a full meal.

✳ Season the lamb with salt and pepper. Line a plate with paper towels. Have a platter ready and a colander for draining the potatoes.

✳ Heat the oil in a large frying pan over medium–high heat. Add the lamb, garlic, bay leaves and chillies (chiles), and cook until the meat changes colour and the garlic is aromatic, about 3 minutes. Transfer the lamb, garlic, bay leaves and chillies to the platter with tongs or a slotted spoon.

✳ In the same pan, fry the potatoes until tender, about 15 minutes. Transfer with a slotted spoon to the colander to drain excess oil.

✳ Return the lamb, garlic, bay leaves and chillies to the pan and fry until the lamb is cooked through, about 4 minutes. Transfer with tongs to the paper towels to wick off some of the excess oil.

✳ Divide the potatoes among 2 plates. Top with the lamb, cloves of garlic, bay leaves and chillies. Sprinkle with coarse salt and serve immediately.

Grilled Goat Chops
with Grilled Tomatoes

Preparation time: 5 minutes,
   plus marinating time
Cooking time: 20 minutes
Serves: 4

1–1.5 kg/2 ¼ lb–3 ¼ lb goat chops
4 cloves of garlic, skins on, lightly
   crushed under the palm
2 tablespoons minced fresh herbs, such
   as thyme and rosemary
Olive oil, for drizzling
8 ripe tomatoes, halved crosswise
Salt and pepper

DF ✳ GF ✳ 5

There is deep pleasure in cooking *a la brasa* – over embers – especially when grilling some of Formentera's excellent goat chops. Goat meat is similar to lamb but a touch deeper red, a touch sweeter. Summer is not just barbecue season, but also tomato season, and grilled tomato halves pair perfectly with the goat chops. In spring, grill whole stalks of asparagus instead. To make this recipe under the oven grill (broiler): preheat the oven grill (broiler) and line a baking sheet with aluminium foil for easier clean-up. Arrange the pieces of meat and tomatoes and brush with oil from the marinade. Broil until richly browned on each side, about 10 minutes, turning as needed.

✳ Generously season the goat with salt and pepper. Set in a bowl, add the garlic and scatter over about half of the herbs. Drizzle with oil and turn to coat. Cover and let marinate in the refrigerator for about 1 hour, turning from time to time.

✳ Prepare the barbecue. Allow the charcoal embers to burn down until surrounded by a layer of greyish white ash, and then rake into an even layer. Brush the grill grate with oil.

✳ Set the tomatoes on the grill cut sides-up. Season with salt, scatter over some of the remaining herbs and drizzle with oil. Grill until the sides begin to split and black marks form on the bottoms, 3–4 minutes. Carefully turn cut-sides down, and grill until some black marks appear on the cut sides, 3–4 minutes. Transfer to a platter. Loosely cover with a tent of aluminium foil to keep warm.

✳ Lay the goat on the grill. Grill, turning a few times, for 6–8 minutes. Do not overcook. The meat should be moist and tender.

✳ Transfer to a platter and serve immediately with the tomatoes and remaining herbs.

Menorcan Meatballs with Sobrassada in Sweet Tomato Sauce

Preparation time: 20 minutes
Cooking time: 1 hour
Serves: 5–6

300 g/11 oz minced (ground) beef
300 g/11 oz minced (ground) pork
100 g/3½ oz sobrassada (see page 208), pulled into small pieces
1 large (US extra-large) egg
65 g/2¼ oz (½ cup) fine dry breadcrumbs
4 tablespoons olive oil
1 yellow onion, finely chopped
2 cloves of garlic, minced
4 ripe plum tomatoes (about 500 g/ 1 lb 2 oz total), halved and grated (see page 25)
2 teaspoons sugar
60 ml/2 fl oz (¼ cup) dry white wine
2 sprigs fresh thyme
2 heaped tablespoons pine nuts, dry-toasted (see page 25)
Salt and pepper

DF ✳

When my two daughters were young and we were renting a small farmhouse outside the village of Es Mercadal, this Menorcan meatball dish became a family favourite, one that is both frequently requested at home and often served when my daughters' friends are visiting as well as whenever we are going to a potluck. The sobrassada in the meatball mixture adds a perfect counterpoint to the sweet tomato sauce. Serve with plenty of bread.

✳ In a mixing bowl, mix together the meat, sobrassada and egg, and season with salt and pepper. Add the breadcrumbs and work into a smooth mixture. With moistened hands, roll into meatballs about 4 cm/1½ inches in diameter, using about 1½ tablespoons of the mixture (about 25 g/1 oz) per meatball. There should be 36 of them.

✳ Heat the oil in a flameproof casserole pan (see page 25), Dutch oven or heavy sauté pan over medium–high heat. Working in 2 batches, cook the meatballs, turning frequently, until browned on all sides, about 5 minutes per batch. Transfer to a platter.

✳ In the same pan, fry the onion until it begins to colour, about 5 minutes. Stir in the garlic and then add the tomatoes and cook until darker and pasty, about 10 minutes. Stir in the sugar.

✳ Return the meatballs to the pan, pour over the wine and cook for about 2 minutes. Add the thyme and cover with 175 ml (6 fl oz/¾ cup) water, then reduce the heat to low and gently cook until the meatballs are cooked through and the sauce reduced but still loose, 20–30 minutes.

✳ Remove the sprigs of thyme. Sprinkle over the pine nuts. Serve at the table from the casserole.

Meatballs in Almond Sauce

Preparation time: 20 minutes
Cooking time: 50 minutes
Serves: 4–5

250 g/9 oz minced (ground) beef
250 g/9 oz minced (ground) pork
1 large (US extra-large) egg
2 tablespoons minced flat-leaf parsley
75 g/2⅔ oz (generous ½ cup) fine dry
    breadcrumbs
4 tablespoons milk
3 heaped tablespoons plain
    (all-purpose) flour, or as needed,
    for dusting
6 tablespoons olive oil
1 yellow onion, sliced
4 cloves of garlic, 2 minced and 2 peeled
60 ml/2 fl oz (¼ cup) dry white wine
80 g/3 oz (about ½ cup) peeled raw
    almonds
½ slice of day-old or toasted bread,
    torn into small pieces
Parsley leaves, to garnish, optional
Salt and pepper

There are two savoury classics in the Menorcan kitchen covered with almond sauce, one from the sea (stuffed squid/calamari) and this farm one with meatballs. While some texture to the final sauce is nice and a touch more rustic, some cooks prefer to remove the sauce at the end, pass it through a food mill or purée until smooth and then return it to the pan. This recipe calls for peeled raw almonds. See page 25 for tips on peeling.

✳ In a mixing bowl, mix together the meat, egg and parsley, and season with salt and pepper. Add the breadcrumbs and milk and work into a smooth mixture. With moistened hands, roll into meatballs about 4 cm/1½ inches in diameter, using about 1½ tablespoons of the mixture (about 25 g/1 oz) per meatball. There should be about 30 of them.

✳ Put the flour in a wide bowl. Roll the meatballs in the flour to lightly coat.

✳ Heat 4 tablespoons of the oil in a large, shallow, flameproof casserole pan (see page 25), Dutch oven or heavy sauté pan over high heat. Working in batches, add the meatballs and cook until browned on all sides, about 5 minutes per batch. Transfer to a platter.

✳ To the same pan, add the onion, reduce the heat to medium and cook until soft, about 8 minutes. Stir in the minced garlic and then return the meatballs to the pan. Pour over the wine, cook for 1–2 minutes and then stir in 250 ml (8 fl oz/ 1 cup) water. When it reaches a simmer, reduce the heat and gently cook until the meatballs are cooked through and the sauce reduced but still loose, about 20 minutes.

✳ Meanwhile, heat the remaining 2 tablespoons of oil in a small frying pan and fry the almonds until golden, turning to ensure even cooking, about 3 minutes. Transfer with a slotted spoon to absorbent paper towels to drain.

✳ In the same small pan, cook the whole peeled cloves of garlic until aromatic and soft, ensuring they do not burn, 30 seconds–1 minute. Remove immediately.

✳ Once the almonds and garlic have cooled somewhat, grind them in a food processor with the bread and 6–8 tablespoons water (or more if needed) to form a paste. Alternatively, pound in a large mortar with a pestle.

✳ Loosen the almond-and-garlic paste with 250 ml (8 fl oz/1 cup) water and stir into the meatball pan. Cook for a final 10 minutes to thicken the sauce. Serve at the table from the casserole, with a few parsley leaves, if desired.

Stewed Meatballs
& Cuttlefish

Preparation time: 30 minutes
Cooking time: 1 hour 10 minutes
Serves: 4–5

250 g/9 oz minced (ground) beef
250 g/9 oz minced (ground) pork
1 large (US extra-large) egg
2 cloves of garlic, minced
1 heaped tablespoon parsley, minced
50 g/2 oz (scant ½ cup) fine dry
    breadcrumbs
4 tablespoons plain (all-purpose) flour,
    for dusting, or as needed
6 tablespoons mild olive oil
800 g–1 kg/1¾–2¼ lb cuttlefish, cleaned
    (see page 25) and cut into 2-cm/
    ¾-inch pieces
1 yellow onion, finely chopped
4 ripe tomatoes, halved and grated
    (see page 25)
120 ml/4 fl oz (½ cup) dry white wine
Parsley leaves, to garnish, optional
Salt and pepper

DF ✳

The stewed dish of cuttlefish and meatballs is one of the most classic *mar i muntanya* (sea and mountain) combinations on the islands. This is one of those saucy dishes that is served with plenty of bread. The combination of flavours might seem surprising at first, but they pair very well together.

✳ In a mixing bowl, combine the meat, egg, garlic, parsley and breadcrumbs, season with salt, and mix to a smooth consistency. With moistened hands, roll into meatballs about 4 cm/1½ inches in diameter, using about 1 heaped tablespoon of the mixture (about 25 g/1 oz) per meatball. Set aside.

✳ Put the flour in a wide bowl. Roll the meatballs in the flour to lightly coat.

✳ Heat 3 tablespoons of the oil in a large frying pan or sauté pan over medium–high heat. Working in batches, add the meatballs to the pan and fry until browned on all sides, turning frequently, about 5 minutes per batch. Transfer to a platter.

✳ Heat the remaining 3 tablespoons of oil in a large, flameproof casserole pan (see page 25), Dutch oven or heavy sauté pan over medium–high heat. Add the cuttlefish and cook until lightly golden and tender, about 8 minutes. Transfer with a slotted spoon to a bowl.

✳ To the same pan, add the onion, reduce the heat to medium and cook until soft, about 8 minutes. Add the tomatoes and cook for about 8 minutes, stirring frequently.

✳ Return the cuttlefish to the pan, pour over the wine and let cook for 2 minutes to burn off the alcohol.

✳ Return the meatballs to the pan, season with salt and pepper, add 250 ml (8 fl oz/ 1 cup) water and jiggle the pan to settle. Reduce the heat to medium–low, partly cover and cook, jiggling the pan again and stirring from time to time, until the sauce has been reduced, the meatballs are cooked through and the cuttlefish is tender, 20–30 minutes. The final sauce should be loose – add a touch of water if needed. Serve with a few parsley leaves, if you like.

CHAPTER 9

POULTRY, RABBIT,
GAME & SNAILS

Stewed Chicken

Preparation time: 10 minutes
Cooking time: 1 hour 5 minutes
Serves: 4

4 bone-in chicken legs (drumsticks
    and thighs, about 1.2 kg/2½ lb total),
    excess fat trimmed from edges
    of skin
4 tablespoons olive oil
1 yellow onion, finely chopped
1 tomato, halved and grated
    (see page 25)
6 cloves of garlic, skins on, lightly
    crushed under the palm
1 tablespoon finely chopped flat-leaf
    parsley
1 bay leaf
½ teaspoon sweet paprika
Grating of nutmeg
15 g/½ oz (2 tablespoons) pine nuts
1 hard-boiled egg yolk
Salt and pepper

DF ✳ GF

While chicken might be one of the most popular meats in the world today, few recipes with it can be found in old Balearic cookbooks. Simply put, chickens were valuable and dishes featuring them reserved for special occasions. In *Bon Profit!*, his classic work on the cooking of Ibiza and Formentera, first published in 1967 with more than 250 recipes, Joan Castelló Guasch included just two recipes for chicken, one in tomato sauce (see page 258) and the other stewed with a *picada* of pine nuts and hard-boiled eggs, a cousin of sorts to the island's famed *borrida de rajada* (Skate & Potatoes with Crushed Almonds & Saffron, page 172). At home, we love this chicken dish, which here is adapted from Castelló Guasch's original recipe. Dry-toasting the pine nuts brings out their nuttiness. Let them cool completely before pounding in the picada. Use toasted almonds if you don't have pine nuts.

✳ Generously season the chicken with salt and pepper.

✳ Heat the oil in a shallow, flameproof casserole pan (see page 25), Dutch oven or heavy sauté pan over medium–high heat. Add the chicken and brown, turning as needed, for 6–8 minutes. Add the onion, tomato, garlic, parsley and bay leaf, and cook for 5 minutes, turning the pieces of chicken from time to time. Add the paprika and nutmeg, then stir in 250 ml (8 fl oz/1 cup) water. Bring to a simmer and cook for 30 minutes.

✳ Meanwhile, heat a small ungreased frying pan over low heat, add the pine nuts and dry-toast until just golden, about 2 minutes. Be careful that they do not burn. Transfer to a mortar and let cool completely.

✳ Remove one of the cloves of garlic from the pan, slip off the skin and add the garlic to the mortar. Pound the pine nuts and garlic with the egg yolk to a smooth paste. Loosen it with a couple of tablespoons of liquid from the pan.

✳ Spoon the paste into the stew, stirring to make sure it integrates thoroughly into the sauce. Simmer over low heat until the chicken is done, about 15 minutes. The final sauce should be loose but not watery.

✳ Serve at the table from the casserole.

Chicken in Herby Tomato Sauce

Preparation time: 10 minutes
Cooking time: 1 hour 20 minutes
Serves: 4

4 bone-in chicken legs (drumsticks
    and thighs, about 1.2 kg/2½ lb total),
    some of the skin removed
3 tablespoons olive oil
2 medium yellow onions, finely chopped
2 cloves of garlic, minced
5 ripe tomatoes (about 650 g/1 lb 6 oz
    total), halved and grated
    (see page 25)
1 heaped teaspoon sweet paprika
Pinch of sugar, optional
2 tablespoons finely chopped flat-leaf
    parsley, plus extra leaves to serve
2 sprigs fresh thyme
Salt and pepper

DF ✳ GF ✳ 1 POT

This classic chicken dish is a celebration of chicken with some key elements from the Balearic kitchen – tomatoes, garlic and fresh herbs. The recipe here calls for bone-in chicken legs, but it can be done with any bone-in cut. Add a generous pinch of sugar to the tomatoes if they are outside their peak sweetness. There is thyme in the ingredient list, but add some rosemary, marjoram and/or other fresh herbs, if desired.

✳ Generously season the chicken with salt and pepper.

✳ Heat the oil in a shallow, flameproof casserole pan (see page 25), Dutch oven or heavy sauté pan over medium–high heat. Add the chicken and brown, turning as needed, for 6–8 minutes. Transfer to a plate.

✳ In the same pan, patiently cook the onions until soft, 10–15 minutes. Stir in the garlic, add the tomatoes and cook for 10 minutes, stirring frequently. Add the paprika, sugar (if using), parsley and thyme.

✳ Return the chicken to the pan and turn the pieces to coat with the tomato sauce. Partly cover the pan and cook over low heat until the chicken is done, about 45 minutes. Stir in a touch of water during cooking, if needed, in order to keep the sauce loose.

✳ Serve at the table from the casserole, scattered with more parsley, if desired.

Braised Turkey Drumsticks & Potatoes with Prunes

Preparation time: 10 minutes,
    plus resting time
Cooking time: 1 hour 30 minutes
Serves: 4

4 smallish turkey drumsticks,
    about 350–400 g/12–14 oz each
2 heaped tablespoons plain
    (all-purpose) flour, for dusting
4 tablespoons olive oil
2 medium yellow onions, chopped
4 cloves of garlic, skins on, lightly
    crushed under the palm
120 ml/4 fl oz (½ cup) white wine
1 tablespoon finely chopped fresh
    marjoram
2 spice cloves
12 prunes, preferably with pits
500 ml/18 fl oz (2 cups) Chicken Stock
    (page 338), Vegetable Stock
    (page 339) or water
Generous pinch of ground cinnamon
4 medium white potatoes (about
    800 g/1¾ lb total)
6 tablespoons neutral oil, for frying
3 heaped tablespoons toasted almonds
    or hazelnuts, finely chopped
Salt and pepper

DF ✳

While this traditional dish can be made with chicken, using (ideally smallish) turkey drumsticks is common. Many Mallorcan cooks like to add prunes to the dish – so do I, and I have included them in this recipe – though there are plenty of versions without. I like the sweetness that they bring.

✳ Season the turkey with salt and pepper. Put the flour in a wide bowl.

✳ Heat the olive oil in a large, shallow, flameproof casserole pan (see page 25), Dutch oven or heavy sauté pan over medium–high heat. Dip the turkey into the flour until lightly coated all over, then shake off the excess. Add the turkey to the pan and brown, turning as needed, for about 8 minutes. Transfer to a plate.

✳ Add the onions to the pan and cook until soft, 6–8 minutes. Add the garlic and cook until aromatic, about 30 seconds. Return the turkey to the pan. Pour in the wine and let the alcohol burn off for 1 minute. Add the marjoram, spice cloves and prunes and cover with 250 ml (8 fl oz/1 cup) of the stock. Bring to a gentle boil, reduce the heat to low and simmer for 30 minutes. Add the remaining 250 ml (8 fl oz/1 cup) of the stock and the cinnamon. Simmer until the turkey is cooked, about another 30 minutes.

✳ Meanwhile, peel the potatoes, halve crosswise and cut each of the halves lengthwise into 4 or 5 pieces. Heat the oil for frying in a frying pan over high heat. Add the potatoes and fry, turning as needed, until golden and tender, 12–15 minutes. Transfer with a slotted spoon to absorbent paper towels to drain.

✳ When the turkey is tender, stir in the almonds or hazelnuts, then arrange the potatoes around the meat in the pan and cook for a final 10 minutes.

✳ Remove the pan from the heat and let rest for 5 minutes before serving.

Braised Rabbit with Onions

Preparation time: 15 minutes
Cooking time: 1 hour 30 minutes
Serves: 4

1 whole cleaned rabbit (about 1 kg/
   2¼ lb), head and liver discarded,
   cut into 8–10 pieces
5 tablespoons olive oil
6 cloves of garlic, skins on, lightly
   crushed under the palm
1 bay leaf
120 ml/4 fl oz (½ cup) white wine
Splash of brandy or cognac, optional
1 kg/2¼ lb yellow onions, thinly sliced
Sprig fresh rosemary or thyme, optional
Salt and pepper

DF ✳ GF ✳ 1 POT

In the past, this Menorcan classic was often prepared using wild hunted rabbit. Today, cooks usually use farm-raised rabbits from the butcher. They are more tender and cook faster. (If using wild rabbit, increase cooking time and add a touch more water.) There is usually white wine added while cooking, but also a splash of brandy. The dish is best left to rest for 10–15 minutes before serving.

✳ Season the rabbit with salt and pepper.

✳ Heat the oil in a large, shallow, flameproof casserole pan (see page 25), Dutch oven or heavy sauté pan over high heat. Add the rabbit and brown on each side, 8–10 minutes total, using a mesh splatter guard if needed.

✳ Add the garlic and bay leaf and then pour over the wine and the brandy (if using). Cook over high heat for 2 minutes to evaporate the alcohol. Scatter the onions over the top and cook, turning from time to time, until they begin to turn transparent, about 15 minutes.

✳ Add the rosemary (if using) and 4 tablespoons water, cover with a lid and cook over medium–low heat until the rabbit is very tender and the onions soft, 45–60 minutes. Add a touch of water if it threatens to dry out.

✳ Uncover the dish at the end of cooking. Remove from the heat and let rest, uncovered, for 10–15 minutes. Discard the sprig of rosemary. Serve at the table from the casserole.

Braised Rabbit
with Roasted Red Peppers

Preparation time: 30 minutes
Cooking time: 1 hour 30 minutes
Serves: 4

3 red bell peppers
4 tablespoons olive oil, plus extra
    for brushing
Generous pinch of sugar
1 whole cleaned rabbit (about 1 kg/
    2¼ lb), head and liver discarded, cut
    into 8–10 pieces
4 cloves of garlic, skins on
60 ml/2 fl oz (¼ cup) brandy
    or white wine
1 yellow onion, finely chopped
1 bay leaf
Sprigs fresh herbs, such as thyme
    or rosemary
Salt and pepper

DF ✳ GF

This Menorcan rabbit preparation is associated with summer fiestas that take place in each village. While hunting has long been prohibited in summer, it was (is) permitted in each village in the week leading up to the fiesta. The rabbit would be prepared with red peppers in season. Even if few rabbits are hunted these days, the dish (with rabbit from the butcher's) remains a key culinary part of the celebrations. The red peppers are traditionally roasted and peeled before being incorporated into the dish. (If using wild rabbit, increase cooking time and amount of liquid used.)

✳ Preheat the oven grill (broiler) to high. Line a baking sheet with aluminium foil. Brush the peppers with oil and set on the baking sheet. Grill (broil), turning as needed, until charred in places and tender, 15–30 minutes. Transfer to a large bowl, cover and let cool in the steam to make peeling easier.

✳ Once cool enough to handle, rub off the blackened skin and discard the stems and seeds. Tear into generous strips and lay out on a plate. Sprinkle with the sugar and season with salt, then set aside.

✳ Meanwhile, season the rabbit with salt and pepper. Heat the 4 tablespoons oil in a large, shallow, flameproof casserole pan (see page 25), Dutch oven or heavy sauté pan over medium–high heat. Add the rabbit and brown on each side, 8–10 minutes total, using a mesh splatter guard if needed.

✳ Add the garlic and pour over the brandy. Scatter the onion over the top, add the bay leaf and herbs and cook, stirring from time to time, for 10 minutes. Add 60 ml (2 fl oz/¼ cup) water, reduce the heat to low, partly cover and gently cook until the rabbit is very tender, 45–60 minutes. Add a touch more water if it threatens to dry out.

✳ Lay the strips of pepper on top, then cook together for a final few minutes. Serve at the table from the casserole.

Braised Rabbit with Wild Mushrooms

Preparation time: 15 minutes
Cooking time: 1 hour 25 minutes
Serves: 4

1 whole cleaned rabbit (about 1 kg/
   2¼ lb), head and liver discarded,
   cut into 8–10 pieces
2 heaped tablespoons plain
   (all-purpose) flour, for dusting
4 tablespoons olive oil
1 yellow onion, thinly sliced
4 cloves of garlic, minced
3 tomatoes, halved and grated
   (see page 25)
1 tablespoon minced flat-leaf parsley
120 ml/4 fl oz (½ cup) white wine
Splash of brandy or cognac
1 heaped teaspoon sweet paprika
350 ml/12 fl oz (1½ cups) Chicken Stock
   (page 338), Vegetable Stock
   (page 339) or water
350 g/12 oz wild mushrooms
Salt and pepper

DF ✳ 1 POT

After the first rains in late summer or early autumn, wild mushrooms begin appearing in forests around the islands. They are cooked in various ways, including being braised with rabbit, perfect for when the days are damp and have begun to cool. Add some fresh herbs – rosemary, thyme, bay leaf, marjoram – when adding the mushrooms to the pot. You can also make this using four whole chicken legs. Separate them between drumstick and thigh, remove the excess fat and some of the skin and reduce the cooking time given below slightly.

✳ Season the rabbit with salt and pepper. Put the flour on a plate.

✳ Heat the oil in a large, shallow, flameproof casserole pan (see page 25), Dutch oven or heavy sauté pan over high heat. Dip the rabbit pieces into the flour until lightly coated all over, then shake off the excess. Add to the pan and brown on each side, 8–10 minutes total, using a mesh splatter guard if needed. Transfer to a platter.

✳ In the same pan, fry the onion until soft, about 8 minutes. Stir in the garlic and then add the tomatoes and parsley, and cook until darker and rich, about 10 minutes. Add the wine and brandy and let the alcohol burn off for 1–2 minutes. Stir in the paprika, return the rabbit to the pan and turn to coat the pieces. Cover with the stock or water and bring to a simmer. Reduce the heat to low and simmer until the rabbit is tender, 30–40 minutes.

✳ Meanwhile, clean the mushrooms following the directions on page 25. Depending on their size, halve or quarter the mushrooms into pieces that are a little larger than bite-size.

✳ Add the mushrooms to the pan, with a touch of water, if needed, to keep it saucy. Cook until the rabbit and mushrooms are tender, 5–15 minutes, depending on the mushrooms.

✳ Serve at the table from the casserole.

Grilled Rabbit with Allioli

Preparation time: 5 minutes,
    plus marinating time
Cooking time: 20 minutes
Serves: 3–4

1 whole cleaned rabbit, about 1.2 kg/
    2½ lb, quartered with any excess fat
    trimmed (ask your butcher to do this)
Olive oil, for brushing
2 sprigs fresh thyme
2 sprigs fresh rosemary
4 cloves of garlic, skins on, lightly
    crushed under the palm
Allioli (page 339), to serve
Salt and pepper

DF ✳ GF

Rabbit stews very nicely in a pan, with the meat becoming incredibly tender.
It is also the perfect meat for grilling, either under the oven grill (broiler) or
(preferably) on the barbecue over embers. Directions for both are included.
I prefer to grill a rabbit that has been cut into quarters, or even halves. Allioli
is a must to dollop onto the grilled meat. To accompany the rabbit, I like to grill
some of Menorca's small yellowish-green courgettes (zucchini) – simply split
lengthwise, brushed with olive oil and seasoned with salt and pepper before
laying on the barbecue. Some stuffed artichokes baked in the oven (page 92)
also make a fine accompaniment.

✳ Brush the rabbit quarters with olive oil and season generously with salt and
pepper. Set in a large dish. Strip the thyme and rosemary branches over the top,
add the garlic and turn. Cover and let marinate in the refrigerator for 1–2 hours,
turning from time to time.

✳ To prepare under the oven grill (broiler): preheat the oven grill to high. Line a
baking sheet with aluminium foil for easier clean-up. Brush the rabbit with the oil
from the marinade and arrange on the prepared sheet with the side that has more
bone facing up. Grill (broil) until richly golden brown on both sides, turning a few
times, 15–20 minutes. It should have an internal temperature of at least 71°C/160°F.
Do not overcook. The meat should be moist and tender.

✳ To prepare on the barbecue: Allow the charcoal embers to burn down until
surrounded by a layer of greyish white ash, and then rake into an even layer. Brush
the grill grate with oil. Brush the rabbit with the oil from the marinade and arrange
on the grill with the side that has more bone facing down. Grill until richly golden-
brown on both sides, turning a few times, 10–15 minutes depending on the heat
of the grill. It should have an internal temperature of at least 71°C/160°F. Do not
overcook. The meat should be moist and tender.

✳ Serve the rabbit with the allioli.

Partridge in Escabeche Marinade

Preparation time: 20 minutes,
    plus cooling and marinating time
Cooking time: 1 hour 15 minutes
Serves: 2–4

2 cleaned partridges (about 350 g/
    12 oz each), split in half lengthwise
250 ml/8 fl oz (1 cup) olive oil,
    or as needed
1 small red onion, thinly sliced
12 cloves of garlic, skins on, lightly
    crushed under the palm
1 carrot, cut into thin circles
1 fresh herb wrap – a few sprigs of
    thyme, marjoram and parsley and
    1–2 bay leaves, tied together with
    cotton string
1 teaspoon black peppercorns
250 ml/8 fl oz (1 cup) white wine vinegar
250 ml/8 fl oz (1 cup) white wine
Salt and pepper

DF ✳ GF

One of the most famous ways to prepare game birds in the Balearic Islands is in *escabetx,* an ancient marinade of olive oil, vinegar and herbs. Sardines are also commonly prepared in *escabetx* (page 181), though in a slightly different manner. For sardines, the hot mixture is simply poured over the top of the fried fish. Here, the partridges are actually simmered in the marinade. The herb wrap here calls for thyme, marjoram, parsley and bay leaves, but use what you have available. You'll need to wait at least one day before eating, to fully enjoy the flavours.

✳ Season the partridge with salt and pepper.

✳ Heat 125 ml (4 fl oz/½ cup) of the oil in a frying pan or sauté pan over medium heat. Add the partridge and brown, turning as needed, for about 5 minutes. Add the onion and garlic and gently cook for 5 minutes. Add the carrot, herb wrap and peppercorns, along with the remaining 125 ml (4 fl oz/½ cup) of the oil. Carefully pour in the vinegar, wine and 200 ml (8 fl oz/1 cup) water. The birds should be nearly covered.

✳ Bring to a simmer over medium–low heat and simmer for 1 hour. The birds should be tender but not breaking apart. A leg should jiggle in the socket. (If using wild game, the birds might take longer.) Remove the pan from the heat and let cool for 30 minutes.

✳ Gently transfer to a clean, wide-mouthed glass canning jar or deep bowl. Remove the herb wrap and pour in the marinade and other ingredients to completely cover. (Top up with more olive oil if needed.) Once completely cool, cover the container and let marinate in the refrigerator for at least 1 day.

✳ Remove from the refrigerator 1–2 hours before serving. Serve at room temperature with a spoonful or two of marinade over the top. Best eaten within 3 or 4 days.

Stewed Snails

Preparation time: 30 minutes
Cooking time: 1–2 hours
Serves: 4

500 g/1 lb 2 oz fresh (live) snails
    or snails in brine
2 sprigs fresh thyme
2 sprigs rosemary
1–2 bay leaves
3 tablespoons olive oil
100 g/3½ oz spring onions (scallions),
    trimmed, white and tender green
    parts cut into 1-cm/½-inch pieces
2 cloves of garlic, minced
100 g/3½ oz diced bacon or salted
    and cured pork belly (pancetta),
    optional
4 tomatoes, halved and grated (see
    page 25)
60 ml/2 fl oz (¼ cup) red or white wine
1 tablespoon sweet paprika
1 dried hot red chilli (chile) or pinch
    of red pepper flakes
1 sprig marjoram, optional
Salt, if using fresh snails

DF ✳ GF

Snails in the Balearic Islands are frequently cooked in a tomato and onion *sofregit* that is flavoured with plenty of herbs and often some bacon or pork belly. While Balearic cuisine generally avoids spiciness, snails prepared like this usually call for a small hot red chilli (chile). Directions follow for using fresh (live) snails as well those in brine. It is done in two steps: first boiling the snails and then stewing them in the sauce. Note that snails in the Balearics are smaller than the classic Burgundy or vineyard escargot snail. The most common type has distinctive brown whirls and is usually known in English by their French name, *petit-gris*. Live snails are traditionally left for a time without feeding before preparing, in order to clean out their systems. Nowadays, snails are often sold in net baskets ready to be prepared.

✳ To prepare fresh (live) snails, begin by washing under running water. Place in a large pot, cover with abundant cold water, cover the pot and bring to a boil. (Never add snails to boiling water; this will make extracting the meat when serving more difficult.) When the water reaches a strong boil, drain. Rinse the snails and wash out the pot.

✳ Return the snails to the pot, add 1 sprig of the thyme and 1 sprig of the rosemary, season with salt and cover with 1.5 litres (50 fl oz/generous 6 cups) water. Bring to a boil, reduce the heat, partly cover the pot and gently boil for 1 hour. Cover the pot and set aside until ready to use.

✳ To prepare snails preserved in brine, rinse thoroughly. Bring a large pot of abundant water to a boil, add the snails with 1 sprig of the thyme, 1 sprig of the rosemary and 1 of the bay leaves, and boil for 10 minutes. Cover the pot and set aside until ready to use.

✳ Heat the oil in a shallow, flameproof casserole pan (see page 25), Dutch oven or heavy sauté pan over medium heat. Add the onions and cook until soft and a touch golden, about 5 minutes. Stir in the garlic and then the bacon (if using). Add the tomatoes and cook, stirring from time to time, until the tomatoes have darkened and the sauce is pasty, about 10 minutes. Stir in the wine, bring to a boil and reduce for 3–4 minutes. Stir in the paprika.

✳ Meanwhile, drain the snails, reserving about 250 ml (8 fl oz/1 cup) of the liquid.

✳ Add the snails to the pan with 1 sprig of thyme, 1 sprig of rosemary, 1 bay leaf, the chilli (chile) and about 120 ml (4 fl oz/½ cup) of the reserved liquid.

✳ Cook, uncovered, over medium–low heat for 10 minutes and then add the marjoram (if using). Cook for a final 10 minutes, until the sauce is thickened and the flavours blended.

✳ Serve with cocktail sticks or toothpicks or small snail forks to extract the meat.

Snails in Aromatic Herbs with Potato Allioli

Preparation time: 45 minutes
Cooking time: 1 hour 45 minutes
Serves: 4–6

750 kg/1⅔ lb fresh (live) snails
    or snails in brine
1–2 bay leaves
1 sprig each of thyme and rosemary
    (if using snails in brine)
1 white potato, with skin, scrubbed
1 onion, halved
1 carrot, halved lengthwise
1 large tomato, quartered
5 cloves of garlic
1 large bunch of various aromatic herbs
    (fennel, mint, marjoram, thyme,
    rosemary, etc.), tied together
    with cotton string
1 large (US extra-large) egg, at room
    temperature
120 ml (4 fl oz/½ cup) mild olive oil
Salt

DF ✳ GF

Rather than cooking the snails in a more typical tomato-based sauce (as on page 272), this stunning version from Mallorca boils them with plenty of mixed aromatic herbs and then serves them with an allioli that has been made using a potato boiled with the snails. The potato here softens the garlic, gives it a luscious body and also adds lovely herby notes. The emulsion is also very good spread on bread. See the note on page 272 about snails.

✳ To prepare fresh (live) snails, begin by washing under running water. Place in a large pot, cover with abundant cold water, cover the pot and bring to a boil. (Never add snails to boiling water; this will make extracting the meat when serving more difficult.) When the water reaches a strong boil, drain. Rinse the snails and wash out the pot.

✳ To prepare snails preserved in brine, rinse thoroughly. Bring a large pot of abundant water to a boil, add the snails with 1 bay leaf, 1 sprig of thyme and 1 sprig of rosemary, and boil for 10 minutes. Cover the pot and set aside until ready to use.

✳ To a clean pot, add the snails, potato, onion, carrot, tomato, and 1 bay leaf, and generously season with salt. Crush 4 of the cloves of garlic in their skins. Cover with 2 litres (generous 2 quarts/8½ cups) water. Bring to a boil, reduce the heat, partly cover the pot and gently boil for 30 minutes.

✳ Add the bunch of aromatic herbs and boil for 1 hour. During cooking, remove the potato from the pot once it is very tender (it should take 45 minutes–1 hour) and set aside to cool.

✳ Remove the pot from the heat. Scoop out a few tablespoons of liquid and set aside.

✳ Prepare the allioli once the potato has fully cooled: peel the potato, then peel the remaining 1 clove of garlic. To a tall, narrow and cylindrical container just wider than the shaft of an immersion hand blender, add the potato, garlic, egg, a pinch of salt, the oil and 2 tablespoons of the reserved liquid from the snails.

✳ With the blender still off, put the blender shaft into the container. Now turn on the blender to full speed and begin blending, pushing down towards the bottom. Once the emulsion begins to form, very slowly bring the blender up through to the surface and then slowly back down to the bottom, and then up and out, about 1 minute total blending time. The allioli should be thick, creamy and white.

✳ Transfer to a small bowl. Cover tightly with clingfilm (plastic wrap) and refrigerate until ready to serve.

✳ To serve, transfer the snails with a slotted spoon to a large serving bowl. Serve warm with the allioli on the side and cocktail sticks or toothpicks or small snail forks to extract the meat.

CHAPTER 10

SWEETS
& TREATS

Fresh Cheese Cake
with Mint

Preparation time: 30 minutes,
   plus resting time
Cooking time: 45 minutes
Serves: 8–10

FOR THE CRUST
1 large (US extra-large) egg
125 g/4¼ oz (generous ½ cup) sugar
2 tablespoons olive oil or lard, plus
   extra for greasing
Zest of ½ lemon
2 tablespoons anise liqueur
Pinch of aniseeds, ideally lightly
   crushed in a mortar
Pinch of salt
250 g/9 oz (1⅔ cups) plain (all-purpose)
   flour, plus extra for dusting

FOR THE FILLING
250 g/9 oz fresh goat's
   (or sheep's) cheese
200 g/7 oz (2 cups) shredded
   semi-cured sheep's (or goat's)
   cheese
4 large (US extra-large) eggs
250 g/9 oz (1¼ cups) sugar
10 fresh mint leaves

Ibiza and Formentera's most famous dessert is undeniably the highly original *flaó*. The filling is a blend of two types of cheese – a fresh one for creaminess and a semi-cured (or even cured) one for flavour – plus eggs, sugar and fresh mint leaves. The cheese is either goat's or sheep's or a blend of the two. The crust offers its own original flavours, with aniseed and anise liqueur blended into the sweetened dough. Once an Easter treat, *flaó* is now enjoyed year-round. In fact, *flaó* is so popular that it has become nearly impossible to buy locally produced cheese on Formentera today. Essentially, the island's entire cheese production goes to bakeries for *flaó*.

✳ Prepare the crust: in a mixing bowl, combine the egg and sugar and beat until the sugar dissolves. Beat in the oil or lard, lemon zest, anise liqueur, aniseeds and salt, and then, gradually, fold in the flour. On a clean counter dusted with flour, knead with your hands until supple, about 10 minutes. Add more flour if needed. Cover and let rest in the refrigerator for 1 hour.

✳ Grease a 25-cm/10-inch quiche pan with oil or lard. On a large sheet of baking (parchment) paper, roll out the dough to about 5 mm/¼ inch thick. Turn the dough over into the pan and pull away the baking paper. Tuck the dough in along the sides on the pan and trim away any excess.

✳ Preheat the oven to 180°C/350°F/Gas Mark 4.

✳ Prepare the filling: in a bowl, mash the fresh cheese with the back of a fork. Add the shredded cheese and blend. In a large mixing bowl, beat the eggs with the sugar until the sugar dissolves. Finely chop 6 of the mint leaves and add. Add the cheese and stir until combined.

✳ Pour the mixture into the crust-lined pan. Decorate the surface with the remaining 4 mint leaves.

✳ Bake in the hot oven until the top is a rich golden brown and a cocktail stick or toothpick poked into the centre comes out clean, about 45 minutes. Store covered snugly with clingfilm (plastic wrap) or in an airtight container in the refrigerator for up to 5 days.

Cheesecake with Fresh Cheese, Cinnamon & Lemon Zest

Preparation time: 10 minutes,
    plus cooling and chilling time
Cooking time: 1 hour
Serves: 6

Butter, for greasing
450 g/1 lb brossat (requesón), cottage
    cheese or ricotta (about 2 cups)
60 ml/2 fl oz (¼ cup) milk
Zest of 1 lemon
Generous pinch of ground cinnamon
5 large (US extra-large) eggs
200 g/7 oz (1 cup) sugar
Honey, for drizzling, optional

VEG ✻ GF

The popular fresh local cheese called *brossat* (or *requesón* in Spanish) is akin to cottage cheese and ricotta. (It is a bit moister and less sweet than many ricottas.) *Brossot* is commonly used for fillings in cookies and pastry turnovers in the Balearics. In Mallorca, one of the most common ways to use it is in a crustless cake called *greixonera de brossat*. The name refers to the terracotta casserole in which it is cooked. A *greixonera* isn't required for this recipe, and it can be made in any deep baking dish. As the cake can be hard to unmould without breaking, it is usually served directly from the baking dish. The cake is sweet enough to not really need honey when serving, but it is a lovely (and typical) touch.

✻ Preheat the oven to 180°C/350°F/Gas Mark 4. Grease the sides and bottom of a 22-cm/8½-inch flameproof casserole pan (see page 25), round cake pan or baking dish with butter.

✻ Drain off the excess liquid from the cheese. In a bowl, combine the cheese, milk, lemon zest and cinnamon, and whisk with a fork until creamy.

✻ In another bowl, mix the eggs and sugar and beat until combined, then pour into the cheese mixture. Blend well. Pour into the casserole.

✻ Bake in the hot oven until the top is a deep golden brown and the cheesecake is cooked through (a cocktail stick or toothpick inserted into the centre will come out clean), about 1 hour. Remove from the oven and let cool for at least 30 minutes.

✻ Cover and refrigerate until chilled. Cut into slices and serve directly from the casserole. Drizzle with a touch of honey (if using).

✻ Store any leftovers covered snugly with clingfilm (plastic wrap) or in an airtight container in the refrigerator for up to 5 days.

Sponge Cake with Apricots

Preparation time: 20 minutes,
    plus rising time
Cooking time: 55 minutes
Serves: 12

1 white potato (about 200 g/7 oz)
2–3 large (US extra-large) eggs
150 g/5 oz (¾ cup) sugar, plus
    (if needed) 3 tablespoons
100 g/3½ oz (½ cup) lard or butter,
    or a 50:50 blend of the two
100 ml/3½ fl oz (scant ½ cup) milk,
    warmed
25 g/1 oz fresh baker's yeast or 8 g/
    3 teaspoons instant (easy-blend)
    dried yeast
½ teaspoon salt
500 g/1 lb 2 oz (about 3½ cups) plain
    (all-purpose) flour, sifted, plus
    extra if needed
6 fresh apricots or 12 canned apricot
    halves (page 344)
Icing (confectioners') sugar, for dusting

While it shares a name (*coca*) with the thin and savoury Balearic flatbreads, this is more of a fluffy sponge cake. In Menorca, where it is one of the island's classic baked goods, the dough usually has boiled potato in it. When apricots are ripe, it is made using fresh fruit. For the rest of the year, people use canned apricot halves.

✳ Bring a saucepan of water to a boil, add the potato and boil until tender, 20–25 minutes. Transfer with a slotted spoon to a plate to cool. When cool enough to handle, peel.

✳ Transfer to a large mixing bowl, then mash the potato with the back of a fork. Stir in 2 of the eggs and the 150 g (5 oz/¾ cup) of sugar, and then work in the lard and/or butter with a spoon.

✳ Pour the warm milk into a separate bowl, add the yeast and stir until dissolved. Add to the potato bowl, along with the salt. Gradually work in the flour. Knead with your hands until the dough doesn't stick to them. It should be softer than bread dough. Add a touch more flour, if needed, or, if too firm, another egg or a few tablespoons of water.

✳ Put the dough into a large, clean bowl, cover with a clean kitchen towel and let rise in a warm place for 1 hour.

✳ If using fresh apricots, halve and remove the pits. Arrange on a plate with the cut sides facing up. Sprinkle with the 3 tablespoons of sugar and let sit to soften for about 1 hour or until the dough is ready. If using canned apricots, drain and reserve some syrup.

✳ Line a baking sheet or pan with baking (parchment) paper. Put the dough in the middle of the tray and spread out with the hands to about 25 × 30 cm/ 10 × 12 inches and just over 1 cm/½ inch thick. Smooth with the fingers. Cover with a clean cloth and let rise for 1 hour.

✳ Meanwhile, preheat the oven to 180°C/350°F/Gas Mark 4.

✳ Arrange the apricot halves, evenly spaced, cut-side up on the dough. Press down slightly to embed in the dough. If using canned apricots, drizzle a touch of the reserved syrup into the cups of the apricots.

✳ Bake until a cocktail stick or toothpick inserted into the middle comes out dry, about 30 minutes. Remove from the oven and let cool.

✳ Dust with icing (confectioners') sugar and cut into pieces, each with a piece of apricot, to serve. It is best eaten within a day. Store covered snugly with clingfilm (plastic wrap) or in an airtight container for up to 3 days.

Spongy Orange, Olive Oil & Yogurt Cake

Preparation time: 15 minutes
Cooking time: 30 minutes
Serves: 10–12

Butter, for greasing
250 g/9 oz (1⅔ cups) plain (all-purpose) flour, plus extra for dusting
3 large (US extra-large) eggs, separated
180 g/6 oz (generous ¾ cup) sugar
120 ml/4 fl oz (½ cup) plain unsweetened yogurt
100 ml/3½ fl oz (⅓ cup) mild olive oil or a neutral oil
Zest and juice (about 100 ml/3½ fl oz/⅓ cup) of 1 orange
1 tablespoon baking powder
Icing (confectioners') sugar, for dusting

VEG ✳

Moist, spongy and easy to make, the basic cake here is known generally as *pa de pessic* (*bizcocho* in Spanish) and uses olive oil and yogurt rather than butter and milk. With the important orange industry around Sóller, on the southern slopes of Mallorca's Serra de Tramuntana range, there is little wonder that some zest and juice would find its way into this home staple. While it gets served usually after lunch or dinner, it is, for me, best for breakfast with my morning coffee.

✳ Preheat the oven to 180°C/350°F/Gas Mark 4. Grease a 25-cm/10-inch round or springform cake pan with butter and dust with flour, shaking out the excess. Alternatively, line with baking (parchment) paper.

✳ In a mixing bowl, beat the egg yolks and sugar with hand-held electric beaters until well combined. Add the yogurt, oil and orange zest and blend in. Add the flour and baking powder and mix until the batter is combined but not overly beaten.

✳ In another bowl, whisk the egg whites to soft peaks. Fold the egg whites into the batter, working the spatula from the bottom up to retain as much volume as possible. Transfer the mixture into the pan.

✳ Bake until cooked through and still spongy (a cocktail stick or toothpick poked into the centre should come out clean), about 30 minutes. Do not open the oven during baking. Remove from the oven and let cool before turning out of the pan.

✳ Dust with icing (confectioners') sugar before slicing and serving. Store covered snugly with clingfilm (plastic wrap) or in an airtight container for up to 5 days.

Almond Cake

Preparation time: 15 minutes,
  plus cooling time
Cooking time: 35 minutes
Serves: 8

Butter, for greasing
6 large (US extra-large) eggs, at room
  temperature, separated
200 g/7 oz (1 cup) sugar
200 g/7 oz (generous 2 cups) ground
  (raw) almonds
Zest of ½ lemon
¼ teaspoon ground cinnamon
Icing (confectioners') sugar, for dusting

VEG ✳ GF

Known as *gató d'ametlla* (or often just *gató*), Mallorca's most famous cake dates back to the seventeenth century. The name likely derives from the French for cake (*gâteau*). It's ideally served in summer with a scoop of almond ice cream (vanilla or hazelnut are also excellent) and in winter alongside a hot cup of thick drinking chocolate (page 335). Fluffy and spongy, it is an extremely delightful gluten-free cake.

✳ Preheat the oven to 180°C/350°F/Gas Mark 4. Grease the bottom and sides of a 22-cm/8½-inch round cake pan with the butter.

✳ In a large bowl, patiently beat the egg yolks with the sugar until they turn pale and double in size.

✳ In a separate bowl, mix the almonds with the lemon zest and cinnamon. Fold into the egg yolk mixture, working the spatula from the bottom up.

✳ In another bowl, beat the egg whites to firm peaks. Carefully fold the egg whites into the almond mixture, working the spatula from the bottom up to retain as much volume as possible. Spoon the mixture into the cake pan.

✳ Bake in the oven until a cocktail stick or toothpick poked into the centre comes out dry, about 35 minutes. Remove from the oven, then let cool for about 20 minutes.

✳ Carefully unmould and turn over onto a plate to serve 'upside down'. Generously dust with icing (confectioners') sugar before slicing and serving. Cover snugly with clingfilm (plastic wrap) and store in the refrigerator and eat within 5 days.

'Quarter' Sponge Cake

Preparation time: 15 minutes
Cooking time: 30 minutes
Serves: 8

6 large (US extra-large) eggs, separated
100 g/3½ oz (¾ cup) icing
    (confectioners') sugar, plus extra
    for dusting
100 g/3½ oz (¾ cup) cornflour
    (cornstarch) or potato starch
Thick Drinking Chocolate (page 335),
    for serving, optional

VEG ✳ DF (if served without drinking
chocolate) ✳ GF ✳ 5

Quartos or *coca de quart* (or *coco de cuarto* in Spanish) is a Mallorcan classic, a type of gluten-free sponge cake made with just three ingredients – eggs, icing (confectioners') sugar and cornflour (cornstarch), or sometimes potato starch. That's it. No flour, oil, butter, baking powder, lemon zest, or cinnamon – and still it is a surprisingly spongy (and tasty) cake. It is usually served with a hot cup of thick drinking chocolate.

✳ Preheat the oven to 165°C/325°F/Gas Mark 3. Line the bottom of a 23-cm/9-inch round cake pan with baking (parchment) paper.

✳ In a large mixing bowl, vigorously beat the egg yolks, sugar and cornflour (cornstarch) or potato starch with hand-held beaters until pale and doubled in size.

✳ In a separate bowl, beat the egg whites to soft peaks. Gradually fold into the other mixture, working the spatula from the bottom up to retain as much volume as possible.

✳ Spoon the mixture into the cake pan. Bake in the oven until a cocktail stick or toothpick inserted into the centre comes out clean, about 30 minutes. Remove from the oven and let cool for about 10 minutes. Loosen the sides and turn out onto a plate or cake stand and let fully cool upside down.

✳ Generously dust the cake with icing (confectioners') sugar before slicing and serving. Serve with cups of hot chocolate. Store covered snugly with clingfilm (plastic wrap) or in an airtight container for up to 5 days.

Petal-shaped Cookies

Preparation time: 30 minutes,
    plus resting and cooling time
Cooking time: 15 minutes per batch
Makes: about 30 cookies

2 egg yolks
200 g/7 oz (1 cup) sugar
200 g/7 oz (1 cup) lard, at room
    temperature
1 tablespoon lemon zest
400 g/14 oz (2⅔ cups) plain
    (all-purpose) flour
Icing (confectioners') sugar, for dusting

DF ✳

The sweet most associated with the summer *festes* in my Menorcan village is a petal-shaped cookie called *pastisset*. The classic cutter has seven petals. *Pastissets* are simple – flour, sugar, lard, egg yolks and some lemon zest, with a dusting of icing (confectioners') sugar before serving – but delicious. For best results, roll out the dough between sheets of baking (parchment) paper or clingfilm (plastic wrap). Be sure to let cool on the cookie sheets before transferring to a platter, as they break easily while still warm. During the *festes*, the cookies are usually offered with a glass of slushy gin-and-lemon *pomada* (see page 332).

✳ In a mixing bowl, beat the egg yolks with the sugar until dissolved. Beat in the lard and lemon zest. Sift in the flour and work into a smooth dough. Cover with a clean dish towel and let rest in a cool place while the oven preheats.

✳ Preheat the oven to 180°C/350°F/Gas Mark 4. Line cookie sheets with baking (parchment) paper.

✳ On a clean work counter, lay out a sheet of baking paper or clingfilm (plastic wrap). Working with about a quarter of the dough at a time, cover with another piece of baking paper or clingfilm and roll out to 1 cm/½ inch thick. Using a flower-shaped cutter or a fluted cupcake mould 5–6 cm/2–2½ inches in diameter, press out cookies. Ease the cookies onto on a cookie sheet. Repeat until you have used all the dough.

✳ Bake in the hot oven until just beginning to turn golden, 12–15 minutes. Do not let them get too golden. Remove from the oven and let cool completely on the baking sheets. They are quite delicate until they are fully cool.

✳ Store in an airtight container. They are best eaten within 4–5 days. Before serving, dust with icing (confectioners') sugar.

Almond Cookies

Preparation time: 30 minutes,
    plus chilling time
Cooking time: 20 minutes
Makes: about 20 cookies

225 g/8 oz (2 cups) ground raw almonds
150 g/5 oz (¾ cup) sugar
Zest of ½ lemon, optional
2 large (US extra-large) egg whites
20 peeled almonds (see page 25), to
    garnish

VEG ✳ DF ✳ GF ✳ 5

In Menorca, the important summer fiestas are associated with *pastisset* cookies (page 291), which call for egg yolks. The egg whites often go into another popular cookie, along with ground almonds and sugar. *Amargos* also have a particular prominence in Menorca at Christmastime. The name refers to the bitter almonds that were once used in making this delightful, chewy-soft cookie. The type of almonds has changed, but not the name of this gluten-free treat. They are completely addictive, and never last long in my kitchen.

✳ In a bowl, combine the ground almonds, sugar and lemon zest (if using).

✳ In another bowl, beat the egg whites to soft peaks. Fold the ground almond mixture into the egg whites, working the spatula from the bottom up to retain as much volume as possible. Cover with clingfilm (plastic wrap) and refrigerate for 30 minutes.

✳ Preheat the oven to 180°C/350°F/Gas Mark 4. Line some cookie sheets with baking (parchment) paper.

✳ Shape the dough into balls, using about 20 g (¾ oz/1½ tablespoons) of dough for each one, and place spaced apart on the baking sheets. Gently press a whole almond into the top of each.

✳ Bake until just golden, 15–20 minutes. Remove from the oven and let cool on baking sheets. Store in an airtight container for 4 or 5 days.

Jam-filled Cookies

Preparation time: 30 minutes,
    plus resting time
Cooking time: 30 minutes
Makes: about 20 cookies

500 g/1 lb 2 oz (about 3½ cups) plain
    (all-purpose) flour
200 g/7 oz (1 cup) lard, at room
    temperature
25 g/1 oz fresh baker's yeast or 8 g/
    3 teaspoons instant (easy-blend)
    dried yeast
120 ml (4 fl oz/½ cup) lukewarm water
Jam, preferably non-runny, for filling
Icing (confectioners') sugar, for dusting

DF ✳ 5

In Menorca, *crespells* are a dryish cookie filled with jam. There is no sugar in the dough itself. That sweetness comes from the filling and a light dusting of icing (confectioners') sugar added before eating. The classic ones are about 7.5 cm/3 inches across and are cut with a flower-shaped cookie cutter with nine petals. (*Pastisset* cookies on page 291 are smaller and have seven petals.) You can use any cutter, or even a fluted flan mould, to cut. The jam should be a thicker-bodied one that will hold most of its volume when baking. As one of my neighbours likes to counsel, the cookies need to be *ben torrades* (well-toasted) in the oven.

✳ In a large bowl, mix the flour and lard until combined (it doesn't need to be smooth).

✳ In a small bowl, mix the yeast and lukewarm water, stirring to dissolve the yeast. Add to the flour and lard. Knead with your hands until you get an elastic dough that does not stick to your hands, about 5 minutes. Cover the bowl with clingfilm (plastic wrap), set in a warm place and let double in volume, about 2 hours.

✳ Preheat the oven to 180°C/350°F/Gas Mark 4. Line cookie sheets with baking (parchment) paper.

✳ On a clean work counter, lay out a sheet of baking paper or clingfilm (plastic wrap). Take two pieces of dough about the size of ping-pong balls (40 g/1½ oz) and roll out until thin (ideally less than 5 mm/¼ inch). In the centre of one, place about 1 generous teaspoon of jam in a single dollop; do not spread. Make a small 'x' in the centre of the other and lay across the top as a cover so that the 'x' falls over the jam. Without smoothing out the jam, gently press the dough around the edges to join the two sheets. Using a flower-shaped cutter or a fluted cupcake mould about 7.5 cm/2 inches in diameter, press out a cookie. Lifting up the baking paper underneath, ease the cookie off the paper and place on a cookie sheet. Repeat until you have used the remaining dough.

✳ Bake in the hot oven until golden, 22–28 minutes. Let cool on the sheets.

✳ Once cool, sprinkle with icing (confectioners') sugar. Store in an airtight container. They are best eaten within 4–5 days.

Pine Nut-covered Marzipan Cookies

Preparation time: 30 minutes
Cooking time: 45 minutes
Makes: about 36 cookies

175 g/6 oz sweet potato or potato
    with peel, scrubbed
225 g/8 oz (2 cups) ground almonds
200 g/7 oz (1 cup) sugar
Zest of ½ lemon
Generous pinch of ground cinnamon
1 large (US extra-large) egg, separated
225 g/8 oz (1½ cups) pine nuts
Salt

VEG ✳ DF ✳ GF

On 1 November, the Balearic Islands celebrate Tots Sants, or All Saints' Day, to honour those who have passed. There are, of course, some traditional foods associated with the holiday. In Ibiza, the star gastronomic treat is the *panellet*, a round marzipan cookie rolled in pine nuts and briefly baked. The marzipan has almonds and sugar but also boiled sweet potato (or potato). While it can be a bit tedious to get all of the pine nuts to stick to the outside, the effort is worth it for these sublime treats.

✳ Bring a pot of lightly salted water to a boil, add the sweet potato and boil until tender, about 30 minutes; potatoes will take less time. Drain, reserving a few tablespoons of the liquid. Let the sweet potato cool. Once cool enough to handle, peel.

✳ Transfer the sweet potato to a mixing bowl, then mash. Add the ground almonds, sugar, lemon zest and cinnamon. Work the mixture together, adding 1–2 tablespoons of the reserved liquid, if needed, to get it to bind. Cover and refrigerate the mixture until chilled, about 1 hour, to help with forming cookies.

✳ Preheat the oven to 180°C/350°F/Gas Mark 4. Line a couple of cookie sheets with baking (parchment) paper.

✳ Put the egg whites in a bowl and lightly whisk. Put the pine nuts in a pie pan or wide bowl.

✳ With moistened hands, roll the chilled mixture into balls about 2.5 cm/1 inch in diameter, using 15 g (½ oz/2 teaspoons) of the mixture per ball. Roll each ball in the egg white and then set in the pine nuts. Patiently cover the cookie balls with pine nuts. Gently set on the cookie sheet. Beat the egg yolk in a cup. Brush the cookies lightly with egg yolk and/or the remaining egg whites.

✳ Bake the cookies until the pine nuts are golden brown, 12–14 minutes, watching that they do not burn. Let cool on the sheets.

✳ Store the cookies in an airtight container and eat within 5 days.

Jam-filled Half-moon Pastries

Preparation time: 30 minutes,
  plus resting time
Cooking time: 20 minutes
Makes: about 14 pastries

100 g/3½ oz (½ cup) sugar
150 g/5 oz (⅔ cup) lard,
  at room temperature
2 egg yolks
60 ml/2 fl oz (¼ cup) orange juice
60 ml/2 fl oz (¼ cup) mild olive oil
500 g/1 lb 2 oz (about 3½ cups) plain
  (all-purpose) flour, sifted
250 ml/1 cup apricot jam
  or another fruit jam
Icing (confectioners') sugar, for dusting

DF ✳

While in Menorca, *robiols* tend to be savoury – usually filled with spinach (page 45) or canned tuna – they are generally sweet in Mallorca, with apricot jam being the classic filling. Made all year round, they are among the most emblematic pastries at Eastertime. A dusting of (confectioners') sugar at the end offers a nice balance to the slight tartness of the apricot jam. The directions below press out the dough using a bowl first and then fold over. Alternatively, after rolling out, add the dollop of jam in the centre, fold over and then cut with a fluted pasta cutter into a half-moon shape.

✳ In a large bowl, combine the sugar and lard and beat until the sugar is completely dissolved. Beat in the egg yolks, one at a time, and then beat in the orange juice and olive oil. Gradually fold in the flour, adding about 60 ml (2 fl oz/¼ cup) water as you work. Knead until the dough forms a smooth and supple ball. Put in a bowl, cover and rest for 30 minutes–1 hour.

✳ Preheat the oven to 180°C/350°F/Gas Mark 4. Line cookie sheets with baking (parchment) paper.

✳ On a clean work counter, lay out a large sheet of baking paper. Take a piece of dough weighing about 70 g (2½ oz/¼ cup) and roll it out on the baking paper to 5 mm/¼ inch thick. Using a round cutter or smallish round bowl that measures 12–13 cm/4½–5 inches in diameter, press out a disc.

✳ Place a tablespoon of jam in the centre. Moisten the edges of the pastry with water and, lifting up the baking paper, fold over to form a half-moon. Lightly press the edges together with your fingers. Using the tines of a small fork, press down along the edges. Gently place on one of the cookie sheets. Be careful not to tear the dough, or some of the jam will bleed out during baking. Repeat until you have used the remaining dough and filling.

✳ Bake until just golden (don't let them darken too much), about 18 minutes. Remove from the oven and let cool.

✳ Once cool, dust with icing (confectioners') sugar. Store in an airtight container. They are best eaten within 4 or 5 days.

The Queen's Bread

Preparation time: 15 minutes
Cooking time: 20 minutes
Serves: 4

350 ml/12 fl oz (1½ cups) milk
2 tablespoons sugar, plus extra
    for sprinkling
½ cinnamon stick
Peel of ½ lemon, white pith scraped
    away
2 large (US extra-large) eggs
Neutral oil, for frying
120–175 g/4–6 oz day-old 'Vienna' bread
    or thick baguette, cut into 2-cm/
    ¾-inch-thick slices
Ground cinnamon, for dusting

VEG ✳

While generally called 'French toast' in English, in the Balearic Islands, where this is a traditional treat (especially around Lent and Easter), this dish goes by a wide range of names, and none of them have anything to do with France. In Ibiza, some call it *pa de la reina* (literally 'the queen's bread') while in Menorca it goes by *sopes de partera. Partera* means 'midwife' and refers to the energy these give to a woman who has given birth, while *sopes* indicates older or drier bread. This offers an important clue to the use of drier bread, which is allowed to fully absorb the milk (rather than being given just a cursory dunk). The soaked bread is then dipped in beaten eggs, fried in oil and sprinkled with cinnamon and sugar. This version includes a few touches to improve on that, such as infusing the milk with lemon peels and cinnamon first.

✳ Put the milk, sugar, cinnamon stick and lemon peel in a saucepan and bring to a simmer over medium heat. Reduce the heat to low and simmer for 5 minutes. Remove from the heat and let infuse as it cools for 5–10 minutes. Remove and discard the cinnamon stick and lemon peel. Pour into a wide bowl.

✳ In another wide bowl, beat the eggs with 2 tablespoons of the infused milk.

✳ In a small frying pan, heat at least 5 mm/¼ inch of oil over medium–high heat until it shimmers. Line a plate with absorbent paper towels.

✳ Working in batches that won't crowd the pan, dip the slices of bread in the milk, turning over to fully soak. Gently remove without breaking, set in the egg, turn over to coat and then gently slip into the hot oil. Fry until richly golden brown on each side, turning once, about 4 minutes total per batch.

✳ Transfer with a slotted spoon to the absorbent paper towels to briefly drain. Generously sprinkle with sugar and cinnamon. Serve.

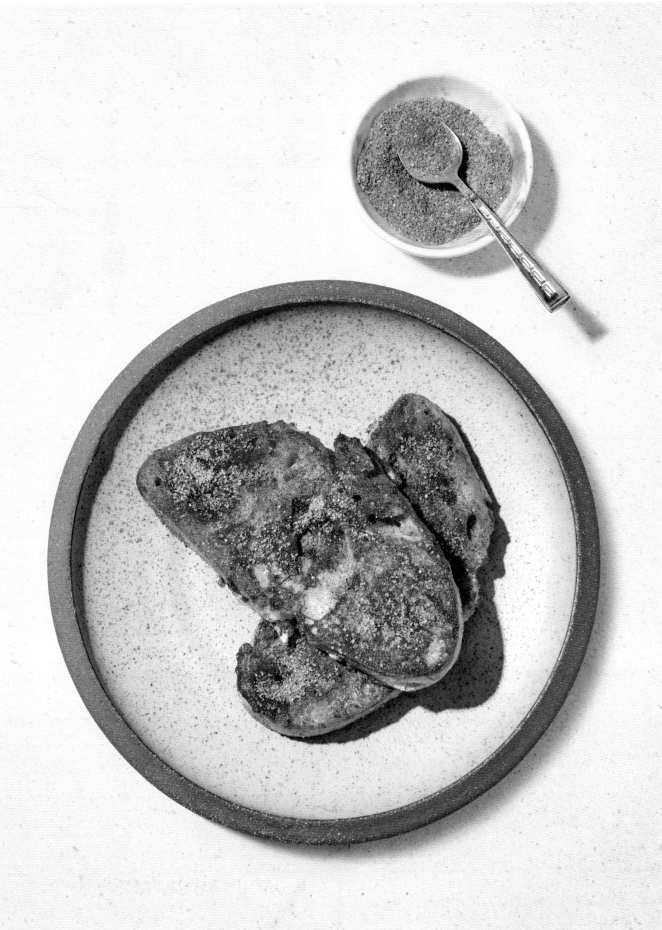

Creamy Orange Pudding

Preparation time: 10 minutes,
    plus chilling time
Cooking time: 20 minutes
Serves: 4

500 ml/18 fl oz (2 cups) freshly squeezed
    orange juice
30 g/¼ cup cornflour (cornstarch)
1 large (US extra-large) egg
150–200 g/5–7 oz (¾–1 cup) sugar
Zest of 2 oranges
Whipped cream, to serve

VEG ✳ GF ✳ 5

From cakes to puddings, there is an abundance of sweet dishes in Mallorca that include oranges or orange juice. One is orange flan, which first appeared in the eighteenth-century recipe book of a Mallorcan friar named Jaume Martí Oliver. This is another, a traditional orange pudding that is easier to prepare than flan, and, as it contains no milk, makes for a light and refreshing dessert.

✳ In a bowl or jug, combine the orange juice with 250 ml (8 fl oz/1 cup) water; there should be 750 ml (25 fl oz/3 cups) total liquid.

✳ In a small bowl, mix the cornflour (cornstarch) with 4–5 tablespoons of the diluted orange juice, stirring to dissolve.

✳ In a mixing bowl, beat the egg. Add the dissolved cornflour mixture and beat to combine. Gradually beat in the sugar, then the orange zest and then the rest of the diluted juice. Transfer to a 2-litre/2-quart saucepan.

✳ Cook over medium heat, stirring without stopping once it begins to heat, until it has thickened and easily coats the back of a spoon, about 20 minutes.

✳ Pour through a strainer into 4 ramekins. Let cool to room temperature, stirring once or twice as it cools to keep a skin from forming on the surface. Cover with clingfilm (plastic wrap), ensuring it is in contact with the pudding to prevent a skin from forming, and refrigerate for at least 2 hours to fully chill.

✳ Serve chilled with whipped cream.

Milk Pudding

Preparation time: 5 minutes,
  plus cooling and chilling time
Cooking time: 15 minutes
Serves: 3–4

500 ml/18 fl oz (2 cups) full-fat (whole) milk
100 g/3½ oz (½ cup) sugar
1 small cinnamon stick
Peel of ½ lemon, white pith scraped away
30 g/4 tablespoons cornflour (cornstarch)
Ground cinnamon, for dusting

VEG ✳ GF

Menjar blanc is a mediaeval dish found in early recipe collections. But while many of those early recipes call for the inclusion of almonds or even chicken broth, *menjar blanc* (literally 'white food') has, over the years, become a milky pudding most often thickened with cornflour (cornstarch). Sweet and creamy, with hints of cinnamon and lemon, it is an ancient delight that continues to please.

✳ Set aside about 120 ml (4 fl oz/½ cup) of the milk.

✳ To a heavy pot, add all of the remaining milk, along with the sugar, cinnamon stick and lemon peel, and slowly heat, stirring frequently, until bubbles start breaking the surface, about 10 minutes.

✳ Meanwhile, add the cornflour (cornstarch) and the reserved milk to a small bowl and stir to dissolve.

✳ Stir the dissolved cornflour into the pot, reduce the heat to low and cook, stirring continually to avoid any lumps forming or the mixture sticking and scorching, for 3–5 minutes until creamy and thick. Remove the cinnamon stick and lemon peel.

✳ Divide among 3–4 dessert cups or small bowls. Let cool to room temperature, stirring once or twice to keep a skin from forming on the surface. Cover with clingfilm (plastic wrap), ensuring it is in contact with the pudding to prevent a skin from forming, and refrigerate until chilled, at least 2 hours.

✳ Before serving, lightly dust with cinnamon.

Ensaïmada

The flat, spiral ensaïmada pastry is the most emblematic food of the Balearic Islands. And while it is found across all four islands, it is most associated with Mallorca.

A loose, open spiral of sweetened, lard-rich dough is left to expand overnight, connecting the whorls. Fresh from the oven, the pastry is a rich golden-brown colour, slightly brittle on the top and light and airy inside. Once cooled, it is generously dusted with icing (confectioners') sugar.

It is an ancient delight, at least according to a rhyming Spanish refrain: *Antes de que hubiera harina, ya existía la ensaïmada mallorquina.* 'Before there was flour, the Mallorcan ensaïmada already existed.' That, of course, is impossible, but it does date quite far back into the history of the island. Just how far back, though, is lost in the yeasty dough of folklore. One legend claims that a Jewish baker presented the Christian *conquistador* Jaume I with an ensaïmada upon his arrival in Mallorca in 1229. Another claims that it was made by Muslim Moors, who ruled the islands for around three centuries preceding the arrival of Jaume I. This often resides on the flimsiest of circumstantial proof – the shape of an ensaïmada is like that of the coiled turbans the Moors wore.

While Muslims introduced numerous dishes, ingredients and crops to the island's culinary repertoire during their rule, it is hard to see the ensaïmada among them, as the name comes from *saïm*, archaic Catalan for lard. This gives the pastry elasticity and flakiness, plus flavour. Considering the ban of pork lard in Islam, it is hard to see a pastry with a name roughly meaning 'enlarded' as having been invented on the island during the period of Muslim rule, at least in its current form.

Dishes rarely appear spontaneously; they usually build on another, drawing in available ingredients, dietary restrictions or new techniques. Perhaps the lard was added to a similar coiled pastry that used a different fat, and the new iteration took on a different name. In Spanish lands recently reconquered by Christians, eating pork or items with lard was a way to demonstrate that you were not a Muslim.

For culinary sleuths, the ensaïmada's origins will remain speculative, as the first written references appear relatively late. Jaume Martí Oliver, an Augustinian friar in Mallorca, mentioned it in his mid-eighteenth-century recipe collection, one of the very first such works from the Balearic Islands. While wheat flour was largely used then for baking breads, he noted that ensaïmades were being prepared for festive and celebratory occasions. A century later, the wealthier classes made them popular to enjoy alongside (or dipped into) hot drinking chocolate, a combination still frequently enjoyed together (page 335). Their popularity spread to the other islands, and references to the spiral pastry have abounded ever since.

In Spain, using fermented dough is rare, and the Mallorcan ensaïmada is considered so unique that the Spanish government awarded the 'Ensaïmada de Mallorca' Protected Geographical Indication status (IGP) in 2003.

Ensaïmades come not only in an individual size but also in larger sizes that serve eight or even twelve people and come packed in an octagonal cardboard box. These are to be cut into wedges and served at gatherings.

The large ones are also a near obligatory souvenir. Many (even, it seems, most) visitors to the islands board their flights or ferries back carrying flat boxes tied with string, a flavourful memory of their island stay and a way of sweetly softening the return home.

Figs

The road from one end of Formentera to the other – some 19 km/12 miles – runs across the Z-shaped island's narrow neck that's just 1,400 metres or so wide (less than a mile). On the southern side of that road, in plots of fertile farmland that slope gently towards the sea, grow numerous sprawling fig trees. They have noticeably low and broad canopies and branches propped up by multiple *estalons* (supporting poles), offering unique silhouettes that have become an emblem of Formentera and appear on various logos. The largest fig tree, found a few minutes down the turnoff for the Es Còdol Foradat beachside *xiringuito*, even has a name: Na Blanqueta de Can Mestre. Planted in 1910, it has an area of over 350 sqm/ 3,750 square feet.

Made from the trunks of *ullastre* (wild olive), pine or juniper trees, *estalons* have an upper end that finishes in a 'Y' for the branches to rest on. These props allow the branches to grow longer, both extending the tree's fruit-bearing capacity and making it easier to pick when the figs are ripe. But there is another important reason. Fig trees tend to be fragile and can break in the strong northern (*tramuntana*) winds that blow across this exposed stretch of island. Lowering the crowns is a way to protect the trees and their fruit crop. These sprawling crowns also create pockets of welcome shade for sheep and goats – and even people – to shelter from the unrelenting summer sun.

Figs are the most important fruit on Formentera, and certainly one of the most important across the Balearic Islands. Every farmhouse has at least one *figuera* (fig tree). They produce fruit for people but also in the past were important for pigs – ones that had fallen were fed to the animals.

In the Balearics, over fifty varieties of figs grow today. Each offers a slightly different taste and texture and colour. Some are green, some are purple and others nearly black. The insides, too, can range from pale pink to ruby red to purplish. While many gardens have a fig tree, there are also plenty of trees that grow semi-wild around the islands. People tend to have their favourite that they head to with an empty bucket at the end of summer. ('The third tree on the right on the road from X to Y,' a neighbour recently divulged, information which I swore not to repeat.) In our Menorcan village, there is a large fig tree near the church for anyone to pick from. I pass it many times a day and, in the August heat, as the fruit begins to ripen, the aromas emanating from it become intense.

When fig trees are fruiting in abundance, we eat dozens a day at home – for breakfast or a snack, as an appetizer or dessert, with fresh cheese or cured ham, in salads... Some of those we have picked, many have been given to us by friends with their own trees and the rest are bought at the Thursday farmers' market or in the village fruit store.

Figs, of course, are not only eaten fresh. Formentera and Ibiza have strong traditions of drying figs. These are known as *xereques*. The figs are cut in half (without separating), opened like a book and dried in the sun. After being placed in the oven for a few minutes to warm and soften, they are packed into terracotta jars, layered with carob leaves and thyme or aniseeds and bay leaves. A staple of the pantry, *xereques* are usually eaten with almonds, a perfect combination of flavours and textures. Many homes wait to begin eating them until Christmastime, when the memory of summer abundance has faded.

Xereques are hard to find these days. So beloved and cherished are they, few make it to the market. In Sant Francesc Xavier, Formentera's main town, the covered Mercat Pagès de Formentera sells out the entire production within a week or two.

From time to time, *xereques* appear in weekly markets in Ibiza, or in certain restaurants that either prepare their own or have sources that they will never reveal.

Baked Ensaïmada Pudding

Preparation time: 20 minutes,
    plus cooling time
Cooking time: 1 hour 30 minutes
Serves: 6

1 litre/34 fl oz (4¼ cups) full-fat (whole)
    milk
250 g/9 oz (1¼ cups) sugar
Peel of 1 lemon, white pith scraped away
1 cinnamon stick
6 large (US extra-large) eggs
4 plain (non-filled) individual day-old
    ensaïmades (about 80 g/3 oz each)

Finding ways to use old bread is universal. Finding uses for old pastries is somewhat less common. This is the local version of bread pudding that uses day-old ensaïmades, the traditional and iconic spiral pastry found around the Balearic Islands (see page 306). The name of the dessert is simply *greixonera*, after the round and deep flame-proof terracotta casserole dish in which it is traditionally baked. The best versions of this extremely popular dessert have (like flan) a layer of caramel in the pan before adding the other ingredients.

✳ In a saucepan, combine the milk, 150 g (5 oz/¾ cup) of the sugar, the lemon peel and the cinnamon stick. Bring to a low boil over medium heat, about 20 minutes. When it reaches a low boil, remove the pan from the heat and let the milk cool and infuse for 20 minutes.

✳ In a large mixing bowl, beat the eggs. Strain in the infused milk and mix well. Tear the ensaïmades by hand into large pieces and add to the bowl, pushing down into the liquid. Let absorb for about 10 minutes.

✳ Preheat the oven to 180°C/350°F/Gas Mark 4. Have a deep baking dish or shallow, flameproof casserole pan (see page 25) ready.

✳ In a small saucepan, combine the remaining 100 g (4 oz/½ cup) of the sugar and 3 tablespoons water, then bring to a boil over medium heat. When it reaches a boil, reduce the heat to medium–low and cook without stirring until it is a rich amber colour, 8–10 minutes. Pour into the baking dish, tilting the dish as needed to evenly coat the bottom.

✳ Spoon the contents of the mixing bowl into the baking dish. Bake in the hot oven until a cocktail stick or toothpick inserted into the centre comes out dry and the top is a touch golden brown, 45–55 minutes depending on the thickness. Remove from the oven and let cool. (The puffiness will deflate slightly.)

✳ Serve at room temperature, cut into wedges with some caramel from the bottom of the dish drizzled over the top.

Aromatic Creamy Rice Pudding

Preparation time: 5 minutes,
     plus chilling time
Cooking time: 40 minutes
Serves: 4

1 litre/34 fl oz (4¼ cups) full-fat
     (whole) milk
Peel of 1 lemon, white pith scraped away
Pinch of salt
100 g/3½ oz (½ cup) short-or
     medium-grain white rice
100 g/3½ oz (½ cup) sugar
1 small cinnamon stick
Ground cinnamon, for dusting

VEG ✳ GF ✳ 1 POT

From Menorca's wet winters and springs comes an important dairy industry, and from that a number of milky desserts, including aromatic rice puddings. This is one of those dishes to prepare in autumn once the weather cools. The smell of milky rice simmering with lemon peels and cinnamon pleasantly fills (and warms) the kitchen: not a small part of the reason I love to prepare it. While the most typical way on the island to eat rice pudding is chilled, I can never resist a first bowl while still warm.

✳ In a large saucepan, combine the milk, lemon peel and salt, then bring to a boil. Stir in the rice and sugar and add the cinnamon stick. When the milk returns to a low boil, reduce the heat and cook, uncovered, at a very gentle boil for 25–30 minutes, stirring frequently to keep the rice from scorching, a skin from forming on the surface or the mixture from potentially boiling over. The rice should be plump and chewy, and the consistency somewhat runny, as it will thicken as it cools. If needed, cook for another 5 minutes or stir in a touch more milk towards the end.

✳ Remove the lemon peel and cinnamon stick. Divide the rice between dessert bowls and let cool to room temperature, stirring once or twice to keep a skin from forming on the surface. Cover with clingfilm (plastic wrap) and refrigerate until fully chilled.

✳ Before serving, dust with ground cinnamon. Serve chilled.

Sant Joan's Sweet Pasta

Preparation time: 5 minutes,
    plus cooling and chilling time
Cooking time: 35 minutes
Serves: 4–6

1 litre/34 fl oz (4¼ cups) full-fat (whole)
    milk
100 g/3½ oz (½ cup) sugar
12 whole saffron threads
1 cinnamon stick
Peel of ½ lemon, white pith scraped
    away
Dash of olive oil
Pinch of salt
150 g/5 oz mafalda corta pasta
Ground cinnamon, for dusting

VEG ✳ 1 POT

This original Ibizan dessert is most associated with the village of Sant Joan de Labritja in the rural north of the island, where it is eaten on its saint's day (23 June). In some ways, it is a distinctive version of the popular rice pudding (page 311) that uses flat ribbons of pasta instead of rice. Most people in Ibiza now use a pasta labelled 'mafalda corta' with ruffled edges. (At around 3 cm/1¼ inches long, it's a short version of mafaldina, a pasta shape of long ribbons with frilly edges.) In the past, the pasta was often cooked in water instead of milk, or just some milk. But the dish has evolved to use exclusively milk, and is certainly better for it. It's creamy and, adding to the richness, has a golden colour from the saffron threads. It is served chilled.

✳ Add the milk to a large pot with the sugar, saffron, cinnamon stick, lemon peel, oil and salt, and bring to a boil over medium heat. Add the pasta, lower the heat, partly cover the pot and gently boil until the pasta is tender (but not mushy) and the milk has thickened, 30–35 minutes, stirring from time to time.

✳ Remove from the heat and let cool. Remove and discard the cinnamon stick and lemon peel. Spoon into a large bowl or divide among individual dessert bowls. Once cooled to room temperature, cover with clingfilm (plastic wrap) and refrigerate until fully chilled.

✳ Serve chilled in bowls and dusted with cinnamon.

Baked Figs

Preparation time: 5 minutes,
     plus cooling time
Cooking time: 35 minutes
Serves: 4–6

50 g/2 oz (¼ cup) sugar
12 fresh figs (about 500 g/1 lb 2 oz total)
juice of ½ lemon
3 tablespoons sweet red or white wine

V ✳ VEG ✳ DF ✳ GF ✳ 5

Sometimes in summer, when figs are in season, plentiful and on the table every day to eat fresh, there is a desire to prepare them in a different manner – especially when company is coming over. Baking figs in the oven with a touch of sweet wine is a favourite local way. They are delightful with plain (unsweetened) yogurt or ice cream, especially with a scattering of toasted pine nuts (or walnuts) and some of the dark, syrupy liquid from the bottom of the baking dish drizzled over top.

✳ Preheat the oven to 180°C/350°F/Gas Mark 4.

✳ Prepare a simple syrup: in a pan, bring 175 ml (6 fl oz/¾ cup) water and the sugar to a boil and boil for 5 minutes. Remove from the heat and let cool for 5 minutes.

✳ Gently rinse the figs and trim the tips from the stems. Set the figs upright in a small baking dish. Juice the lemon over the top and pour in the syrup. Bake in the oven for 15 minutes. Drizzle over the wine and bake for another 15 minutes, or until the figs are tender. Watch that the tops of the figs don't burn.

✳ Serve warm with some of the syrup spooned over the top, or allow them to fully cool and chill. Store in a covered dish in the refrigerator. It is best eaten within 3 days.

Baked Quince with Brandy & Spices

Preparation time: 5 minutes
Cooking time: 1 hour 30 minutes
Serves: 4

4 quinces (about 350 g/12 oz each)
8 spice cloves
8 heaped teaspoons sugar, for
  sprinkling
Brandy, for dashing
Ground cinnamon, for dusting
Sweet white wine, such as muscatel,
  for dashing

V * VEG * DF * GF

Despite their wonderful, perfumed fragrance when picked, fresh quince are too tough and woody to eat raw. But once cooked, their flesh becomes tender and sweet. The most common way to eat them in the Balearics is baked in the oven, and there are various ways to do this. One simple way is to roast (or boil) them whole in the oven, then peel and slice and serve dusted with cinnamon and sugar. The typical method below is a touch more special – fitting for an autumn treat when quince begin arriving in the markets.

* Preheat the oven to 180°C/350°F/Gas Mark 4.

* Halve the quince lengthwise and remove the hard cores. Arrange on a baking dish cut-sides facing up.

* Into each half, put 1 spice clove and 1 heaped teaspoon of sugar. Moisten each with a dash of brandy and dust with cinnamon. Pour about 150 ml (5 fl oz/⅔ cup) water into the base of the dish.

* Bake, uncovered, in the oven until tender (a cocktail stick or toothpick will go in with little resistance), 1 hour 15 minutes–1½ hours. (If the top is getting more than browned along the edges but the centre is still not done, loosely cover with aluminium foil.)

* Remove from the oven, sprinkle with sweet wine and let cool a little. Serve warm with a drizzling of the liquid in the dish.

Baked Apples with Walnuts

Preparation time: 10 minutes
Cooking time: 1 hour
Serves: 4

4 tart green apples or golden ones
   tinged with green
6 pieces of lemon peel, white pith
   scraped away
4 tablespoons sugar, preferably brown
4 generous pinches of ground cinnamon
6 tablespoons white wine
   or sweet white wine
4 heaped tablespoons chopped
   walnuts, hazelnuts or almonds
   (about 40 g/1½ oz total)
120 ml (4 fl oz/½ cup) hot water

V ✳ VEG ✳ DF ✳ GF

Slightly tart or acidic green apples – or golden ones with touches of green to them – baked in the oven are a traditional weeknight dessert in Menorca. But with a few additions, cooks here easily turn them into something more special. They are often cored and filled with chopped nuts, a piece of lemon peel, sugar and some wine. So, on a chilly weeknight, this dessert feels somewhat festive.

✳ Preheat the oven to 180°C/350°F/Gas Mark 4.

✳ Using a corer or a paring knife and small spoon, remove the core and seeds of the apples, working from the top, leaving the bottoms intact. Set the apples side by side in a baking dish. Into the hollowed core of each apple, put, in this order: a piece of lemon peel, 1 tablespoon of sugar, a generous pinch of cinnamon, 1½ tablespoons of wine and, finally, 1 heaped tablespoon of chopped nuts. Pour the hot water around the base of the apples, and then set the remaining 2 pieces of lemon peel in the water.

✳ Bake in the oven until the apples are soft but not mushy (a cocktail stick or toothpick will go in with little resistance) and their sides are beginning to crack, 45 minutes–1 hour. Remove from the oven and let cool until warm.

✳ Set on dessert plates, spoon any juice from the baking dish over the top and serve.

Oranges with Sweet Wine

Preparation time: 10 minutes,
    plus chilling time
Serves: 4

4 ripe oranges
Sugar, for sprinkling, optional
4–6 tablespoons sweet white wine
    or red wine

V ✳ VEG ✳ DF ✳ GF ✳ 5 ✳ 30

In the Balearics, after the main lunch or dinner course comes fruit, with some pears or figs or whatever fruit is in season usually just set out in a bowl with small plates and sharp knives to peel as needed. But sometimes the fruits get a little twist – strawberries with a dash of vinegar and generous pinch of sugar, pomegranate seeds with a moistening of wine (page 323) or orange slices with a drizzle of honey. Another delicious way to transform oranges into something a bit more special is sprinkling them with sweet wine (or table wine with some generous pinches of sugar). Both white and red wine are popular. These orange slices are excellent served with cookies like soft and chewy almond *amargos* (page 292).

✳ Peel the oranges and remove as much of the white pith as possible. Using a serrated paring knife, cut the oranges crosswise into slices about 1 cm/½ inch thick. Remove any pips. Reserve any juice.

✳ Arrange the slices overlapping in a wide bowl, sprinkling with the sugar (if using) and drizzling over the wine as you work. Cover with clingfilm (plastic wrap) and refrigerate until chilled.

✳ Turn over the slices before serving. Serve chilled on dessert plates with any juice from the bowl spooned over the top.

Pomegranate Seeds
with Wine

Preparation time: 15 minutes,
  plus chilling time
Serves: 3–4

1 ripe pomegranate
1 teaspoon icing (confectioners') sugar
2 tablespoons red wine

V ✳ VEG ✳ DF ✳ GF ✳ 5

When pomegranates are at peak season in October and November in Ibiza, a bowl of seeds drizzled with some red wine and a touch of sugar makes a lovely dessert. You can also use a sweet wine here; if you do, just reduce (or omit) the sugar. Pomegranates were introduced on Ibiza by the Phoenicians, who settled on the island around the seventh century BCE. The genus of the fruit – *punica* – reflects its origins.

✳ Seed the pomegranates and remove any pieces of white pith.

✳ Put the seeds into a large bowl, sprinkle with the icing (confectioners') sugar, add the wine and toss to blend well. Cover with clingfilm (plastic wrap) and refrigerate for at least 30 minutes to chill. Before serving, toss again. Divide among small dessert bowls and serve.

CHAPTER 11

DRINKS

Chilled Aromatic 'Prepared' Milk

Preparation time: 5 minutes,
    plus cooling and chilling time
Cooking time: 15 minutes
Makes: 1 litre (1¾ pints/34 fl oz/
    4¼ cups);
Serves: 4

1 litre/34 fl oz (4¼ cups) full-fat
    (whole) milk
Peel of 1 lemon, white pith scraped away
1–2 cinnamon sticks
50 g/2 oz (¼ cup) sugar
Ground cinnamon, for dusting

VEG ✳ GF ✳ 5

On the Spanish peninsula, this is sometimes called *leche mallorquina* – Mallorcan milk. But in Mallorca, this chilled, refreshing drink, with the milk infused with lemon peel and cinnamon, is known as *llet preparada* ('prepared milk') or, in some places, *llet freda* ('cold milk'). While that last name gives a sense of how it is served – always cold! – there is little hint of the aromatics that make it special. It is frequently served with either of Mallorca's two most famous cakes, *coca de quart* ('Quarter' Sponge Cake, page 288) or *gató d'ametlla* (Almond Cake, page 287). When the days are warm it is nice to stick it in the freezer for about an hour, shaking from time to time, to get it nearly icy.

✳ Bring the milk, lemon peel and cinnamon stick(s) to a slow boil in a large saucepan over medium heat without letting it scorch, 10–15 minutes. Add the sugar and stir until it dissolves. Remove the pan from the heat and let infuse as it cools, stirring from time to time, to room temperature.

✳ Strain into a glass pitcher and chill in the refrigerator until very cold. To serve, pour into tall glasses, lightly dust with cinnamon and serve very cold.

Almond Granizado

Preparation time: 10 minutes,
    plus cooling and freezing time
Makes: 2 large glasses

100 g/4 oz (1 cup) finely ground almonds
100 g/3½ oz (½ cup) sugar
Zest of ½ lemon
Generous pinch of ground cinnamon

V ✳ VEG ✳ DF ✳ GF ✳ 5

A glass of slushy almond *granissat* (*granizado* in Spanish) is both refreshing and a touch filling. It is common during summer, especially in a certain type of old Mallorcan café, enjoyed with a slice of *quartos* ('Quarter' Sponge Cake, page 288) or *gató d'ametlla* (Almond Cake, page 287) or an ensaïmada. Use finely ground almonds that are sometimes sold as 'almond flour'. Don't use almond meal, which is coarser ground. The final texture is grainy enough as it is.

✳ Bring the almonds, sugar, lemon zest, cinnamon and 500 ml (16 fl oz/2 cups) water to a boil in a saucepan over high heat, stirring to dissolve the sugar. Remove from the heat and let cool for a few minutes. Pour into a freezer-proof container with a tight-fitting lid and let cool completely with the lid off, stirring from time to time.

✳ Once cool, put on the lid and put in the freezer until it is partially frozen, about 2 hours, shaking the container from time to time to break up the frozen crystals. It should be slushy.

✳ If it freezes completely, remove from the freezer about 2 hours before serving, breaking up with a fork and shaking once it begins to thaw. Divide between 2 large glasses to serve.

Left to right: Almond Granizado,
Chilled Aromatic 'Prepared' Milk.

Almonds in Ibiza & Mallorca

While the coastal landscape of the Els Amunts region of northwestern Ibiza is marked by spectacular wild cliffs and hidden coves, the interior has limestone mountains that rise some 300–400 m/1,000–1,300 feet high. Covered with juniper and pine trees and separated by small valleys and plateaus, they contain some of the most fertile land on the island. Els Amunts is the centre of Ibiza's almond growing.

Pulling off the road on a sunny, early-February day on a plateau known as the Pla de Corona near a traditional flat-roofed, whitewashed farmhouse, the breezy air is fragrant with a subtle, sweet and floral aroma, and the almond trees are awash with delicate white and pink flowers.

Typically starting in late January and peaking around mid-February, the almond blossoms transform the landscape and offer a decisive seasonal marker that emphatically says: Winter has ended! Spring has arrived!

In the past, selling almonds from the August harvest was of utmost importance for many families in Els Amunts. Before the arrival of (and dependence on) tourism, Ibiza exported a significant amount of *ametlles*. Today production is lower than it once was, with a maximum harvest of around 65,000 kg/143,300 lb. But while paltry on the global or even national scale – depending on the year, that's a mere 0.05 per cent of Spain's total – Ibiza's almonds are appreciated for their quality and command high prices.

Even if families don't rely on the almonds financially as they once did, they remain important to the island's identity and key to its cooking. In Ibiza, almonds are eaten out of the hand (especially tasty with dried figs called *xereques*, see page 307) but also found in numerous dishes, both sweet and savoury. One of the most famous is *borrida de rajada* (Skate & Potatoes with Crushed Almonds & Saffron, page 172). As in this dish, almonds are often pounded into a *picada* (see page 175) and added to stews, a culinary technique that dates back to the Middle Ages.

In neighbouring Mallorca, almonds appear with even more frequency in the kitchen. A slice of spongy almond cake (*gató d'ametlla*, page 287) with almond ice cream is the most classic way to finish a meal. There is almond nougat at Christmas, various biscuits made with ground almonds (such as *amargos*, page 292) and drinks made from almonds, including a refreshing and somewhat filling *granizado* (page 326).

With its much larger and better developed industry, Mallorca's almonds have Protected Geographical Indication status (IGP). This official certification guarantees the quality of the island's almonds by ensuring the link between the almonds, their origin and the methods used in producing them.

There are some four million almond trees in Mallorca – by some accounts, that's over half of all fruit trees on the island. That statistic sounds almost unbelievable, at least until their white and pink flowers blossom from late January into February. Then that number seems wholly realistic.

Some six months later, the trees will need to be fully picked during the harvest, or rather, almost fully picked. A few almonds must be left on each tree to ensure the quality of the next harvest. According to tradition, it should be a dozen.

Menorcan Gin & Pomada

While the Netherlands is generally credited as the birthplace of gin, the spirit had already become one of Britain's national drinks by the eighteenth century when the Royal Navy was helping spread its popularity around the globe in various ports of call. Among them was Menorca.

Menorca is the only one of the Balearic Islands to have historical links to the British, who captured the island in 1708 during the War of Spanish Succession and then negotiated to keep it afterwards with the 1713 Treaty of Utrecht. The capital of the island at the time was Ciutadella, and the British shifted it to Maó, built above one of the most protected ports in the Mediterranean. From here, the British ruled the island for about a century. Gin was distilled for the Royal Navy, who sheltered in Maó's port. After the island returned to Spanish control with the 1802 Treaty of Amiens, the navy left, but the tipple continued to be produced in Maó.

Today the main manufacturer is the Pons family, who have been bottling and selling gin under the Xoriguer label since the 1940s. Their modest factory is located at the end of the city's narrow port, just across from where the large ferries from Barcelona, Valencia and Palma de Mallorca dock and near the cruise ship berth. Xoriguer continues to use copper stills from the late-eighteenth century, and uses salt water from the harbour to cool the stills.

One key difference between Xoriguer gin and the original Dutch and British versions is that it uses wine alcohol rather than grains such as wheat, barley and/or rye. Along with a heady infusion of juniper berries from the Catalan Pyrenees, which are allowed to dry in baskets for a couple of years on the floor above the stills, there is a range of herbs – perhaps rosemary, thyme and sage. The overall composition remains a closely guarded family secret. The gin is bottled in distinctive green glass bottles with a small handle on the neck and a label that carries an image of the family's eighteenth-century windmill that gives its name to the brand.

Xoriguer's flavour is of juniper, fresh green wood and some citrus notes, along with the herby bouquet. The wine-based spirit gives it softer notes – smoother, fruitier – than most grain-based gins.

While gin and tonics are as popular here as anywhere, today most of the island's gin goes into Menorca's iconic drink, *pomada* (page 332). The single most common piece of advice given for preparing not just a good version but simply any *pomada*? 'You have to use Xoriguer gin.' Made with fresh lemon juice and sugar, sometimes lemon soda and occasionally a few fresh mint leaves, *pomada* is popped in the freezer and served slushy. Drinking small cups of *pomada* is synonymous with summer and the fiestas when each town celebrates its patron saint, from the end of June through to September.

Mixing gin with lemon juice is hardly original, but what is remarkable is how quickly the drink became a summer staple. Asking around the island, no one remembers *pomada* before the 1970s. But by the end of that decade, it was ubiquitous. The most repeated story is of a barman in Maó who hid his penchant for gin from his wife by secreting it into carbonated lemon soda. He christened it *pomada* ('ointment') and began offering it in his establishment. The name has stuck, even if it's a bit nonsensical, everywhere on the island apart from Ciutadella. Ask for a *pomada* there, and you will be directed to the pharmacy, in a joke that never seems to grow old. In Ciutadella, the drink is called, more prosaically, *gin amb llimonada* (gin with lemonade).

Redolent of the sunny Mediterranean, it's refreshing and icy-cold, fragrant with local lemons and the herby, light-bodied gin. And importantly, it's a social drink. While *pomada* can be made for an individual glass – some bars simply pour gin and lemon soda over ice and garnish with a lemon slice – I don't know anyone here who prepares it at home for themselves. It's made in a batch and enjoyed with others.

Bottling Ibiza

Back in antiquity, islanders on Ibiza began picking the ample Mediterranean herbs that grew wild and brewing medicinal infusions, which were later sweetened to take away some of the bitterness. At some point, people began making medicinal herbal liqueurs using anisette as a base and to macerate chamomile, fennel, sage, rosemary, lemon verbena, wild thyme, eucalyptus, orange and lemon leaves, occasionally sage or bay leaves, and even juniper bark. The drink was first commercialized in 1880 by Hierbas Familia Marí Mayans, which remains the largest and best-known brand today. In 1997, the Spanish government bestowed Protected Geographical Indication status (IGP) on 'Hierbas Ibicencas', giving the product a level of protection and certain guarantee of quality. (In the local language, it is called *herbes eivissenques*.)

There are a couple of smaller producers with strong local followings. Many have been preparing *herbes* for generations. One of these is Herbes Can Vidal, which is sold from the family's *estanco* (tobacconist shop) in Sant Joan de Labritja, in the north of the island. Among cartons of cigarettes, packs of gum and lottery tickets in the *estanco*, sits a selection of different-sized and shaped bottles filled with *herbes*. Each of the bottles has been painstakingly filled with herbs that the family has gathered and topped up with anisette following a generations-old recipe. Another delicious local brand comes from Ca n'Anneta (also known as Bar Anita), a popular bar in the northeastern interior of the island that opened in 1942. Many consider this among the best and stop by for a glass that can be either an *aperitivo* or a *digestivo*.

But while it is easy to buy on the island, it remains popular to prepare homemade versions on Ibiza and neighbouring Formentera. Each is distinct, both for its balance of sweet-to-dry anisette used and the selection of herbs macerated in the bottle.

The main time to prepare is late spring, when chamomile is flowering, and thyme and fennel are abundant. Families head out into the countryside with baskets to collect these in the wild. With the help of a skinny stick, a dozen or more different herbs get pushed down into bottles, which are then filled with anisette. Sweet anisette is the typical base, though people generally mix in some dry anisette, too, so that it is not overly sweet; the balance is to their taste. The bottles are left for at least three months to macerate, to take on the flavours of the herbs and to slowly turn a yellowish colour from the chamomile as it ages.

The most common way to enjoy this drink is in a small glass and chilled. (Some even add ice, though purists scoff at the drink being diluted in any way.) In recent years, *herbes* has also become a popular shot in clubs and chic bars.

A short glass of the yellowish drink captures the flavour of Ibiza's countryside, with a nice little kick.

Ibizan Herb Liqueur

Preparation time: 20 minutes,
    plus steeping time
Makes: 1 litre/1¾ pints

Mix of fresh sprigs of thyme, rosemary,
    mint, spearmint, lemon verbena and/
    or fennel fronds
Bay leaf
Lemon and/or orange leaves
Piece of lemon and/or orange peel,
    white pith scraped away
750 ml/25 fl oz (3 cups) sweet anisette,
    or as desired
250 ml/8 fl oz (1 cup) dry anisette,
    or as desired

V * VEG * DF * GF

A dozen or more herbs often go into Ibiza's iconic liqueur, *herbes eivissenques*, literally 'Ibizan herbs', or simply *herbes*. (It is called *hierbas ibicencas* in Spanish.) This recipe gives the standard herbs. Add others – lavender, rue, juniper bark – as desired. For anisette, the typical ratio is three parts sweet to one part dry, though adjust based on personal taste and the sweetness of the brand of anisette. The herbs depend largely on what you have – or can find. (See opposite for more on *herbes*. Photo on page 333.)

* Clean and trim the herbs so that their length will fit beneath the neck of the bottle.

* Feed the herbs, leaves and peels into 1 or 2 sterilized glass bottle(s), pushing down with the end of a wooden spoon.

* In a jug, add the sweet anisette and begin blending in the dry, adding more as needed until you get your desired taste. With the help of a funnel, pour into the bottle(s) over the herbs.

* Firmly cork and label the bottle(s). Store in a cool, dry place for at least 3 months before serving. Served chilled.

Menorcan Gin & Lemon Slushy

Preparation time: 15 minutes,
    plus freezing time
Makes: about 1 litre/34 fl oz (4¼ cups)

3–6 fresh mint leaves
6 tablespoons sugar, or as needed
180 ml/6 fl oz (¾ cup) fresh lemon juice
    (from about 3 ripe lemons),
    or as needed
180 ml/6 fl oz (¾ cup) light-bodied gin
    (I like Menorcan Xoriguer),
    or as needed

V ✳ VEG ✳ DF ✳ GF ✳ 5

Nothing says Menorcan summer (or summer village *festes*) more than a gin-and-lemon drink called *pomada* (see page 329). While *pomada* is often made using some carbonated lemon drink, this version is made using only fresh lemonade (lemon juice, sugar, water), plus a handful of mint leaves for flavour. The standard ratio is one part gin to three parts fresh lemonade or lemon soda. But this one – the one we prepare at home – calls for slightly less gin. Taste before freezing and add a touch more gin (or sugar) if desired. A speedy quicker (but non-slushy) version can be made by simply mixing and then serving over plenty of large cubes.

✳ To a clean 1.5-litre (50 fl oz/6-cup) (or larger) disposable plastic water bottle or Tupperware container with tight-fitting lid, add the mint leaves, sugar, lemon juice and gin. Screw on the lid tightly and vigorously shake the bottle. Unscrew the lid, add about 600 ml (1 pint/2½ cups) water, replace the lid tightly and vigorously shake again. The sugar should be dissolved. Taste and adjust the gin, lemon juice and sugar if needed.

✳ Put the bottle or container in the freezer until frozen. For the first 1–2 hours, shake it from time to time.

✳ Remove from the freezer 1–2 hours before serving. If using a disposable bottle, carefully cut in half using heavy kitchen scissors and transfer the block of frozen drink to a bowl. Use a fork to break it up as it gradually thaws. It should be just slushy when serving. Using a ladle, serve in small glasses.

Gin & Soda Cocktail

Preparation time: 5 minutes
Makes: 1 glass

1 organic lemon, scrubbed
Large ice cubes
60 ml/2 fl oz (¼ cup) light-bodied
    aromatic gin (I like Menorcan Xoriguer)
120 ml/4 fl oz (½ cup) soda water or *sifó*
    (siphon)

V ✳ VEG ✳ DF ✳ GF ✳ 5 ✳ 30

Before the *pomada* took over the island as the most popular gin drink of choice (see page 329), Menorcans often enjoyed their gin *a palo seco* (straight), or like this, with a lemon peel and shot of soda water from a *sifó* (siphon). The spiral of lemon peel lends the drink its name.

✳ Cut a long, curling strip of lemon peel. If there is an abundance of white pith, gently scrape it away with a knife without breaking the peel. Add to a tall glass with ice cubes. Pour in the gin, spritz with the soda water and stir. Serve immediately.

Left to right: Gin & Soda Cocktail, Ibizan Herb Liqueur (page 331),
Menorcan Gin & Lemon Slushy.

Preparation time: 5 minutes
Cooking time: 10 minutes
Serves: 4

2 teaspoons cornflour (cornstarch)
500 ml/18 fl oz (2 cups) full-fat
    (whole) milk
50 g/2 oz (¼ cup) sugar, or as needed
175 g/6 oz dark (semisweet) cooking
    chocolate (50–70 per cent cocoa),
    grated or finely chopped
Pinch of ground cinnamon
Pinch of salt

VEG ✳ GF ✳ 5 ✳ 30

Preparation time: 5 minutes
Cooking time: 25 minutes
Serves: 4

1 (750 ml/25 fl oz) bottle full-bodied red
    wine
4 tablespoons sugar, or as needed
Peel of 1 orange or lemon, white pith
    scraped away
1 cinnamon stick
Pinch of freshly grated nutmeg

V ✳ VEG ✳ DF ✳ GF ✳ 5 ✳ 30

Thick Drinking Chocolate

While this hot, thick drinking chocolate 'in the cup' is enjoyed on its own once the weather cools, it is frequently also served alongside pastries. If ensaïmada is king, then *xocolata a la tassa* is the iconic pastry's frequent companion in Mallorca. It is also part of a classic duo with spongy *coca de quart* cake (page 288). While there are a number of ready-to-make powder mixtures, it is easy enough to prepare from scratch. The amount of sugar depends on taste but also on the chocolate used. Begin with just a small amount, taste at the end and add more if needed.

✳ Dissolve the cornflour (cornstarch) in a couple of tablespoons of the milk and set aside.

✳ In a saucepan over medium heat, bring the remaining milk and the sugar to a low boil. When it breaks a boil, stir in the chocolate and then the dissolved cornflour, along with the cinnamon and salt. Cook, stirring continually, until it thickens and heavily coats the back of a spoon, about 5 minutes. Taste for sweetness, and add more sugar if desired. Pour into cups and serve.

Hot Mulled Wine

While there has been wine in Menorca likely since the Roman era, this mulled tipple dates back to only the eighteenth century, during the British rule of the island. It was drunk very hot on cold days (and nights). Its popularity has faded greatly in recent years, but some families still retain the tradition of drinking it around Christmastime. This classic Menorcan version skips the most exotic spices (star anise, cloves) and uses what goes into so many local desserts and is always on hand – a cinnamon stick and some orange (or lemon) peel, plus a grating of nutmeg. The name is an anglicism of sangaree, the mulled drink that the British brought from the tropics. It is a tasty reminder of those years when the British controlled the island.

✳ Combine the wine, sugar and 250 ml (8 fl oz/1 cup) water in a pot or large saucepan and bring to a near boil over medium heat, stirring to dissolve the sugar. Add the orange or lemon peel, cinnamon stick and nutmeg, then reduce the heat to low and simmer for 20 minutes. Taste and add more sugar if needed. Ladle into glasses and serve immediately. Drink it when very hot.

Top to bottom: Thick Drinking Chocolate,
Hot Mulled Wine.

CHAPTER 12

BASICS

Fish Stock

Preparation time: 10 minutes,
    plus cooling time
Cooking time: 1 hour
Makes: 2 litres/2 quarts

1–1.5 kg/2¼–3¼ lb small fish or
    assorted heads and bones of firm,
    white-fleshed non-oily fish
1 tablespoon olive oil
1 clove of garlic, peeled, optional
1 yellow onion, roughly chopped
1 leek, trimmed and roughly chopped
1 celery stalk, roughly chopped
2 tablespoons roughly chopped parsley
2 tomatoes, roughly chopped
12 black peppercorns
Salt

DF ✳ GF

There are two common ways to make fish stock (broth) in the Balearics. While they have similar ingredients, one sautés the ingredients first before adding water and bringing it to a boil while the other does not. The second 'raw' version yields a clearer and softer broth. This is the sautéed version, which gives a denser final stock. Add some shellfish, such as small crabs or shrimp, if you like.

✳ In a stockpot or another large pot, heat the oil over high heat. Add the garlic (if using), onion, leek, celery and parsley, and cook for 5 minutes, stirring frequently. Add the tomatoes and peppercorns, season with salt and cook for 2–3 minutes. Add the fish and cook, gently turning over a few times, until the fish takes on some colour and begins to break apart, about 5 minutes.

✳ Pour in 2 litres (68 fl oz/8½ cups) water. Bring to a boil (this will take about 15–20 minutes), reduce the heat to low, partly cover the pot and gently simmer for 20 minutes.

✳ Remove the pot from the heat and let cool, uncovered, for about 20 minutes. Strain the stock (broth) through a sieve or colander. Gently press the remaining liquid from the fish and vegetables. Discard any solids. Store in the refrigerator for up to 3 days or freeze for longer storage.

Chicken Stock

Preparation time: 5 minutes,
    plus cooling time
Cooking time: 1 hour
Makes: about 2 litres/2 quarts

1 kg/2¼ lb bone-in chicken legs, backs,
    wings and/or necks, excess fat
    trimmed (leave skin)
1 celery stalk
2 carrots
2 sprigs fresh thyme
1 leek, trimmed and cut into a few pieces
1 turnip, scrubbed and quartered
1 parsnip, scrubbed and halved
10 black peppercorns
10 sprigs flat-leaf parsley
Salt

DF ✳ GF

When making chicken stock (broth) in Menorca, many pick up at the produce stall what is called '*sopa verde*', a bundle of carrots, celery, turnip, parsnip and plenty of fresh thyme.

✳ Season the chicken with salt. Gather the celery, carrots and thyme together and tie with cotton string.

✳ To a stockpot or another large pot, add all the ingredients except for the parsley. Cover with 2 litres (generous 2 quarts/8½ cups) cold water. Bring to a boil over high heat, skimming any foam that floats to the surface, if desired. Reduce the heat, cover the pot and gently boil for 45 minutes. Add the parsley and let cool, uncovered.

✳ Strain the cooled stock (broth) through a sieve or colander, gently pressing any liquid from the chicken and vegetables. Store the stock in the refrigerator for up to 3 days or freeze for longer storage.

Vegetable Stock

Preparation time: 10 minutes,
    plus cooling time
Cooking time: 1 hour 15 minutes
Makes: about 2 litres/2 quarts

3 tablespoons olive oil
2 medium yellow onions, roughly chopped
1 leek, trimmed and roughly chopped
3 cloves of garlic, skins on, lightly
    crushed under the palm
2 carrots, roughly chopped
2 turnips, peeled and roughly chopped
1 parsnip, peeled and roughly chopped
1 celery stalk, roughly chopped
10 black peppercorns
1 small bay leaf, optional
10 sprigs flat-leaf parsley
2 sprigs fresh thyme, optional
Salt

V ✳ VEG ✳ DF ✳ GF

A good vegetable stock (broth) improves rice dishes, stews and soups. It can also be enjoyed on its own as a broth, with or without some small soup pasta boiled in it. Rather than adding the vegetables raw to the pot, sautéing them in the beginning for a short time adds to the depth of flavour in the stock.

✳ Heat the oil in a stockpot or another large pot over high heat. Add the onions, leek and garlic, and cook for 5 minutes. Add the carrots, turnips, parsnip and celery and cook, stirring frequently, until they begin releasing their juices, about 5 minutes.

✳ Season with salt, add the peppercorns and bay leaf (if using), and cover with 2.4 litres (generous 2½ quarts/10 cups) water. Bring to a boil over high heat, skimming any foam that floats to the surface, if desired. Reduce the heat, cover the pot and gently boil for 1 hour. Remove from the heat, add the parsley and thyme (if using) and let cool, uncovered.

✳ Strain the cooled stock (broth) through a sieve or colander, gently pressing any liquid from the vegetables. Store the stock in the refrigerator for up to 3 days or freeze for longer storage.

Allioli

Preparation time: 5 minutes
Makes: about 250 ml/8 fl oz (1 cup)

1 small clove of garlic, peeled, germ
    removed if needed, and sliced into a
    few pieces
1 large (US extra-large) egg, at room
    temperature
Pinch of salt
1 teaspoon white wine vinegar or fresh
    lemon juice
175 ml/6 fl oz (¾ cup) mild olive oil or a
    blend of olive oil and sunflower oil

VEG ✳ DF ✳ GF ✳ 5 ✳ 30

This deeply popular, iconic garlicky emulsion is eaten with scores of dishes in the Balearic Islands, from black rice (page 134) to grilled rabbit (page 269) to being slathered on brown bread. The name means 'garlic and oil', which describes the ingredients used (plus a pinch of salt). Traditionally it was made in the mortar with a pestle, with the oil added quite literally drop by drop. Today it is nearly always made using a hand blender with an egg and some vinegar to help bind it. Use lighter olive oil or a blend with sunflower oil to keep it from being too heavy. The method using a food processor is similar, though can require a bit more oil (use 250 ml/8 fl oz/1 cup). If you are using a food processor, add all of the ingredients except for the oil to the food processor, pulse until blended and then blend while slowly adding the oil.

✳ In a tall, narrow and cylindrical container just wider than the shaft of an immersion hand blender, combine the garlic, egg, salt, vinegar and about 120 ml (4 fl oz/½ cup) of the oil.

✳ With the blender still off, put the blender shaft into the bottom of the container. Turn on the blender to three-quarter speed and begin blending. Don't move the shaft. Once the emulsion begins to form, very slowly bring the blender up through the oil to the surface and then slowly back down to the bottom, while very slowly adding the remainder of the oil. Bring the blender up once more and out, 30 seconds –1 minute total blending time. It should be thick and creamy. If there is any oil pooled on the surface, turn the blender back and lower the shaft slowly back to the bottom and out again.

✳ Transfer to a small bowl. Cover tightly with clingfilm (plastic wrap) and refrigerate until ready to serve. Use the same day.

Homemade Mayonnaise (Traditional Way)

Preparation time: 20 minutes
Makes: about 250 ml/8 fl oz (1 cup)

1 large (US extra-large) very fresh egg
    yolk, at room temperature
Pinch of salt
175 ml/6 fl oz (¾ cup) mild olive oil
White wine vinegar or fresh lemon juice

VEG ✳ DF ✳ GF ✳ 5 ✳ 30

Mayonnaise is Menorca's most widely spread culinary export – even if credit is rarely given to the island. (See page 209 for more on the history of mayonnaise.) There are two ways to prepare it: the quick and now most common way (see below) or like this, the laborious and traditional way, in a mortar with a pestle or wooden spoon, adding the oil drop by drop as it is incorporated into the growing emulsion. Spread it on bread, or eat it with mussels (page 218) or dolloped on cooked fish or steamed vegetables. Fresh mayonnaise does not keep well. It is best to use it all on the day it is made. Use a mild or refined olive oil. Using a very fresh egg at room temperature is key to getting the emulsion to form. It takes patience – add the oil too quickly and it will 'break' – and (usually) a few tries to master.

✳ To a mortar, add the egg yolk and salt. Break the yolk with the pestle and begin mixing, always moving in the same circular direction, until creamy and beginning to thicken.

✳ Very slowly, drop by drop, add the oil, always moving the pestle in the same direction. As it begins to bind and thicken, shake in some drops of vinegar. Continue adding oil – which can be added slightly faster towards the end – until it is finished. The mayonnaise is ready when it cannot take more oil and it pools on the surface, 15–20 minutes.

✳ Serve immediately or cover tightly with clingfilm (plastic wrap) and refrigerate until ready to serve. Use the same day.

Homemade Mayonnaise (Quick Way)

Preparation time: 5 minutes
Makes: about 175 ml/6 fl oz (¾ cup)

1 large (US extra-large) very fresh egg,
    at room temperature
Pinch of salt
1 teaspoon white wine vinegar or lemon
    juice
120 ml/4 fl oz (½ cup) mild olive oil or a
    blend of olive oil and sunflower oil

VEG ✳ DF ✳ GF ✳ 5 ✳ 30

Preparing mayonnaise using a hand blender is quick and easy. It requires more oil and the entire egg (not just the yolk) than the traditional method in a mortar (see above. It is also far less likely to 'break' (i.e. fail to hold its emulsification). Use the tall, narrow container that came with your hand blender for best results. The method using a food processor is similar, though can require a bit more oil (use 250 ml/8 fl oz/1 cup). If you are using a food processor, add all of the ingredients except for the oil, pulse until blended and then blend while slowly adding the oil.

✳ In a tall, narrow and cylindrical container just wider than the shaft of an immersion hand blender, mix the egg, salt and vinegar, and slowly pour in the oil.

✳ With the blender still off, put the blender shaft into the bottom of the container. Turn on the blender to three-quarter speed and begin blending. Once the emulsion begins to form, very slowly bring the blender up through the oil to the surface and then slowly back down to the bottom, and then up once more and out, about 30 seconds of total blending time. The mixture should be thick and creamy. If there is any oil pooled on the surface, turn the blender back on and lower the shaft slowly back to the bottom and out again.

✳ Transfer to a small bowl. Cover tightly with clingfilm (plastic wrap) and refrigerate until ready to serve. Use the same day.

Preparation time: 10 minutes
Makes: enough for a coca approximately
    30 × 40 cm/12 × 16 inches

60 ml/2 fl oz (¼ cup) olive oil
50 g/2 oz (¼ cup) lard, at room
    temperature
1 teaspoon salt
120 ml (4 fl oz/½ cup) warm water
350 g/12 oz (2⅓ cups) plain (all-purpose)
    flour

DF ✳ 5 ✳ 30

Preparation time: 10 minutes
Makes: enough for a coca approximately
    30 × 40 cm/12 × 16 inches

350 g/12 oz (2⅓ cups) plain (all-purpose)
    flour, plus extra for dusting
60 ml/2 fl oz (¼ cup) olive oil
50 g/2 oz (¼ cup) lard, at room temperature
1 teaspoon salt
120 ml (4 fl oz/½ cup) lukewarm water
25 g/1 oz fresh baker's yeast or
    8 g/3 teaspoons instant (easy-blend)
    dried yeast

DF ✳ 5 ✳ 30

Preparation time: 5 minutes,
    plus overnight soaking time
Cooking time: 1 hour 30 minutes–2 hours
Makes: about 1 kg/2¼ lb (generous 6
    cups) cooked chickpeas

500 g/1 lb 2 oz (about 3 cups) dried
    chickpeas (garbanzo beans)
1 heaped teaspoon bicarbonate of soda
    (baking soda), optional
½ onion, peeled
3 cloves of garlic, skins on, lightly
    crushed under the palm
1 teaspoon salt

V ✳ VEG ✳ DF ✳ GF ✳ 5

Dough for Coca Flatbread Base (Unleavened)

The classic baker's *coca* does not include yeast in the dough, although many home cooks (and many bakeries now, too) include it. The standard ratio is even parts olive oil and lard and twice the water. Lard gives the dough its flaky texture. This base will work for all of the *coca* recipes included in this book. Kneaded dough can be made 1 day in advance and stored in the refrigerator. Lightly brush with oil and completely cover with clingfilm (plastic wrap).

✳ To a large mixing bowl, add the oil, lard, salt and warm water and stir to blend. Gradually add the flour, working by hand until it is fully incorporated. Knead until soft and it easily comes away from the hands while still being just a touch sticky. The dough is now ready to roll out on a baking sheet and be topped.

Dough for Coca Flatbread Base (Leavened)

Many people (and bakeries) now make leavened bases for their *coca* flatbreads. The results are thicker and slightly fluffier. This base will work for all of the *coca* recipes included in this book. Kneaded dough can be made 1 day in advance and stored in the refrigerator. Lightly brush with oil and completely cover with clingfilm (plastic wrap).

✳ Sift in the flour into a large mixing bowl and make a crater. Add the oil, lard, salt and lukewarm water. Crumble in the yeast. Begin mixing with a spatula until it starts to form a ball. On a lightly floured work counter, knead until the dough detaches from the fingers and is manageable (it has to be a little sticky and soft). It is now ready to roll out on a baking sheet and be topped.

Cooked Chickpeas

Cooked chickpeas (garbanzo beans) are easy to find in jars or cans, and some shops in the Balearics sell them freshly boiled by weight. You can also boil dried beans at home. They need to be soaked overnight. If you have 'hard' water, add some bicarbonate of soda (baking soda) while they soak to help soften them. A piece of onion and cloves of garlic add flavour during the boiling stage.

✳ Rinse the chickpeas (garbanzo beans). In a large bowl, dissolve the bicarbonate of soda (baking soda), if using, in abundant cold water. Add the chickpeas and soak overnight. Drain the beans and rinse thoroughly under running water.

✳ Bring a generous amount of water to a boil in a large, heavy pot. Add the chickpeas, onion and garlic. Return to a boil, then reduce the heat to low, cover the pot with a lid and cook without losing the boil until the beans are tender, 1½–2 hours. Add the salt only once the beans begin to soften. If the pot needs more water during cooking, add boiling water. Remove the pot from the heat and let cool for at least 15 minutes. Discard the aromatics. Drain. If not using immediately, store in the refrigerator and use within 3 days.

Tomato Sauce

Preparation time: 15 minutes,
    plus cooling time
Cooking time: 1 hour
Makes: about 500 ml/18 fl oz/2 cups

1.2 kg/2½ lb ripe plum tomatoes
4 tablespoons olive oil
2 cloves of garlic, peeled
1 small bay leaf, optional
Sugar, optional
Salt and pepper

V ✳ VEG ✳ DF ✳ GF ✳ 5

Numerous Balearic recipes call for tomato sauce, including, in Mallorca, *tumbet* (layers of fried vegetables topped with tomato sauce and often a fried egg, page 105) and stuffed aubergine (eggplant) (page 87). This version passes the cooked sauce through a food mill. To skip this step, either peel the tomatoes first or grate them on a box grater (see page 25).

✳ Working over a bowl to capture all of the juices, halve the tomatoes, remove the seeds and cut each tomato into about 8 pieces. Strain the seeds, pressing out and reserving any liquid.

✳ Heat the oil in a heavy pot or Dutch oven over medium heat. Add the garlic and cook for 30 seconds. Add the tomatoes, along with any reserved juices and the bay leaf (if using), and season with salt and pepper. Cook over low heat for about 1 hour, stirring from time to time. Remove from the heat and let cool for about 10 minutes. Remove and discard the bay leaf.

✳ Pass the mixture through a food mill. Taste for sweetness and stir in some sugar if needed. Store in the refrigerator and use within a few days or freeze for longer storage.

Tomato & Pepper Sauce

Preparation time: 20 minutes
Cooking time: 1 hour 15 minutes
Makes: about 500 ml/18 fl oz/2 cups

1 kg/2¼ lb ripe plum tomatoes
3 tablespoons olive oil
1 red (or green) bell pepper or 2 long
    sweet green peppers, stemmed,
    seeded and finely chopped
2 cloves of garlic, minced
1 heaped tablespoon minced flat-leaf
    parsley
Sugar, optional
Salt

V ✳ VEG ✳ DF ✳ GF ✳ 5

This popular Ibizan *salsa* can accompany just about anything – it is delicious over cooked meats, fried fish, on pasta and so on. Depending on the tomatoes, and your taste, it might require a touch of sugar stirred in at the end. While this is an all-round recipe, we tend to like it best with grilled fresh sausages or sardines that have been fried (see Fried Sardines with Sweet Tomato-and-Onion Sofregit, page 182) or grilled on the barbecue.

✳ Halve the tomatoes and remove the seeds, reserving any juices. Grate on a box grater (see page 25), discarding the peel.

✳ Heat the oil in a heavy pot or Dutch oven over medium heat. Add the pepper(s) and cook until soft and a deeper colour, about 20 minutes. Add the garlic and parsley and cook for 30 seconds. Add the tomatoes, along with any reserved juices, then season with salt, cover the pot and cook over low heat for about 50 minutes.

✳ Taste for sweetness and stir in some sugar if needed. Store in the refrigerator and use within a few days or freeze for longer storage.

Tomato Jam

Preparation time: 20 minutes,
    plus cooling time
Cooking time: 1 hour
Makes: generous 2 × 380 ml/1 lb jam jars

1 kg/2¼ lb ripe plum tomatoes
400 g/14 oz (2 cups) sugar
3 tablespoons lemon juice
½ orange peel, white pith scraped away
1 small cinnamon stick

V ✳ VEG ✳ DF ✳ GF ✳ 5

Made with the abundance of the end-of-summer crop, tomato jams are common across the islands. There are simple versions, with little more than ripe tomatoes and sugar, and slightly more elaborate ones, like this one from Ibiza with cinnamon and orange peel. This version purées the jam with a hand blender for a smoother consistency, but that step can be skipped. The jam is especially nice with goat's cheese or cured Menorcan cheese.

✳ Core, deseed and chop the tomatoes, reserving all juices.

✳ In a heavy saucepan, combine the tomatoes and their juices, the sugar, lemon juice, orange peel and cinnamon stick. Bring to a boil, then reduce the heat and gently boil, stirring from time to time (more frequently towards the end), until thick, glazy and jammy, 1 hour.

✳ Remove the pan from the heat. Remove and discard the orange peel and cinnamon stick. Let cool for a few minutes. Purée with an immersion hand blender.

✳ Spoon the hot jam into 2 sterilized (380 ml/1 lb) jam jars, leaving about one finger space at the top. Wipe clean.

✳ If the jam will be used within 2 weeks, cover and store in the refrigerator. To keep longer, process the jars by boiling in a water bath for 15 minutes with at least 2.5 cm/1 inch water above the top of the jars. Label. Stored in a cool, dry place, it will keep this way for 1 year.

Fig Jam

Preparation time: 10 minutes,
    plus cooling time
Cooking time: 45 minutes
Makes: 1 × 380 ml/1 lb jam jar

500 g/1 lb 2 oz fresh ripe figs
100 g/3½ oz (½ cup) sugar
¼ teaspoon aniseed

V ✳ VEG ✳ DF ✳ GF ✳ 5

Figat is Menorca's classic fig jam. It's simple, with just figs and sugar – and sometimes a spoonful of aniseed as in this recipe or a piece of dried orange peel for a touch of additional flavour. This makes a single (380 ml/1 lb) jam-jar batch that is meant to be eaten within a week or two. While some pass their *figat* through a food mill or blend it with an immersion hand blender before putting into the jar for a smooth texture, most – myself included – prefer the jam a touch textured and don't bother with that step. On the island they say patience, and plenty of stirring, is key to a good *figat*. It is delicious with fresh or cured cheese or yogurt.

✳ Rinse the figs. Trim the stems and peel about half of each fig. Chop.

✳ Put the figs into a heavy saucepan with the sugar. Bring to a boil over high heat. Reduce the heat to low and cook, stirring frequently, until the jam is pasty, a deep-rich colour and falls heavily from a spoon, 20–30 minutes. Stir in the aniseed and remove from the heat.

✳ Spoon the hot jam into a sterilized 380 ml/1 lb jam jar, leaving about one finger space at the top. Wipe clean and let cool.

✳ Once cool, cover and store in the refrigerator. Use within 2 weeks.

Canned Apricots in Syrup

Preparation time: 20 minutes,
    plus cooling time
Cooking time: 5 minutes
Makes: 2 × 1 litre/1 quart jars

1.2 kg/2½ lb ripe but firm apricots
400 g/14 oz (2 cups) sugar

V ✳ VEG ✳ DF ✳ GF ✳ 5

Apricots are a key fruit to add to pastries, and halves commonly top ensaïmades and spongy *coca* (page 283). To use beyond their May to June season, some of the fruit gets preserved. This recipe uses a light syrup, and the 'raw pack' method of pouring the syrup over the raw fruit already packed into sterilized jars.

✳ Rinse the apricots. Cut in half vertically following the line of the pit and remove the pit. Gently and attractively pack into sterilized wide-mouthed glass canning jars as you work, with the cut sides of the apricots facing down. Pack as tightly as possible without crushing the fruit. Leave more than 1.25 cm/½ inch of headspace.

✳ In a saucepan, mix 1 litre (34 fl oz/4½ cups) water with the sugar and bring to a boil, stirring to dissolve. Immediately remove from the heat and let cool for a few moments. Pour over the apricots, leaving 1.25 cm/½ inch of headspace. There may be some syrup remaining; either discard or use for another purpose.

✳ Remove any air bubbles by running a knife around the insides of the jars. Seal with lids. Sterilize by covering with water and boiling in a water bath for 30 minutes (for 1 litre/1 quart jars) or 25 minutes (for 500 ml/1 pint jars). Remove the jars and let fully cool. Label and store. They will keep for 1 year.

Pomegranate Syrup

Preparation time: 15 minutes,
    plus cooling time
Cooking time: 50 minutes
Makes: 250 ml/8 fl oz (1 cup)

2 plump ripe pomegranates (about
    500 g/1 lb 2 oz total)
120 ml/4 fl oz (½ cup) freshly squeezed
    lemon juice
200 g/7 oz (1 cup) sugar
¼ cinnamon stick, optional
1 or 2 cloves, optional

V ✳ VEG ✳ DF ✳ GF ✳ 5

With its deep, fruity flavour and honey-like consistency, pomegranate syrup is a delicious and traditional accompaniment to *porcella rostida* (roast pork, page 230) or roast turkey at Christmas, and is also served drizzled over pork tongue. At home, I most frequently enjoy it with a roasted pork loin (Roasted Pork Loin with Onions & Pomegranate Syrup, page 225). Among the numerous varieties of pomegranates in the Balearic Islands, a sour pomegranate was usually used for this syrup. These have become hard to find, and this recipe calls for a common variety of the fruit plus some lemon juice to give it a hint of that sourness. (If using the sour variety of pomegranate for this recipe, omit the lemon juice.) Some cooks add a cinnamon stick, a couple of cloves and/or a piece of lemon peel. One kilo/2¼ lb of pomegranates yields about 500 ml/18 fl oz/2 cups of syrup. This is a small batch, meant to be used within a week or two. But double it if you have more pomegranates – and company coming over.

✳ Juice the pomegranates. This is most easily done by halving crosswise and gently pressing each half with a manual juicer. Alternatively, purée in a blender. Strain through a cheesecloth, pressing out all of the liquid. There should be about 350 ml (12 fl oz/1½ cups) of juice.

✳ Pour the juice into a heavy saucepan, and add the lemon juice, sugar, cinnamon stick and cloves (if using). Bring to a low boil, stirring frequently, then reduce the heat to low and gently boil until reduced by just over half (to about 250 ml/ 8 fl oz/1 cup), about 45 minutes. Remove the cinnamon stick and cloves (if using). Remove from the heat and let cool.

✳ Pour the syrup into a sterilized 250 ml (8 fl oz) canning jar while still warm. Let cool, seal, label and store in the refrigerator. Use within a few weeks.

INDEX

About the Author

Jeff Koehler, winner of a James Beard award, two International Association of Culinary Professionals (IACP) awards and two Gourmand World Cookbook Award 'Best in the World' prizes, is an American writer and cook. He is the author of eight critically acclaimed books, most recently *The North African Cookbook* (Phaidon 2023). His other books include *Where the Wild Coffee Grows*; *Darjeeling: A History of the World's Greatest Tea*; *Spain: Recipes and Traditions*; *Morocco*: *A Culinary Journey with Recipes*; and *La Paella*. His writing has appeared in the *Washington Post*, NPR.com, BBC *World's Table*, *Wall Street Journal*, *Saveur*, *Food & Wine*, Eater.com*, Fine Cooking, Taste, Punch, Vogue Arabia, Harper's Bazaar Arabia, South China Morning Post* and the *Times Literary Supplement*. Originally from near Seattle, Washington, he did his postgraduate studies at King's College London and settled in Barcelona in 1996. He divides his time between Barcelona and his home in Menorca.

AUTHOR ACKNOWLEDGEMENTS

This book has relied on years of conversations with countless people, from farmers, producers and bakers to numerous others met on the four islands. There are also a number of people who have taught me much about the islands – especially Menorca. *Un gran agraïment a*: Cesc Segura, Joan-Enric Prats and Dolors Cubilo, Oriol Segura and Gemma Pons, and Mireia Segura and Oscar Marx; Nel Pons and Gemma Soler; Cati Albalat, Maria Alles and Juanjo Alles; Pere Pons, Maria Pons and Sara Pons; Marc Pons and Mabel Oliva; Margarita Gomila and Martí Pons; Joan Pallisser; Pere Vinent; *la família* Pons Burillo (Pilar, Lumi, Bep, Toni, Lluisa, Jordi and Ana); Joan Febrer, Tolo Pons, Bep Riudavets and Clara Pons; Mònica Martí and Trini Carreras; Isabel Jubert; Toni Guàrdia; Julio Sintes and Lilian Quiroz; Claudia Amil and Jochen Danzer; Pascal Poignard and Valeria Judkowski; Naomi Duguid; Virginia Irurita; and Rebecca Staffel.

Un agraïment molt especial als de Es Mercadal que ens han fet sentir tan acollits i tan part de la comunitat, i per ensenyar-nos tant sobre la (bona) vida del poble i de l'illa.

I want to offer a deep thank you to agent Maria Whelan at InkWell Management and to Kimberly Witherspoon and the rest of the team at InkWell.

At Phaidon, I have been extremely lucky to have such incredible support, starting and ending with my amazing editor, Emily Takoudes. Project editor Claire Rogers shepherded it through the process from manuscript to finished book with care and skill – many thanks for your incredible attention to detail. A huge thank you to the rest of the Phaidon team, including managing editor Ellie Smith, photographer Simon Bajada and his team for such stunning images, Astrid Stavro for her thoughtful designs, Alex Coumbis, Ellen Bashford, Ellie Levine, Pedro Martin, Jean-François Durance and Anna Lund.

Finally, my deepest debt of gratitude goes to the three around the table at home, Eva, Alba and Maia.

Phaidon Press Limited
2 Cooperage Yard
London E15 2QR

Phaidon Press Inc.
111 Broadway
New York, NY 10006

phaidon.com

First published 2025
© 2025 Phaidon Press Limited

ISBN 978 1 83866 949 2

A CIP catalogue record for this book is available from
the British Library and the Library of Congress.

Commissioning Editor: Emily Takoudes
Project Editor: Claire Rogers
Production Controllers: Lily Rodgers and Gary Hayes
Design: Astrid Stavro Studio
Recipe photography: Simon Bajada
Photos on pages 6, 11, 21 and 24: Jeff Koehler

Publisher's Acknowledgements
Phaidon would like to thank Vanessa Bird,
Tara O'Sullivan and Ellie Smith.

Printed in China

RECIPE NOTES

* Butter is salted butter, unless otherwise specified.
* Eggs are UK size medium (US size large), unless otherwise specified.
* Herbs are fresh, unless otherwise specified.
* Milk is full-fat (whole) or semi-skimmed (reduced-fat) milk, unless otherwise specified.
* Olives can pitted or unpitted, unless otherwise specified.
* Pepper is freshly ground black pepper, unless otherwise specified.
* Salt is fine sea salt, unless otherwise specified.
* Sugar is white granulated or table sugar, unless otherwise specified.
* Lemons and oranges should be organic and unwaxed when zest or peel is used.
* Individual vegetables and fruits, such as carrots and apples, are assumed to be medium, unless otherwise specified, and should be peeled and/or washed unless otherwise specified.
* Where neutral oil is specified, use vegetable, rapeseed (canola), grapeseed, sunflower, corn or light olive oil.
* Some alcohol is processed using animal-derived products; if you follow a vegan or vegetarian diet, please check the label for certification when using alcohol in these recipes.
* Some cured meats include gluten-derived products for binding; if you follow a gluten-free diet, please check the label when using cured meats in these recipes.
* Metric, imperial and cup measurements are used in this book. Follow one set of measurements throughout, not a mixture, as they are not interchangeable.
* All tablespoon and teaspoon measurements given are level, not heaped, unless otherwise specified.
* 1 teaspoon = 5 ml; 1 tablespoon = 15 ml. Australian standard tablespoons are 20 ml, so Australian readers are advised to use 3 teaspoons in place of 1 tablespoon when measuring small quantities.
* When no quantity is specified, for example of oils, salts and herbs used for finishing dishes or for deep-frying, quantities are discretionary and flexible.
* Cooking and preparation times are for guidance only. If using a convection (fan) oven, follow the manufacturer's instructions concerning oven temperatures.
* When deep-frying, heat the oil to the temperature specified, or until a cube of bread browns in 30 seconds. After frying, drain fried foods on paper towels.
* When sterilizing jars for preserves, wash the jars in clean, hot water and rinse thoroughly. Heat the oven to 140°C/275°F/Gas Mark 1. Place the jars on a baking sheet and place in the oven to dry.
* Exercise a high level of caution when following recipes involving any potentially hazardous activity, including the use of high temperatures and open flames and when deep-frying. In particular, when deep-frying, add food carefully to avoid splashing, wear long sleeves, and never leave the pan unattended.
* Some recipes include raw or very lightly cooked eggs, meat, or fish and fermented products. These should be avoided by the elderly, infants, pregnant women, convalescents and anyone with an impaired immune system.
* Do exercise caution when foraging for ingredients, which should only be eaten if an expert has deemed them safe to eat. In particular, do not gather wild mushrooms yourself before seeking the advice of an expert who has confirmed their suitability for human consumption.
* As some species of mushrooms have been known to cause allergic reaction and illness, do take extra care when cooking and eating mushrooms and do seek immediate medical help if you experience a reaction after preparing or eating them.